# Eleanor Roosevelt

# J. William T. Youngs

Eastern Washington University

# Eleanor Roosevelt

*A Personal and Public Life*

*Third Edition*

## THE LIBRARY OF AMERICAN BIOGRAPHY

*Edited by Mark C. Carnes*

PEARSON
Longman

New York    Boston   San Francisco
London   Toronto   Sydney   Tokyo   Singapore   Madrid
Mexico City   Munich   Paris   Cape Town   Hong Kong   Montreal

Executive Editor: Michael Boezi
Executive Marketing Manager: Sue Westmoreland
Production Coordinator: Virginia Riker
Electronic Page Makeup: Alison Barth Burgoyne
Senior Manufacturing Buyer: Mary Fischer
Text and Cover Designer: John Callahan
Cover Photo: Courtesy of the Franklin D. Roosevelt Library, Hyde
    Park, New York
Photos courtesy of the Franklin D. Roosevelt Library at Hyde Park
Printer and Binder: R.R. Donnelly & Sons
Cover Printer: Coral Graphics

Quotations from papers in the Franklin Delano Roosevelt Library at
Hyde Park, New York used by permission of Nancy Roosevelt Ireland.

Library of Congress Cataloging-in-Publication Data

Youngs, J. William T.,
    Eleanor Roosevelt: a personal and public life / J. William T.
        Youngs; edited by Mark C. Carnes.—3rd ed.    p. cm.
    Includes index.
    ISBN 0-321-34232-1
    1. Roosevelt, Eleanor, 1884–1962. 2. Presidents' spouses—
United States—Biography. I. Marc, Carnes, 1915– II. Title.

E807.1.R48Y68 2005
973.917'092—dc22                                    2005012944

**Please visit our website at http://www.ablongman.com**

ISBN 0-321-34232-1

1 2 3 4 5 6 7 8 9 10—DOH—08 07 06 05

*For my daughter*
*Hope Eleanor Youngs*
*and*
*in memory of my friend*
*Samuel G. Engel*

# Contents

# Editor's Preface

Eleanor Roosevelt and Franklin, the future president, were honeymooning in northern Italy. Biographer Youngs portrays a romantic idyll as the young couple traveled by carriage to the resort town of Cortina in the heart of the Dolomite mountains of northern Italy. "Eleanor and Franklin looked out on meadows speckled with wildflowers and saw barefooted farm women with bright handkerchiefs around their heads working in the fields beside their men." He describes how the couple stayed in a quaint hotel, where they drank tea, took walks, and gazed at distant peaks that "glowed in the late afternoon sun." But Eleanor's insecurities shadowed the story. While Franklin was gregarious and self-confident, Eleanor was shy and insecure. Her anxieties mounted when, while playing cards at the inn, Franklin became friendly with Kitty Gandy, a young New York businesswoman and hiking enthusiast. The two agreed to climb the mountain above the inn the next day; Eleanor, deemed too fragile, was left behind to fret. Eleanor needed "to be comforted and reassured," Youngs concludes, yet "that day she felt more like a wallflower than a bride."

This story illustrates Youngs' art. He evokes Eleanor's world with vivid details that reveal her insecurities and foreshadow the psychological incompatibilities that characterized her marriage. The episode also makes Eleanor's transformation into an ardent social reformer and assertive statesman all the more remarkable.

As a student at Harvard College, Youngs aspired to write historical novels; he especially admired Joseph Conrad and Willa Cather. Instead of becoming a novelist, however, he pursued a career as an historian, taking a doctoral degree from Berkeley. Yet he seeks to imbue his nonfiction with the "evocative quality of historical novels." *American Realities* (2004), another of his books, consists of thirty essays on telling moments in American history, each episode conveying "the flavor of something larger."

The present book represents the culmination of his approach. In addition to the usual research, Youngs scoured the archives for telling novelistic details. Having never been to Cortina, for example, he studied Baedeker's travel guides of the early 1900s.

In consequence of his diligence and skill, this powerfully evocative biography reads like a novel.

MARK C. CARNES

# Preface to the Third Edition

Most biographers emphasize the years of their subject's greatest influence, moving quickly through the apparently less important childhood years. This telling of the story of Eleanor Roosevelt is different. I have chosen to give roughly equal time to Roosevelt's childhood in New York and to her career as first lady; in this volume Eleanor's adolescence looms as large as her years as a widow. The name by which she was known hints at the suitability of this approach: in my previous sentence the more formal "Roosevelt" gave way to the more intimate "Eleanor." Although Eleanor Roosevelt was an aristocrat at birth and a Very Important Person during her later years, she was generally known as "Eleanor" in both periods. Her relatives called her Eleanor or by a nickname when she was a little girl; half a century later the American public thought of her as "Eleanor" when she was the First Lady. In her life the child and the adult were inextricable.

This then is the story of a woman whose personal and public personas were closely intertwined. Or more correctly, it is the story of a woman who strove to live a full and honest inner life, while struggling with the forces in her public life that sometimes threatened, and occasionally overwhelmed, her inner core. At times Eleanor felt lost in her public persona, whether the persona was there to serve the demands of an overbearing mother-in-law or the expectations of the American public. But on those occasions where the public and private self were one, as in her comforting wounded soldiers in the South Pacific during World War II, her presence was quite remarkable. And there were many such occasions.

Another consideration I have brought to this story is the importance of immediacy. At times, certainly, a historian needs to present the big picture, to give some idea, for example, of the general impact of the Great Depression. But we experience our kinship most abundantly with other lives and other times when we are brought close to the realities of those other worlds. Through archival research and by visiting sites once known to Eleanor, I have attempted to tease out these realities. In some cases the sources "spoke" for themselves. I wanted to convey the texture of Eleanor's friendship with Lorena Hickok by describing a trip they took together around Canada's Gaspée Peninsula. Eleanor's own account of the trip presented ample information.

But often the historical research was more demanding. I wanted to describe fully the day of the marriage of Eleanor's parents, Anna Hall and Elliott Roosevelt. The society page of a contemporary newspaper described the wedding and the reception that followed. That helped me get started. Then various books on New York City helped me reconstruct the route the carriages took with the wedding party from the church where the service took place to the house where the reception was held. But I hoped to find more information about Calvary Church itself, the scene of the wedding. Fortunately, the church is still there. From an old newspaper I learned that the day of the Roosevelt wedding was sunny. By visiting Calvary Church in New York during the same season and at the same time as the wedding, I was able to say with certainty that at the conclusion of the service the couple did indeed turn to "the sunshine pouring through the windows at the rear of the church." Why do such details matter? For me, the answer is simple. They contribute to the authenticity of the story. They help us realize that this and this *really* did happen.

When I was unable to visit an actual setting, other sources helped flesh out the story. After Eleanor married her fifth cousin, Franklin Roosevelt, they visited Cortina in the Italian Dolomites. Although I did not travel to these mountains in person, I was able to journey them in thought by reading several wonderful travel guides describing the Dolomites in the early twentieth century. I wanted to embellish this particular scene because this honeymoon interlude indicates so much about the character of both Eleanor and Franklin, and it suggests the attractions and the tensions in their relationship. Eleanor's letters to Sara Roosevelt, her mother-in-law, helped me describe the honeymoon journey. Using the guidebooks, I could visualize Cortina more fully.

In such ways I have attempted to reconstruct various scenes in the life of the leading lady of twentieth-century America. Because this is a short book I have needed to be selective in choosing episodes in Eleanor Roosevelt's story. Fortunately, other authors have written a multitude of books about her life. I have listed many of these in the bibliography. There the reader who wants to learn more about Eleanor's role in the UN, her friendship with Lorena Hickok, her marriage to Franklin, and many other subjects will find scores of informative books to expand this account.

My own telling of Eleanor Roosevelt's life is as much a work of evocation as explanation. I invite the reader to know Eleanor by carrying the impression of her childhood forward to her adult life. Realize that the Eleanor who met with an orphan at a European refugee camp, shortly after World War II, was herself orphaned in childhood half a century before. Recognize that the Eleanor Roosevelt who coaxed and cajoled Communists and Muslims and Christians in the United Nations to set aside their differences and agree upon a "Universal Declaration of Human Rights" was the same woman who, in her childhood after the death of her parents, part of a wildly diverse community of individuals at her grandmother's house. Thus, Eleanor Roosevelt's youth was not simply a prologue to her adult life, a set of booster rockets to be jettisoned as the trajectory of her career carried her far away from home. Eleanor was in important ways *the same person* as a child and as an adult. And accordingly I have attempted to tell her story in a way that, while brief, creates an impression of her life *as a whole*.

J. WILLIAM T. YOUNGS

# Acknowledgments

One of the greatest pleasures of being a writer is the opportunity to indulge one's reflective instincts; for hours at a time the author shuts the door on the world and contemplates in solitude the joy and sorrow, the humor and triumph of human existence. To the historian these reflective moments can bring a compelling sense of communion with the past and a wondrous feeling of purpose. But in writing, as in other creative activities, moments of inspiration must be paid for with hours of perspiration. Then the isolation of writing may lose its charm and the inwardness of the craft become a burden. In such moments the human contacts available to the lawyer, politician, doctor, or journalist can seem far more appealing than the author's private world.

But if a writer is fortunate, he or she will find companions who become an audience of listeners, advisers, and supporters during the long months and years of research and composition; and communion with these friends will help sustain him or her during the search for a more elusive communion with the life of the past. I have been fortunate in the number of people who have shared in some measure in the composition of this book. Many are individuals whom I met by chance on planes or at parties whose faces lit up when I told them I was writing about Eleanor Roosevelt—they too admired this remarkable woman. Among the friends and acquaintances whose advice and reminiscences were most valuable were Arjai Barrington, Dale Davis, Florence Frost, Madeleine Freidel, Charles Horowitz, Kathleen Nichols, John Elwood, Marie Salisbury, Carola Norton, Linda Stowe, Karen Blair, John Allen, Gina Hames, Andrea Beatty, Earl Davis, Ruth Engel, Michael Fronmueller, Emory Bass, Carolyn Ennis, James Gale, Kathy Fridstein, Ted Morgan,

Blanche Cook, Phil Ashby, Louise Lindgren, David McCracken, Margot Knight, Jim Tabilio, Kay Austin, Dana Cooley, William Kidd, Richard Donley, Charles and Ann Yonkers, Marian Ferguson, Helen Pastor, Lori Barnett, C. J. Maupin, and my mother, Marguerite Youngs. I was fortunate to have the help of two fine research assistants—Susan Metzler and Merri Morash. Jenny Ahrend assisted me with many valuable suggestions for the second edition of the book and with revisions to the bibliography. I appreciate the advice and encouragement of many people at Little, Brown, especially Bradford Gray, David W. Lynch, Mary Tondorf-Dick, and Barbara Breese. And I owe the previous longtime Library of American Biography series editor, Oscar Handlin, my thanks for encouraging me by example, while I was in college, to see the value of evocation as well as analysis in history. I also appreciate the work of the staff at Longman in preparing the third edition for publication.

I am grateful for the assistance of the staffs of the Franklin D. Roosevelt Library at Hyde Park, Kennedy Library at Eastern Washington University, and Suzzallo Library at the University of Washington. Wilton Fowler and Donald Treadgold kindly appointed me Visiting Scholar at the University of Washington while I was working on the book. My students in two seminars on Eleanor and Franklin Roosevelt at Eastern Washington University were unfailingly interested in the Roosevelts and in their professor's work. The members of Eastern Washington's chautauqua kept me on my toes for three hours one evening with a spirited discussion of Eleanor Roosevelt's parents. Samuel G. Engel, who shares the dedication to this book, helped Clare Boothe Luce come to appreciate Eleanor Roosevelt and helped me recall—if I needed reminding—that I was writing about one of the great leaders of the twentieth century. The other person on the dedication page, my daughter, Hope Eleanor Youngs, and her twin brother Theodore (who will have his own dedication someday) gave me insights into Eleanor Roosevelt's childhood feelings—simply by being themselves.

Three people have been especially close to my work. Linda Youngs, had to suffer with me through the fallow periods when the writing went more slowly than either of us would have wished. Nonetheless, she has always been ready to evaluate my innumerable rough drafts and to provide criticisms that are unfailingly thorough and perceptive. Frank Freidel, who came to the University of Washington from Harvard just as I was beginning work on Eleanor Roosevelt, has shared with me his encyclopedic knowledge of the Roosevelts; our conversations about Eleanor and Franklin inspired many of my own insights into the character of each. Another friend, Catherine Porter, worked with me for many hours as editor, researcher, and colleague; her involvement in my work gives me a sense of creative partnership—surely the best antidote to writer's isolation. She and the other "assistants" named here contributed greatly to my pleasure in writing about a woman who understood, as few have, the importance of friendship.

# Eleanor Roosevelt

# Prologue:
## The South Pacific, 1943

From the window of an Army transport plane Eleanor Roosevelt gazed down at the blue waters of the South Pacific. In the vast ocean the occasional islands seemed so remote that she "wondered how our planes found them or that the waves did not wash them away." The very names of the islands suggested something distant and exotic: Bora Bora, Tutuila, Samoa, Fiji, New Caledonia, Espiritu Santo, Guadalcanal. Until recently these specks of land had been some of the most peaceful places on the globe, the subject of romantic tales by Stevenson, Melville, and London. Eleanor Roosevelt came to the South Pacific, however, not to find peace but to study war. Her trip would cost her dearly in mind and body, stripping thirty pounds off her graceful frame and leaving her so tired that friends would worry about her health.

For the past two years the South Pacific had been a huge war zone. Fleets of battleships, carriers, and destroyers maneuvered across the waters and fought one another at places like Midway and the Coral Sea. Swarms of planes screamed over the islands, blasting rival bases. And on some islands, occupied by both armies, gunfire sounded in the tropical air, and men died horribly on beaches and in jungles.

Eleanor Roosevelt had already seen the results of this carnage during her visits to hospitals on the West Coast, where she walked miles of corridors talking to wounded men. War was no abstraction to her; it was as palpable as a medical report on the men she saw in a San Francisco hospital: "Fractured skull, fractured vertebra. . . . Severe avulsed wound, left leg. . . . Amputation, left leg. . . . Gunshot wound, face. Ruptured eye, right. . . . Multiple machine-gun bullet wounds, legs and arms." Each wound touched her as if her own child had been injured.

Eleanor's four sons were in the armed forces, and she had felt as they left that she "might be saying goodbye for the last time." Her son Franklin was wounded when his ship was bombed in the Mediterranean. His injury was slight, but at any moment Eleanor might learn that one of her boys had been killed. "Life had to go on," she later wrote, "and you had to do what was required of you, but something inside of you quietly died." She knew that millions of other American mothers were "going through the same slow death," and she was angry. She could not accept war as a necessary element in human affairs. It was wrong, and she must publicize the wrongness of it. She was determined, she said, "to prevent a repetition of this stupidity called war."

And so she went to the South Pacific in 1943. The First Lady had a number of "practical" reasons to tour the region. She planned to visit Australia and New Zealand, where her presence would symbolize the wartime alliance between those countries and the United States. She intended to visit women's groups in both places to see how they were contributing to the war effort. And as an official representative of the Red Cross she would report back to its chairman, Norman Davis, on conditions in the South Pacific. But above all Eleanor felt that in order to oppose war, she must know war. She could not, of course, enter a battle zone while the bullets were flying, but she was determined to come as close to the fighting as possible.

During her tour of the South Pacific she would travel 23,000 miles, spending more than a hundred hours aloft in a four-engine Liberator bomber equipped as a transport, and visiting Australia, New Zealand, and seventeen smaller islands. Eleanor traveled in spartan simplicity in planes crowded with soldiers. When island natives bedecked her with floral wreaths, she passed them on to the enlisted men. Like the other passengers, she carried only forty-four pounds of luggage, and because some of her allotment went for the typewriter on which she wrote her newspaper column, "My Day," her wardrobe was plain. She wore a crisp blue-gray Red Cross jacket and skirt over a white blouse, a "uniform" that symbolized well the austerity of a world at war.

Eleanor was fifty-nine in 1943. She had been First Lady of the United States for a full decade—longer than any woman before her—and had attained a reputation as a uniquely energetic woman. She had given more teas, shaken more hands, written more articles, delivered more addresses, and held more press conferences than any other First Lady. She was virtually an assistant President, traveling around the country and the world on Franklin Roosevelt's behalf, proposing legislation to him and to his advisers, and publicizing programs she favored. She was known as a friend of the poor and the oppressed: one of the most popular magazine cartoons of the 1930s showed her deep in a coal mine; "Oh, my God," says a miner, "it's Mrs. Roosevelt!"

Eleanor Roosevelt's personality was never revealed more dramatically than during her South Pacific tour of

1943. There was, first, her public persona: the impression she created on people she met. She was a master politician—charming journalists, soldiers, legislators, housewives, farmers, and factory workers with her grace and capturing their imaginations with her vision of a better world. Beneath the surface of this public performance—always serene and orderly—was the private Eleanor Roosevelt, more vulnerable than the public figure. While the First Lady met generals and prime ministers and delivered public addresses, the more reclusive Eleanor was profoundly troubled by the brutal inhumanity of war. Her anxiety was deepened by the presence of one of her best friends, a young sergeant named Joseph Lash, in the war zone, on the island of Guadalcanal. Eleanor's affection for Lash had begun five years before when he was a leader of the American Youth Congress and Eleanor was looking for ways to help the nation's young people. They had become political collaborators, friends, intimates. When he was shipped overseas, she wrote him, "All that I have is yours always, my love, devotion and complete trust follow you."

The First Lady's famous warmth owed much to her communion with men like Lash. She could project herself compellingly to humankind en masse: to blacks, Jews, the poor, the oppressed; she could shake a hundred hands in a receiving line and seem interested in everyone she met; she could sign and send a hundred letters a day. But in order to deal with the generalities she needed particularities. She understood the suffering of millions of American blacks because she knew a few blacks well. She understood the plight of unemployed coal miners because she visited and revisited one mining community. And above all she understood people because she had come to love a few people as much as life itself. Joseph Lash, a weatherman on Guadalcanal, was one of those friends.

Christmas Island was one of the first places to receive the First Lady. The Liberator dropped out of the sky, taxied along the runway, and came to a halt before a small cluster of buildings. A man fixed a short ladder to the passenger door at the rear of the aircraft, and Eleanor Roosevelt stepped onto the tarmac. On such islands men often felt that their country had forgotten them, caring only about the big battles in Europe and Africa. Simply by her presence the First Lady gave the men a sense of importance. But more than that, an island journalist reported, she "soon won the admiration and eternal friendship of every man she contacted."

Mrs. Roosevelt attended a base movie, "a Betty Grable epic," and visited every corner of the island, seeing the radio station, newspaper offices, the mess tent, and the camp laundry. She chatted with wounded men in hospital tents and "signed autographs by the thousands." How did Broadway look, some of the men wondered, and she described for them "the Great White Way" with the lights covered for wartime defense. The men who put together a report on the visit for the soldiers' *Pacific Times* were struck by two seemingly contradictory qualities in the First Lady. She was an aristocrat, a "gracious lady," and yet she was warm and approachable. "She reminded one more of some boy's mother back home," wrote Corporal Terry Flanagan, "than the wife of the President of the United States—and we all loved it."

The First Lady went from Christmas Island to New Zealand and Australia, where she planned to visit American hospitals and to see factories and farms where women had taken over men's jobs because of the war. In New Zealand, according to her temporary secretary, George Durno, she took the country "by storm." She was equally successful in Australia. Thousands of people flocked to Canberra to hear her speak, renting every available room in and near the city and camping in tents and cars. In Melbourne three thousand people came to the town hall to hear her, and another ten thousand gathered on the streets outside. In Sydney people climbed telephone poles, awnings, and car roofs to watch her go by, and twenty thousand gathered for her speech. A reporter who followed her around Canberra collecting people's reactions heard her described, in the Australian dialect, as a "corker," a "beaut," a "real aristocrat," and "all wool and a yard wide."

They came to see Eleanor Roosevelt in part because she was the wife of a famous American and in part because she represented an important wartime ally. But they also came because she had attained an international reputation in her own right. The *Auckland Star* described her as a woman dedicated to "the quest for a better way of life, not only for her own people of the United States, but for all the peoples of the world." Eleanor Roosevelt's name "carries its own title," the *Star* asserted: "There is no better known woman in all the world . . . and that includes all the most glamourous film actresses."

The journalists Down Under were accustomed to notable visitors who had little time for reporters. But Eleanor always made time. At airports she would pose until the photographers were satisfied. In press conferences she established a friendly, informal tone. She met with forty reporters in Canberra; they expected to be kept at a respectful distance, but she invited them to sit nearby. "As she sat on a rose brocade settee," a journalist wrote, "with a large bowl of white blossoms in the background, and the press representatives on the floor at her feet, she looked just like most people's dream aunt—understanding, good-natured, yet worldly wise." Mrs. Roosevelt's topics ranged from family life to foreign affairs. She replied to the hardest questions "with a gunshot quickness, and a clarity that showed a thorough grasp of what she was discussing." What did she think of the Soviet Union, she was asked. This was a hard question. She must not appear too pro-Soviet, for Russia was a Communist country, but she could not be anti-Russian, either, because Russia was fighting against Germany. She placed the question in a personal context: she would "love" to have Soviet Premier Joseph Stalin visit the White House.

Several reporters tried to capture Eleanor Roosevelt's physical presence. "She was completely charming to look at," wrote one. "Her blue eyes were always alight with interest; her fair skin was pale but clear, and framed by soft, silver hair worn in a small bun." Sometimes she leaned forward with her elbows on her knees as if she were talking to a class of students. Her "beautiful hands, long and slim and brown," were wonderfully expressive. Her speech was soft and her enunciation clear; she emphasized certain words, particularly at the ends of sentences. She seemed completely relaxed.

Many of the reporters who listened to Eleanor Roosevelt were struck by a quality they had difficulty in describing. Sometimes they resorted to hyperbole: she was "a very great woman," a "great and gracious person," and America's "Public Energy No. 1." Or they tried to describe some fundamental attribute: one reporter admired "her alert, lively independent mind, her quick sympathy for ordinary people, . . . her inexhaustible curiosity about the world." Several journalists remarked that in spite of her many activities she remained preeminently "feminine" and "motherly." Above all she was natural: she was "a confident woman who appears completely oblivious of her own terrific personality." She carried herself with a dignity that was "so constant and effortless that you feel it would still be there if she stood on her head."

During her tour of Australia the First Lady could do no wrong. She met with the Prime Minister and Members of

Parliament, and she visited farms, hospitals, and factories. She held a koala bear in Sydney's Taronga Park Zoo and delivered speeches on the postwar world. George Durno was staggered by her energy. Durno wrote Malvina Thompson, Mrs. Roosevelt's secretary in Washington, "Mrs. R. keeps telling people Down Under about that secretary of hers who has been with her for twenty-odd years. I don't believe it. Long before twenty years anyone in that job would have to be in an insane asylum." He told her, "When this tour is over, I am going to return to one of the convalescent officers' retreats we have visited and catch my breath."

Despite her great success, however, Eleanor was strangely restless in Australia. One reporter discerned tension beneath the placid exterior. "Her hands gave her away," the journalist wrote. "One of them is nearly always in the air, but when it isn't, she clasps them nervously, rubs them together, moves a finger or thumb of one hand around the palm of the other." Eleanor felt oppressed by the continual "pomp and ceremony"; she did not enjoy being on display. The world was at war. Only a few hundred miles off the coast of Australia men were locked in deadly combat. Her friend Joseph Lash was among them. She could not be content to bask in public adulation while they were fighting.

She must have felt better when she was delivering speeches. An idealist, she sought to move people with her concept of global justice. In a radio address in New Zealand she declared, we "want a world which is peaceful because people have enough to eat, shelter for themselves and their families, enough clothes to wear, and above all, work to do which will pay a decent living wage. We want a world which is peaceful because all people have hope—hope that they can grow and build increasingly for themselves the kind of life of which they dream." In a better world women would achieve equality with men. When Eleanor saw women at work in factories, replacing men who were at war, she used the opportunity to speak on behalf of women's rights. In Sydney she declared, "Perhaps here is the germ of an idea that in the postwar period women will be encouraged to participate in all activities of citizenship."

Eleanor Roosevelt wanted to believe that men were fighting at this very moment in the South Pacific for a more just world. But even in Australia the war seemed remote. She longed to be nearer to the actual front and was deeply moved when she met men going to the battlefields. In the north of Australia outside Townsville she encountered men in combat dress heading down a dusty road for a disembarkation point; they were on their way to the bloody fighting in New Guinea. Eleanor walked down the line wishing the men good luck, her voice quavering with emotion. The First Lady wanted to visit New Guinea, but General Douglas MacArthur would have no woman, not even the President's wife, in his war zone. It looked as if Eleanor would be denied the chance to see the actual battlefields.

But then word came that Admiral Halsey had approved her visit to Guadalcanal, which had seen some of the bloodiest fighting of the war and was still being bombed almost daily by Japanese aircraft. The First Lady arrived in the early morning and breakfasted with General Nathan Twining. Eleanor told the general that she wanted to see Sergeant Lash, and soon the soldier and the First Lady met, upsetting military protocol with a warm embrace. Joseph Lash accompanied Eleanor as her driver during much of her island tour.

Guadalcanal was a large island, some two thousand square miles in area, where only a year earlier the Americans had launched their first major offensive against the Japanese. During six months of fighting in the jungles that covered the island the two sides suffered more than twenty-five thousand casualties. The Japanese had withdrawn from the island, but they still attacked daily from the air.

After breakfast the First Lady began a grueling visit to the island hospitals. In the past few weeks she had talked to thousands of soldiers. And yet she retained an ability to treat each new patient as if he were the first wounded man she had seen. One reporter who had watched her meeting people wrote, "Every time she grasps a new hand her face lights up with a resolute effort to feel sincere, not to leave this a mere empty gesture. She tries to feel a genuine impulse of friendship towards the person she is greeting."

Eleanor Roosevelt had a feeling for the needs of the soldiers. "One boy told me his wife is expecting a baby in November," she later wrote, "and you could see longing in his eyes. Another one said, 'I am just going to get married and I wrote my girl that I want her dressed in frills and chiffon when I get home.'" Most of the men she met had longings like these. At each bedside Mrs. Roosevelt paused and talked. A tough officer who had been assigned to accompany her against his will was soon won over by her manner. He reported: "When she chatted with the men, she said things mothers say, little things men never think of and couldn't put into words if they did. Her voice was like a mother's too."

In public Eleanor was unfailingly cheerful, but she realized that many of the men she saw would never again see their homes. "Hospitals and cemeteries are closely tied together in my head on this trip," she wrote, "and I thought of them even when I talked to the boys who were well and strong and in training, ready to go wherever they had to go to win the war." Eleanor had been seeking the meaning of the war, trying to find some place that might evoke for her the fundamental message in the whole sordid business.

She came finally to a chapel and a graveyard on Guadalcanal that touched her more than any place before. The chapel had been built of wood by the natives and given to the Americans. Its steep, thatch roof sloped almost to the ground. A thatch-covered cupola rose above and was topped by a cross. Eleanor reported that the local residents "even made the altar and the altar vessels, carving them beautifully, decorating the church with symbols which have special meanings for them—fishes of various kinds which mean long life, eternity, etc."

Outside in the cemetery wooden crosses marked the graves of men killed in the fighting on Guadalcanal. Perhaps the simplicity of the markers most affected Eleanor. Mess kits and sometimes helmets hung on the crosses, and at the base of each marker friends had carved their prosaic tributes: "He was a grand guy" or "Best friend ever." That was all, but here was war reduced to its plainest, the destruction of a young man, a great guy, a friend. In her diary Eleanor wrote, "I said a prayer in my heart for the growth of the human spirit so that we might do away with force in settling disputes in the future."

That evening the First Lady sat on a screened porch talking with Joseph Lash. They discussed the war and their friends back home. Eleanor was helping Trude Pratt, the woman Lash would marry, decorate their apartment. Relieved to be with such a good friend after a month among strangers, Eleanor may have let him see the fatigue that she tried to hide from others. He wrote Trude telling her he had seen "a very tired Mrs. Roosevelt, agonized by the men she had seen in the hospitals, fiercely determined because of them to be relentless in working for a peace that this time will last."

Few people realized that Eleanor was "agonized" by her contact with wounded men or that she lost thirty pounds under the strain of her tour to the South Pacific. Many politicians had made similar trips without being deeply affected. But it was precisely because she was profoundly moved when she met a soldier who longed to see his sweetheart in "frills and chiffon" or saw a grave marker for the "best friend ever" or embraced a sergeant whom she knew back home—it was, in short, because she knew the war through personal contact that she was able to project a sympathy that came, quite literally, from the heart.

Eleanor left Guadalcanal and began the long trip back to the United States. Most of the area commanders in the South Pacific had been apprehensive about her visit, anticipating that they would waste time entertaining the First Lady. By now it was apparent that she had worked wonders. Admiral Nimitz's flag officers came in from their various posts "singing her praises and reporting on the beneficial effect she had had on the morale of the men." In the South Pacific she acquired almost legendary status. The actress Una Merkel, touring the area shortly afterward, heard about a boy whose stomach had been all but destroyed. He was kept alive by blood plasma and tubular feedings and had lost the will to live, but he began to recover after Eleanor, like a mother, kissed him.

A few weeks later a well-rested Eleanor Roosevelt received a guest at the White House, a reporter named Ernie Pyle, who was the best-known journalist covering the war. Pyle had been in London during the great firebombing of 1940, and he spent the early part of 1943 with the U.S. infantry covering the fighting in North Africa and Sicily. Like the First Lady he instinctively appreciated the sacrifice of the common soldier, and his articles sang their praises.

But despite his breadth of experience, he was overawed at the idea of meeting Eleanor Roosevelt. He had only an old jacket to wear because he had just returned from the front. Somewhat shyly he greeted the First Lady and sat down to tea. The only other person in the room was the First Lady's secretary. Eleanor immediately made Pyle feel at ease, asking him with interest about the soldiers in Europe and telling him about her own observations in the

South Pacific. He found in her a person who cared as much as he did for the common soldier. At last he felt that he should leave. Outside he walked across Lafayette Park, opposite the White House. The air was chilly in the late afternoon, and Pyle felt "as light as a feather."

Eleanor Roosevelt affected people that way. For the wounded soldier and the battle-hardened journalist, and for the thousands of other men and women who met her and the millions who heard her speak or read her articles, she seemed an unfailing source of courage and inspiration. She was virtually an American saint, able to move with a grace that seemed otherworldly and to heal a dying soldier with a kiss. Her achievements as First Lady seemed so effortless that it is difficult to imagine the anxieties that followed her through life or to see her as anyone other than the legendary figure of her mature years. Could she have been a child who cried when she fell, a painfully shy adolescent, a bride who doubted her husband's affection, and a mother troubled by her failure as a parent?

Surely these youthful worries were only masks that hid the *real* Eleanor Roosevelt. Beneath all these guises must have been the incipient adult: self-assured, invulnerable. But for Eleanor the worlds of the 1880s and the 1910s were as real as the world of the 1940s. They were different worlds, and she was a different person. There was nothing inevitable about her later triumphs. And yet both the suffering and the achievements of her early years made possible the person whom many regard as the greatest American woman of the twentieth century.

# 1

# A Victorian Family

*My father . . . married Anna Hall, and, as is so often the case in
life, tragedy and happiness came walking on each other's heels.*

Eleanor Roosevelt, *This Is My Story*

During the summer of 1883 Anna Hall wore the tiger-claw
necklace Elliott Roosevelt had given her. Elliott shot the tiger
himself, and the weight of its claws around her neck reminded Anna that her fiancé was a sportsman, an adventurer, a
hunter. Elliott was wonderfully handsome, with short dark
hair parted smartly in the middle, twinkling eyes, and a neat-
ly trimmed moustache. Anna was equally attractive. One of
New York's most beautiful debutantes, she was tall and slender and carried herself with graceful self-confidence. Her
light brown hair framed a lovely oval face; her eyes were
bright and her lips full.

Anna's beauty was both ethereal and fleshly: a whimsical
smile revealed a hidden thoughtfulness, while her lovely figure won admiring glances. Elliott was at first drawn to
Anna's looks and described her to a friend as a "slender fair-
haired little beauty." A century later the two might soon have
become lovers, but respectable couples in Victorian America
did not kiss until engagement or undress together before marriage. Elliott and Anna obeyed the rules: their ardor was contained, channeled, and intensified by convention.

If convention was a jailer, however, holding their passions in check, convention also played cupid in drawing

them together. They were bluebloods and were expected to marry aristocrats like themselves. On her mother's side Anna was a Livingston, descended from land-rich colonial grandees who had ruled the Hudson River Valley like feudal barons. Her ancestors signed the Declaration of Independence and administered the oath of office to George Washington. Her upbringing was characterized by tradition and supervision. Every morning and evening the family prayed together, and on Sunday afternoons they sang hymns. Her father, Valentine Hall, required Anna to take daily walks with her shoulders held back by a stick in the crook of her arms. The training had been painful, but like a formal garden, Anna accepted discipline gracefully. When she entered society, she was frequently praised for her upright bearing. The training in posture could be enlarged into a lesson on life: success came through self-discipline.

If Anna's household can be compared to a well-cultivated garden, Elliott's was more like a wilderness park, where orderly paths merge with scenes of nature and mystery. Certainly the Roosevelt lineage met the conventional requirements of New York society. Elliott was an eighth-generation American whose Dutch ancestors had breathed American air and hunted American game long before the Livingstons left their English hearths. Elliott's grandfather, Cornelius Roosevelt, made a fortune in banking and left his son, Theodore, two million dollars.

Elliott's father was a big-chested, square-jawed bear of a man with firm convictions and a generous spirit. One of New York's leading philanthropists, he helped found the Metropolitan Museum of Art, the Museum of Natural History, and the Orthopedic Hospital. He also established the Newsboys' Lodging House and spent many hours there visiting the street waifs who came for food and shelter. Theodore Roosevelt presented the world to his children as a place of infinite possibility. When Elliott was twelve the family went to the Near East, where they sailed in a native boat twelve hundred miles up the Nile and rode horseback through the Holy Lands. They saw the great temple of Karnak by moonlight, slept in monasteries, and bathed in the Jordan River. When he was twenty Elliott began a sixteen-month journey around the world on his own, continuing the education with travel encouraged by his father.

Elliott returned from his global tour in March 1881. Barely twenty-two years old, he had already seen more of the world than most men could imagine. Feeling the need to settle down, he joined his brother-in-law, Douglas Robinson, in a real estate firm. The partners recognized the value of the Roosevelt connection and changed the firm name to Robinson, Russell and Roosevelt. Elliott spent his working days in their offices at 106 Broadway.

The young Roosevelt was less interested in business, however, than in the social world. He joined the fashionable Meadowbrook Country Club on Long Island, played polo, rode to hounds, and quickly established himself as one of New York's finest horsemen. Brave to the point of recklessness, he injured himself at polo several times during his first year.

He entered friendship with the same intensity he displayed in riding. With many adventures to recount, he was a good talker, but unlike many garrulous men, he also listened well. By the fireside at Meadowbrook, at dinner parties, and at dances, the handsome young man was immensely well liked. One of the many women he charmed said he could make anyone he talked to feel they were the most important person in the world. Elliott's charm extended to everyone he met. He was so popular with the poor youngsters in the Newsboys' Lodging House that they clapped and stamped their feet whenever he came to visit.

In the small circle of New York society it was inevitable that Elliott would meet Anna Hall. Perhaps she already knew of the young man-about-town just returned from a world tour. And he must have known about her: a debutante with a stunning figure and a beautiful face. Anna sailed through dances and supper parties as impressively as Elliott rode across the polo field. They began their first animated conversations in ballrooms and parlors. During the winter of 1883 they began to see one another regularly. Elliott showered Anna with invitations to go riding and took her to visit the Newsboys' Lodging House. He sent her bouquets, telling her, "Even the flowers are happier at being your servants."

As the months passed Anna and Elliott became intimates, exchanged words of love, agreed to marry. Happiness, that most elusive of human sentiments, came for each to center in the affection of the other. The young couple were not, however, merely dewy-eyed romantics. They came to know one another not only as love objects but also as human beings, and they began to recognize each other's hopes and needs. Anna was a beautiful and popular young woman, but she harbored doubts about herself. Could she be a good wife and mother? "Oh! Elliott," she wrote, "I do want to be worthy of you." Elliott reassured his young bride-to-be, making light of her worries. But he was plagued by worries of his own. The real estate business was slow, and although he could live on inherited wealth, he wanted to support Anna in luxury. Moreover, despite his sportsman's demeanor, he was often nervous and sickly. Many years later his daughter Eleanor said of her father: "He had a physical weakness he himself probably never quite understood."

Anna sensed Elliott's weakness and urged him to reveal all his fears to her. "If you do not show them to me," she scolded, "how am I to learn to help you?" From frivolous conversations matching his charm and her coquetry, Elliott and Anna entered that disquieting realm of human discourse where one being feels the presence of another and seeks to respond. In a motion of her spirit that must have frightened her, Anna embraced Elliott, became responsible for him. "All my love and ambition are now centered in you," she wrote her fiancé, "and my objects in life are to keep and be worthy of your love, to aid you in the advance of all your projects in life, and to lead myself and aid you in leading a life worthy of God's children."

In September 1883 Elliott joined Anna at Oak Terrace, a Hall family estate at Tivoli on the Hudson, for a month's vacation. As summer gave way to fall, Elliott and Anna took long walks alone in the woods, where the leaves were beginning to turn, and by the river, where a chilly breeze made ripples on the water in the afternoon sun. In two short months they would be man and wife. The days passed; then came the last night in September. The next morning Elliott would take the train to New York, and then he and Anna would be separated. They had grown closer, and yet Elliott still felt a barrier between them. Could they not exchange some further token of affection, share some act that would confirm their bond? Convention dictated that they should not make love until they were married, but Elliott had probably known women during his days as a world traveler. On that last night Elliott must have yearned to make love to his beautiful fiancée. In the quiet house after the family had gone to bed Anna wavered. She did love Elliott, she would marry him, and he did need her. He *needed* her.

The next day Elliott was at work again in New York. "My heart has been sorrowful today," he wrote Anna, "and the week before me looks very long and dreary." He missed his "little Baby girl" and longed to hold her. At the same time he was elated by the memory of their closeness. "Do not forget last night," he wrote, "we can neither of us ever recall [change] it. *I* do not wish to and never shall, being oh *so* happy and proud as I think of it, and the heart beat loyal and true my sweet, that pressed to yours." She was really his. "My dear love," he concluded, "God bless you, your lover Elliott."

In her letter that day Anna was constrained. She made no allusions to heartbeats or touching or lovers. "I feel so lonely without my tender, loving boy," she wrote. She wished they could have a "long chat over the fire." What more could she say? What *should* a woman say? She thought about Elliott's anxieties. "I do so hope you will not have any more horrible nights," she wrote, "and no more dreams which make my boy so wretched." Then shyness returned. She ended simply, "Devotedly, Anna R. Hall."

Anna spent the following morning in the sitting room with her family, reading in front of the fire. Later she wrote Elliott again, more confiding this time. How had she really felt after he left? She would tell him. "Yesterday," she wrote, "somehow I felt nearer [to] Christ, as though he were really going to take me into his army and make me his. It made me so *peaceful* and happy. I felt as though all my struggles would be ended." Giving herself to Elliott had assumed a spiritual quality in her imagination. She was less constrained now, even brash, as she signed her letter, "*your ever loving,* Baby."

Elliott rejoiced in Anna's closing. In Victorian America women were taught restraint. But still a man wanted to be cherished. Elliott savored the words "your ever loving, Baby," repeated them, and told Anna he longed to "kiss the hand that wrote them." Encouraged by her openness he told her that when he contemplated their next meeting, "my heart beats with the thought and the hot blood rushes to my head."

Hot blood, heartbeats, a vision of Christ's army: Elliott's and Anna's romance had reached a culmination, and now came the turmoil of new feelings. Anna encouraged Elliott to find confidence and stability in God. Don't worry if business is bad, she told him. "Remember that you are God's child and he will do what is best for you." God had been good to them: "It is wrong for us to be unhappy," she said, "when he has given us each other—what more can we ask for!" If only Elliott could put away his worries.

"Do be happy, my beloved," she coaxed him.

On the afternoon of December 1, 1883, a long line of carriages stood outside of New York's Calvary Church as several hundred of New York's most prominent citizens gathered to attend the wedding of Anna Hall and Elliott Roosevelt. A reporter would call this wedding "one of the most brilliant social events of the season." It was that and more. The marriage was both a love match between a passionate man and a beautiful woman and a dynastic alliance joining two of the most respected families in New York.

As Elliott waited self-consciously for his bride at the altar, one could imagine him standing more comfortably beside a fire in a hunting lodge after a day in the woods, his hands pressed into his pockets, his booted feet spread at a jaunty angle as he laughed and told stories about guns and horses. There was nothing frivolous, however, in his demeanor today. He looked upon marriage as a sacred commitment and must have been deeply moved when he first caught sight of his bride.

Anna entered the church, her soft figure robed in a white satin dress. She walked slowly to the altar and stood beside her handsome groom. Then the minister, Henry

Saterlee, began to intone the wedding service. As he listened, Elliott may have glanced down at the tiny mosaic tiles in the floor, while Anna looked past the minister to the statue of Christ, arms outstretched, calling the beholder to salvation. The minister paused, allowing Elliott and Anna to make their wedding vows, then pronounced them husband and wife. Elliott lifted Anna's veil, glanced at her face, and brushed her lips with his. They turned toward the sunshine pouring through the windows at the rear of the church and walked down the aisle.

Outside the air was crisp and clear. In the street the young couple and other guests climbed into fine carriages. Drivers urged horses forward, and soon the wedding procession rolled into the busy confluence of Broadway and Fifth Avenue. Flanked by elegant hotels, this was the most fashionable crossroads in New York. A tall white-gloved policeman from the elite "Broadway Squad" waved a rattan stick over the traffic, guiding the carriages through the favored crossing with a bandmaster's crisp precision. Signaled on, the coaches moved up Fifth Avenue, where New York society was made tangible in monuments of stone: A. T. Stewart's column-studded marble palace and the Astor mansions, their solid walls built on profits from western furs. Here stood New York's most fashionable clubs: the Calumet, the Knickerbocker, the Union, and the Manhattan. The wedding guests knew them well; these clubs, this avenue, were their private realm within the city.

The carriages rattled north past fine brownstone houses, side by side in orderly rows, and turned left on Thirty-Seventh Street to a house just off the avenue where Anna's family lived and where now Elliott and his bride would greet fashionable New York. It was cold outside in the late afternoon, but inside the air smelled of spring. Roses hung over chandeliers, door frames, and windows; palms and ferns decorated rooms. Lander's string orchestra, the favorite of society, filled the house with music. Men and women chatted about opera, the theater, and the social season. While they talked, a pink sun sank beyond New York harbor and the soft hills of New Jersey, and darkness fell over the city. At last Anna and Elliott embraced their mothers, said goodbye, and went out into the night.

Mrs. Hall was eager that Anna and Elliott make a good start in life, and so she sent her daughter away with a letter telling her how she and Elliott should behave on their first night as husband and wife. "Go to God," she said, "before retiring and in His presence read your Bible and kneel together and ask Him to guide you both through this world which has been so bright to you both, but which must have some clouds."

Did Anna and Elliott indeed fall down before God on that first night? Elliott hastened to reassure his mother-in-law: "We both knelt before the Giver of every good and perfect gift and thanked him . . . for his tender loving kindness to us." "Dear Lady," he continued, "do not fear about trusting your daughter to me. It shall be my great object all my life to comfort and care for her."

The sportsman and the socialite were serious about their marriage. They would try, with God's help, to be good partners.

Anna and Elliott took a brief honeymoon and settled into a brownstone house in mid-Manhattan. Theirs was one of many fine houses clustered around Fifth and Madison Avenues between Washington Square and Central Park. In these houses and in larger mansions built by business tycoons lived the elegant members of an increasingly select New York society. During the past half century businessmen had made astonishing fortunes in railroads, steamships, retailing, and banking, enabling them to enjoy the conspicuous display of wealth and to seek admission to the inner circles of New York society—a society that defined itself by those it excluded as well as by those it accepted. A few families with distinguished colonial lineages and substantial property clearly belonged. Others, like the descendants of the fur trader-capitalist John Jacob Astor and shipping magnate Cornelius Vanderbilt, eventually won places among the elect.

Anna and Elliott belonged. They were not as wealthy as the Astors or the Vanderbilts, but the blue blood of New York's "best" families flowed in their veins, and fifteen thousand dollars a year from inherited wealth poured into their bank accounts. These assets allowed them to enjoy life to the fullest: in the 1880s enjoying life in New York meant living in a fine house well staffed with servants, owning imported dresses for Anna and polo ponies for Elliott, and attending the fabulous Vanderbilt ball on December 11, 1883.

On that magical night a thousand guests alighted from carriages in front of the Vanderbilt mansion at Fifty-Second Street and Fifth Avenue. Inside the house they were surrounded by flowers. In the entryway stood immense twenty-five-foot towers of roses. Guests received hats filled with red roses and Indian baskets with carnations. They then passed into the main hall, where they saw garlands of tulips, jonquils, and lilies of the valley. Elliott and Anna, the newlyweds, spent the evening enjoying their opulent surroundings, strolling from room to room and eating food catered by Delmonico's. They viewed the magnificent library, its high ceiling embellished with cut glass, and they danced on a floor polished like ivory while Lander's orchestra played in a balcony above. A journalist observing the scene wrote, "The effect of the brilliant jewels and dresses, not to speak of the handsome faces, with the brilliant surroundings, was charming in the extreme."

Finally in the early morning the guests began to depart. Anna and Elliott said their farewells and returned to the private world of their marriage. Elliott enjoyed parties but may have felt uneasy that night. He did belong to the world of the Vanderbilts: after all, they had invited the young Roosevelts to their ball. But his own house was so unassuming, so humble, really, in comparison to the Vanderbilt mansion. Nor could Elliott buy Anna jewels to match those worn by the great ladies of society. Now that he was married Elliott fretted about his meager earnings. Anna urged him not to worry. "As for money and luxuries," she wrote him after one of his bouts of depression, "we cannot expect to live extravagantly when we start. Don't think of the future. Let it take care of itself, or better, trust to God. Let's live in the present and be happy and enjoy what we have."

Anna was right, of course, but Elliott did worry. His Anna deserved to live in luxury. He wanted her to.

The week of January 6, 1884, brought winter to New York. An ocean steamer came into port from the icy North Atlantic, her sides covered with a frozen waterfall of spray, her ice-coated rigging sparkling with rainbow colors. On the streets omnibus drivers shivered in the open air beneath blankets, overcoats, caps, and mittens. Newsboys poorly clad, some wearing carpets, sacking, or newspapers bundled around their waists for insulation, danced the sailor's hornpipe for warmth while waiting for the wagon with the five o'clock edition.

Anna and Elliott left no written record of their activities during the week of January 6, 1884. But the weather must have drawn them out to enjoy sleigh-riding on colder days and pressed them closer to the fire in the evenings. They had been married for six weeks and had begun to know one another as lovers. Anna may have been frightened by the strangeness of sex—Victorian women were not expected to enjoy love as unabashedly as their great-granddaughters of a century later. But physical contact must have extended the personal intimacy of previous months, and during the winter of 1884 they conceived their first child.

The days grew longer. Crocuses and sweet-smelling hyacinths pushed through the ground. On Bedloe's Island an army of Italian workmen raised blocks of stone onto a huge pedestal. For eight years there had been stories about a gigantic statue coming to New York from France. Curiosity had turned to skepticism, but now the platform made tangible the promise of a figure representing liberty soon to grace the harbor.

In June the muggy heat of summer enveloped New York. Anna and Elliott attended horse shows and polo matches, visited friends on the Hudson, and vacationed in Newport. In that favored place they sipped tea with the Vanderbilts and dined aboard the Morgan yacht. Anna's pregnancy was beginning to show, and during the summer she and Elliott began to feel the child's movements. As the days shortened and the time for Anna's delivery drew near, the young couple's anticipation was tainted with fear. Children were still delivered at home in the 1880s, and death in childbed was common. Only a few months before, Elliott's sister-in-law, Alice Roosevelt, had died after giving birth to a baby girl.

On October 11 Anna's frame was wracked with pain. Elliott must have waited apprehensively outside the room where his wife, attended by a physician or midwife, struggled with the delivery. Elliott may have heard frenzied movements and a baby's cry. Finally he was told: he was the father of a baby girl, and mother and child were doing well. Relieved, he was allowed to see his daughter, soon to be known as Eleanor. He called her "a miracle from heaven."

The infant Eleanor was probably turned over to a wet nurse, for children of the upper classes were usually not nursed by their own mothers. A few days later she was clothed in a long white christening dress and baptized. Elliott's brother, Teddy, was her godfather.

On the day when Eleanor Roosevelt was born the Civil War was only two decades past, Custer's defeat at the Little Big Horn had occurred only eight years before, and the last Indian Wars had yet to be fought. There were no automobiles and few telephones or electric lights, and New York was a city of five-story buildings lit by gas. A schooner coming into New York would have found a harbor full of sails. Fishing sloops darted across the bay; majestic iron ships under billowing canvas glided on the breezes; and flat side-wheeled ferry boats crowded with horses and carriages paddled back and forth between New York and New Jersey. Manhattan appeared as a wedge of land in the emerald waters of the bay. On the waterfront a latticework of timber, the spars of ships, framed row upon row of warehouses, stores, and office buildings. Flat façades of wood and brick rose to five stories above the water as far as the eye could see. No Empire State Building or other towers broke the horizon. The skyline belonged to church steeples and to the Brooklyn Bridge, completed a year before Eleanor's birth.

New York and America as a whole would change rapidly in the early years of Eleanor's life. During the 1880s and 1890s millions of immigrants came to the United States from southern and eastern Europe. Often poor, they crowded into places like New York's Lower East Side, where each acre of dingy tenements contained more than seven hundred people. They worked in sweatshops in the city or went west to labor in coal mines and steel mills. Other Americans, the former slaves, had been free for about twenty years. After a few years of enjoying the fruits of American citizenship, the blacks were now losing much of their freedom with the rise of "Jim Crow laws" barring them from the voting booth and segregating them in inferior schools. Eleanor Roosevelt's life would some day involve her in the broad currents of history and bring her into contact with immigrants and blacks. But she lived her childhood in the narrow world of the New York aristocracy. Her life was shaped by that world and by the peculiar tragedy of her own family.

The tragedy unfolded slowly; the aristocratic lifestyle was there from the start. Elliott continued to devote his attention to the gentlemanly sports of foxhunting and polo. On a typical hunt at the Meadowbrook Country Club thirty to forty brightly clothed riders would set forth on the trail of the fox, cantering over farmland and jumping hedges and fences. As horses fell or faltered at the jumps, the ranks of the hunters thinned, but Elliott was almost always there to the end. The pleasure of chasing a red fox across Long Island's countryside was exceeded in Elliott's imagination only by the joy of chasing a small white ball across a polo field. In the elite company of Meadowbrook polo players Elliott was competitive, making up in hard riding what he lacked in finesse.

Toward the end of the year the polo ponies were stabled for the winter at Meadowbrook. Then another, more feminine element of society came into play. The world of sport on horseback was primarily a man's world. In the fall, however, the social "season" began, consisting of dinner parties, dances, theater, and the opera. Men were the essential partners in these activities, but women were in command. During the 1880s New York society was dominated by Mrs. William Astor. She determined who belonged in society and planned many of the most elegant social events.

Anna and Elliott could not afford to entertain on the scale of the Astors, but their personal charm and aristocratic lineage compensated for their modest fortune. In their early years as husband and wife they were among the most popular young couples in New York. They counted the Astors and Vanderbilts among their friends and played a role themselves as leaders in the young social set known as the "swells." Anna quickly established herself as one of society's most popular ladies. Her "presence was a blessing," a friend declared. "She never entered a room as others did—she seemed almost to float forward, with upraised hand and cordial greeting." Her smile was described as "the sweetest play of light upon the features, . . . an expression of sweetness and of sympathy sometimes so intense that one knew it was never to be forgotten." In 1887 a national news magazine assigned a reporter to interview New Yorkers and discover the most popular and influential society women. Anna was the subject of one of their sketches, "A leader in the exclusive circles she adorns."

The young Roosevelts had friends, social prestige, a modest fortune, and a romantic attachment that grew stronger each year. Elliott had never hesitated to express his passionate fondness for Anna; with marriage she grew more openly loving. Missing Elliott during a visit to her family at Tivoli, she wrote him, "I am crazy to hear from you and wish you were here. We could have such nice times going around together."

Elliott and Anna did have "nice times" together. Sailing, riding, dancing, lying in one another's arms. Their warmth extended naturally to their daughter. Eleanor learned to crawl, to walk, and to talk. She became a little girl with light brown hair cut straight across her forehead and rolling in long waves to her shoulders. Her large blue eyes were quizzical and alert. Elliott began to call her "Little Nell," a nickname taken from the heroine of Charles Dickens's *Old Curiosity Shop* but also Elliott's own childhood nickname.

In the fashion of the times they often left Eleanor with relatives when they went visiting and with servants during their days at home; in fact Eleanor's first language was French, which she learned from her nurse. But they also shared many tender moments with their daughter. During a winter evening snowflakes would fall over the city, dancing like moths before the gaslights, clinging to window ledges and cornices, and laying a soft quilt over the cobblestone streets. Eleanor, three or four years old, might peek out of her bedroom window at the quiet, swirling flakes and return thrilled to the delicious coziness of blankets. In the morning the streets seemed immense in their whiteness, and Elliott would fairly dance with excitement, eager to finish breakfast and go outside.

Bundled in long coats, scarves, and gloves the family would set out in their sleigh for Fifth Avenue; Eleanor, nestled between her parents, looked over the horse's rump at an enchanted world. On Fifth Avenue Elliott would coax his horse into a fast trot and join the sleighs speeding along in stately haste. On such mornings the air danced with the music of hundreds of harness bells, and horsemen sought good-naturedly to outpace one another. The sleighs swished north into Central Park, where the road curved through white hillsides and trees heavy with snow. On crisp, clear days when the sun shone brightly through a pale blue sky, Elliott might take the family round the snowy course two or three times. Then he would drive home, and a chilly Eleanor would stamp snow from her boots, brush her coat, and rush to the sitting-room fire.

Eleanor was confident of her parents' love. Mornings she came to her father's dressing room and chattered to him and danced in circles. Then he complained that she made him dizzy and tossed her high in the air. She called herself "father's little golden hair." As Elliott tucked her into bed on the night of her fourth birthday, she told him, "I love everybody, and everybody loves me." Such a cunning, funny little tot, Elliott thought.

On October 1, 1889, when Eleanor was nearly five, Anna gave birth to a second child, Elliott Jr., who was nicknamed Ellie. Eleanor learned about her new brother while visiting her grandmother at Tivoli. Undeterred by this possible rival, she dictated a letter to her father. What did her brother look like, she asked. Some people said a bunny, others an elephant. She hoped he did not cry, but if he did, she advised, Elliott should have the nurse "give him a tap, tap." She closed, "I love you very much and mother and brother too if he has blue eyes."

"If he has blue eyes . . ." With supreme self-confidence the child Eleanor came to terms with her world. But her perceptiveness enabled her to discern a flaw in that world. Despite all his success as a sportsman, Elliott Roosevelt was a deeply disturbed young man. Eleanor unwittingly hinted at her father's weakness when she told her Aunt Pussie, Anna's sister, "You would be unhappy if you were a man, because your wife would send you down to town every day." A woman sent a man to work: how many times had Eleanor seen her mother chastise Elliott because he did not apply himself? Eleanor even acquired the habit herself. In his dressing room she cheerfully scolded her father in the mornings, telling him he would be late for breakfast. When she was five Eleanor was shown in a painting with a finger pointing accusingly. Elliott called the picture "Eleanor Scolding Daddy."

Elliott should have enjoyed life: What greater pleasure could he imagine than hunting and playing polo and being with Anna? But he was dissatisfied. The nature of his malady was elusive. He may have suffered from an obscure "Indian fever" contracted in the Orient or from mild epilepsy or a brain tumor, but his difficulty was probably more psychological than physiological. He was simply unable to live up to a standard of achievement inculcated by his family, his friends, his society. "I must try to get wealth for my little wife's sake," he told Anna. But he was strangely uncomfortable with the business world. He declared, "How I covet, yet how I hate" the almighty dollar.

Victorian culture set clearly defined roles for men and women. Men were expected to be dynamic, aggressive, independent. In Charles Darwin's *Origin of Species* they found evidence that men were belligerent, passionate, selfish, competitive. From Herbert Spencer they learned that man's competitive instinct ultimately benefited society as a whole. Andrew Carnegie was a good example. He was tough, even unscrupulous. He paid his workers a pittance, spread rumors about his rivals' goods, and amassed a fortune of four hundred million dollars. One of his foremen said Andrew was "born with two sets of teeth and holes drilled for more." Was he then a social pariah? Hardly, for while pursuing his own self-interest, Carnegie created a huge steel company, and the nation needed steel.

The Victorian ethic demanded much of men in the marketplace, but it did not stop there. Effectiveness in the business world demanded, in turn, that a man be in control of himself. His very psyche must be honed to a competitive edge. The passions, mercurial and untrustworthy, were the greatest enemy. In an age of scientific management the mind itself must be carefully managed. The classic statement of this position was John Harvey Kellogg's *Man, the Masterpiece,* published in 1886. Kellogg argued that men should not only avoid sexual excesses but should even attempt to eliminate erotic dreams.

Women too had rigorously defined roles in Victorian America. Even as men were being encouraged to be ambitious and competitive, more genteel values were inculcated into women, and "American culture," according to one historian, "seemed bent upon establishing a perpetual

Mother's Day." Women were associated with the home, which reflected different values than those of the business world. Nineteenth-century literature set forth norms for the way a "true woman" should behave. The true woman must be pious: "a woman never looks lovelier," a contemporary tract declared, "than in her reverence for religion." She must also be pure. Man was impulsive and sometimes could not help sinning, but a woman was endowed with greater reserve—some doctors even claimed that woman had no sexual passions. And, of course, a woman must be domestic. In the home she provided a cultivated atmosphere to nourish her children and relax her husband. A popular guide for young brides described home as "this sanctuary" and the wife as a "priestess at its altar." Finally, a woman must be submissive, subjecting herself to her husband.

Men and women were thus bound together in a carefully defined partnership. These ideas circulated widely in newspapers, magazines, sermons, and private letters. Elliott's Aunt Anna Bulloch, for example, expressed the Victorian ideal in femininity and marriage when she wrote Elliott before his wedding, calling Anna "a pure and holy woman" who would "keep and strengthen" him in all his activities. She told Elliott that now that he had found Anna, he should "always be tender to her and regard her as something holy." Men and women were different but complementary. Aunt Anna imagined the young couple as a perfect pair: "It is a most restful sweet harmonious little picture I hold of her womanliness giving your busy active life its even balance and filling in all the chords of fullest meaning—the calm and peace and love and tenderness and the quiet womanly strength upon which the strongest men love to lean."

Husband and wife, each with a role to perform in the ideal Victorian family: Anna suited the picture well. Her spirituality was so refined that she had sublimated her encounter with Elliott on their last night at Tivoli into a religious experience. Her friends' statements about her sound like descriptions of a Victorian saint: "She ever strove to be faithful to God"; she was "the light of her home"; "her virtues were most truly womanly in being little known by the outside world"; she "grew into lovely and noble womanhood."

Anna fit the mold of Victorian respectability, but Elliott did not. He simply could not apply himself to his work. His problem was not uncommon in Victorian America. Ministers, journalists, and politicians might praise a spirit of "rugged individualism," but many men lacked the willpower to play the aggressive "manly" role. This difficulty was so widespread that in 1880 a New York neurologist, George Miller Beard, invented a new disease that he called "neurasthenia." Its symptoms included insomnia, fear of responsibility, desire for stimulants and narcotics, morbid self-consciousness, and above all paralysis of the will. Miller attributed the disease to the peculiar tensions of industrial culture, especially to "constant inhibition, restraining normal feelings, keeping back, covering, holding in check atomic forces of the mind and body."

Elliott showed many of the symptoms of "neurasthenia." His inability to succeed may have reflected a personality that simply was not made for the business world; he may have had to restrain too many "normal feelings." His greatest successes lay in personal relations. He was loved for his spontaneous goodwill and kindness. He liked flowers and enjoyed giving them to friends. His sister, Corinne, credited him with "a devotion which was so tender that it was more like that of a woman."

Elliott's difficulties were compounded by his relationship with his father and his brother. Elliott had adored his father, calling him "just my ideal." But in the winter of 1878 he saw Theodore Roosevelt reduced to a pathetic shadow of himself by a cancerous stomach tumor. On Theodore's last day of life, he was almost incoherent in his agony. His face pathetic with fear, he clasped Elliott hard each time the pain seized him, as if trying to press his life into his son. Late that night he died. A few days later Elliott wrote a description of his father's last hours. "Oh my God, my father," he wrote, "what agonies you suffered."

God and father: the two persons could easily merge in Elliott's mind. Theodore Roosevelt had been a kind of patron saint of the whole city, pouring himself into his charities. On Sunday mornings he taught Sunday school for Italian children, and on Sunday evenings he went to the Newsboys' Lodging House to instruct the boys in religion. Years before, in a moment of inspired playfulness, Theodore's sister-in-law had dubbed him "Greatheart." The chivalric title was so appropriate that it became Theodore's nickname. As he lay dying, newsboys and other children gathered on the front stoop of his house waiting for reports of the man who "meant more to them than any other human being." The newspapers showered the deceased patriarch with praise, and two thousand people attended his funeral.

Long after his death Theodore Roosevelt's children wrestled with the legacy of their larger-than-life father. In his shadow they were compelled to demand much of themselves. His eldest son and namesake, Teddy, was afflicted with asthma and a weak body. So "Greatheart" turned the upper floor of his house into a gymnasium, and slowly Teddy built his body to a weightlifter's proportions. Years later this son's fame would eclipse the father's, and Teddy Roosevelt would be President of the United States. Throughout his life, however, Teddy held his father in awe. He claimed he never made a presidential decision without considering first what his father would have done, and in his final years Teddy Roosevelt regretted that he had not been more worthy of his father, who was, he said, the only man he was "ever afraid of."

Teddy Roosevelt was one of the most dynamic men of his time and was much tougher than his brother in facing life's challenges. Elliott played with the idea of writing a book based on his world tour but never did. Teddy completed an exhaustive naval history of the War of 1812. When Elliott started out in business, Teddy, only sixteen months his senior, was already serving his first term in the New York Assembly. Elliott admitted that he "lacked that foolish grit of Theodore's." Teddy Roosevelt tried to live up to his father; Elliott, less fortunate, lived in the shadow of both his father and his brother.

During his early years of marriage the flaws in Elliott's character could be overlooked. He drank too much, played too much, and worked too little, but he lived a comfortable life. In 1888 he and Anna built a house in Hempstead near the Meadowbrook Country Club on ten acres of land. There they could entertain friends on their own country estate. Eleanor, then four, loved the new house, enjoyed watching it built, and called it her own. She could play with cats, dogs, and chickens on the estate, and she had her own kitten, an angora—which she called an "angostura." The house was a retreat from the city, decorated with trophies from Elliott's hunting expeditions; one room was lined with Japanese panels. Anna and Elliott called the house "Half-Way Nirvana."

Despite Elliott's weaknesses, the Roosevelts might have lived out their years happily in Hempstead and New York. Elliott might have learned to work just hard enough to satisfy his conscience and make peace with himself. But in the spring of 1889 an accident altered forever the delicate balance of his personality. While practicing for an amateur circus sponsored by a friend, he attempted a double somersault and fell hard on his ankle. The ankle was broken, but the doctor assumed it was only strained, and so Elliott went without proper attention for several weeks. Finally he saw a second doctor who declared that the first "ought to be hung" and told Elliott he was "on his way to getting a fine club foot."

Eleanor was not yet five when her father's ankle was rebroken and set, but the memory of his suffering during the summer of 1889 remained with her for the rest of her life. In the past she had cried many times in front of her parents after banging her shin on a table or falling on icy pavement. She cried and sought comfort in her parents' arms: that was only natural. Now, however, the natural order was reversed, and night after night her father's pathetic cries echoed through the house. For days on end he lay in bed, unable to eat. Eleanor must have been puzzled and distraught: How could a small child comfort a parent?

Elliott spent much of the summer in bed and found solace in medicines more poisonous than the hurt ankle: morphine and laudanum. These drugs, prescribed freely in Victorian America, carried Elliott into a pleasant oblivion where neither the pain of the ankle nor the mortification of his personal failures could touch him. During the summer and fall of 1889 his ankle slowly healed, but his drug dependence increased. Anna begged him to give up narcotics. He refused, and in December he abruptly left the family and went south, ostensibly to seek a rest cure.

Anna, left at home with Eleanor and baby Ellie, was disconsolate. She hoped Elliott would return one afternoon shortly after Christmas, and when he did not she went to her room, lay on the bed, and sobbed. In the evening she wrote Elliott, beseeching him to come home and be well. Sentence by sentence she drew a picture of a bereaved household. She and Eleanor had opened Christmas presents alone. She had gone by herself to a holiday party but was so "wretched" she came home after a few minutes. Whenever the postman came Eleanor rushed down the stairs, hoping for word of her father. Anna told Elliott, "I do nothing but think of you and pray you will come back. . . . I am so *terribly* lonely without you." "Dearest," she wrote, "Throw your horrid cocktails away and don't touch anything hard. . . . Remember that your little wife and children love you so tenderly and will try to help you in every possible way they can to conquer in the hard hard fight." The "hard fight"—self-discipline was what Elliott needed. "Nell," she said, "it must be an entire conquest, a partial one is *no good.*"

There, she had done her wifely duty; she had preached the doctrine of self-control. But she could not end on such an austere note; she was a wife, not a schoolmistress, and she needed him. "Don't leave us again," she implored. "We can't do without you."

Elliott did come home to New York that winter, but he was not cured. He continued to drink heavily and had difficulty settling down to work and to Anna. She tried to help him, but in her arms he must have felt reproach. She was his heaven, the angel of his house, his pure Anna. How could he, a sinner, make love to an angel? Elliott wanted sex, plain and simple, without restraint or reproach, and so he sought the embraces of one of the servants, Katy Mann. Impressed by his charm or his power, she accepted his advances. With Katy he must have felt bitterly divided, craving her flesh but lamenting his betrayal of Anna—more hopelessly lost than ever.

# 2

# The Legacy

*The Christian life and spirit of the parents, which are in and by
the Spirit of God, shall flow into the mind of the child.*

Horace Bushnell, *Christian Nurture*

By the summer of 1890 Elliott was desperate. His face
was bloated with drink, and his eyes were haunted with
inner torment. He was so distracted that at times he had
difficulty connecting words into sentences. Seeing no
chance for recovery in New York, he fled once more, seeking solace in travel. Anna, Eleanor, and Ellie came this
time, and for a full year they wandered through Germany,
Italy, and France.

Fall found them in Venice, where Elliott was momen-
tarily caught up in the beauty of that most beautiful of
cities. He and Anna took the children on the canals, where
white buildings and statues reflected in the water. They
went to Saint Mark's and stood beneath its soaring domes
and pinnacles while little Ellie, barely able to walk but
growing "stronger and fatter and rosier every day," fed
the pigeons that strutted in hordes over the broad plaza.

Elliott went with Eleanor on a boat to the Lido, the
long spit of land protecting Venice from the sea. Father
and daughter walked along the shore, where waves green
and blue beat upon the sands. Eleanor watched tiny crabs

scurrying across the beach and hiding in holes. "Little funny crabs," she called them. She reached down and caught one, then another. Eleanor loved being with her father, loved his voice, loved the way he treated her. He had even played boatman for her, poling a gondola on the Venetian canals and singing lustily with the other gondoliers while she looked up at him with "intense joy." She did not know him as an adulterer, a drunkard, a problem. He was simply her father.

A few weeks later the family moved south to Sorrento, a small village set among chestnut trees and perched on a cliff above the Bay of Naples. Their rooms in an inn looked over the bay, and from the piazza they could see in the distance the terraced city of Naples rising tier upon tier from the sea. A few miles inland Mount Vesuvius stood high above the rolling plain, sometimes crystal clear, sometimes capped in billowing clouds of volcanic smoke.

Elliott had not touched liquor for weeks, and yet he was still disturbed, still fragile. He spent much of each day alone in restless introspection. In the afternoons he took a small sailboat out into the bay and drifted by the hour, sometimes napping, sometimes watching the fishing boats, the blue waters, the enfolding shores. At night he usually slept a few hours, then awoke and went out alone onto the piazza. In the darkness the bay was outlined with village lights, sentinels of other lives, tokens of the sorrow and mystery of life.

As he lay beneath the autumn sky in his sailboat or paced back and forth beneath the stars on the piazza, Elliott fought his own desperation. Here he was an exile, afraid to return home. In his confusion he had even struck out at his daughter, punishing her when she seemed to lack "grit." They had been riding donkeys on the country roads outside Sorrento; Elliot slid his donkey down a steep bank and beckoned Eleanor to follow. She was eager to please, but only six years old, she was frightened by the drop and refused to plunge down after him. He shouted at her and rode off alone, leaving Eleanor to find her way home with her nurse.

Deeply confused, Elliott was acutely sensitive to criticism. One day a letter arrived from one of his aunts, encouraging him to overcome his problems. Anna thought it was a "sweet" note, but Elliott cried, then flew into a rage and said he would never go home. The next morning he had to get away from the inn and woke Anna to tell her he was taking Eleanor and her nurse to ride up Mount Vesuvius.

Late that afternoon Elliott had not returned, and Anna, full of worry, poured out her feelings in a letter to Elliott's sister. Anna declared that she was "nearly dead" from watching over Elliott day and night. He seemed well, but she was "dreadfully worried" that he would begin drinking again. When he went sailing in the afternoons, Anna saw him off at the dock and then watched him from the piazza until he returned. "I know he could stand no temptation," she wrote.

While Anna was fretting in Sorrento, Elliott and Eleanor had ridden the twenty miles up to the summit of Vesuvius. They threw pennies into the bubbling lava and were given them back encased in stone. This had been fun for Eleanor. But then began an endless ride back. The little girl, bone tired, was hard pressed to "bear it without tears." Long after dark Elliott and Eleanor arrived at the inn. Anna was relieved at this temporary respite in her ordeal: this time Elliott had come home safely.

Six months later Anna and Elliott were in Paris, awaiting the birth of their third child. Elliott wrote Anna's mother enthusiastic accounts of the "deliciously beautiful" Paris spring and assured her, "I will take care of your sweet daughter." In June he wrote, announcing the birth of a child named Hall. "The little boy is the biggest thing you ever saw," he said, "and he kissed me like a little bird the first hour of his life."

Although Elliott tried to convey an impression of domestic peace, his life with Anna was becoming less and less tenable. During the summer of 1891 he resumed drinking, stayed away from home for days at a time, and began an affair with an American woman living in Paris. For several months Elliott's brother Teddy, now a member of the United States Civil Service Commission, had been urging Anna to leave him. Elliott's servant-girlfriend, Katy Mann, had contacted Teddy, claiming that she was pregnant by Elliott and demanding ten thousand dollars for her silence. Elliott denied the accusation, and Teddy tried to call Katy's bluff.

The girl stuck to her story, however, claiming she could produce a locket and love letters Elliott had given her. Other servants, she said, would testify to having heard Elliott's voice in her room. Within a few weeks of Anna's delivery in Paris, Katy Mann gave birth to a baby boy. Teddy secretly visited the child and was dismayed to see in Katy's arms a child with distinctly Rooseveltian features— an unwanted nephew.

Teddy probably arranged a payment for Katy; he then turned his attention to Elliott and Anna. He and his brother had been close friends and hunting companions as young men, but Teddy would not excuse what he called Elliott's "hideous depravity," and he decided to rescue Anna and the children from his brother's influence. He persuaded a reluctant Anna to leave Elliott and return to New York with the children. While they were separated, Elliott would have to live alone for "two or three years of straight life" in order to prove that he was worthy of being received back into the family.

Elliott's probation would be served in the hills and mountains of southwestern Virginia, where his brother-in-law, Douglas Robinson, owned a vast estate. Robinson operated several coal mines, but most of the land was wilderness: tens of thousands of acres of forests, laurel thickets, wildflowers, and cool mountain streams. Robinson intended to develop these lands and decided to take a chance on Elliott as his supervisor. Elliott's center of operations would be Abingdon, Virginia, a county seat with fifteen hundred residents on the edge of Robinson's holdings.

Abingdon's people were at first wary of Elliott Roosevelt. Mainly plain folk—small merchants, farmers, and craftsmen—they expected this aristocrat from the big city to look down on them. But Elliott's flaws did not include condescension. He took an apartment above a store in Abingdon and quickly won the people's affection with his warm personality. Buoyed up by his initial success in making friends and determined to prove himself to Anna, he threw himself into his work. In the delicate affair of negotiating with squatters on the Robinson lands and with workers in the coal mines he was an able diplomat. He also joined with local businessmen to set up a bank in Abingdon. Within six months he was more solidly established in his work in Virginia than he had ever been in New York. In November 1892 he could write Anna's mother, telling her, "If you put yourself in communication with those who have been my daily associates for the past ten months, I think you would only hear good of me." He claimed he had shown the "very powers of self-control and purpose" Anna wished him to have.

Elliott longed to hear Anna confirm this view, but she and Teddy insisted that his period of repentance and hard work must last more than a few months. He was not even allowed to visit Anna. This continued rejection was hard for Elliott, a man who loved the company of a family. At times his homesickness nearly overwhelmed him, but instead of giving in to despair, he did a remarkable thing: he treated the whole people of Abingdon as a kind of adopted family.

Elliott hid his sorrows from the people of Abingdon, riding through town in a two-seated yellow carriage pulled by two fast-stepping trotters. He entertained the townspeople with his horsemanship, riding across a railroad trestle before a cheering crowd. Missing his family, he surrounded himself with local life. His companions at home were an assortment of dogs, including a host of fox terriers and a puppy named "Little Nell Dog" after Eleanor. Elliott knew every child in Abingdon; they flocked to his rooms when he had new puppies and sang for him when he was sick. On morning rides through the countryside he took along his fox terriers and half a dozen youngsters. "We rarely fail to secure some kind of game," he told Eleanor, "and never return without roses in the cheeks of all those I call now, my children." The youngsters were devoted to Elliott. He came back from a trip to New York and was surprised to find Miriam Trigg, a girl Eleanor's age, waiting for him at the station with his terriers. How had she known which train to meet, he asked. It was easy, she told him; she had simply met every train into Abingdon for the past two days.

The adults of Abingdon could hardly object to their children's devotion to Elliott, for they too were captivated by him. He drank apple cider at their firesides, read them his favorite poems, and invited them to his rooms to sing songs around the piano. In winter, when snow lay deep on the hillsides around Abingdon, Elliott organized sledding parties for the whole town. He joined the local Episcopal church, sang in its choir, and was soon made a member of its vestry. Like his father, "Greatheart," Elliott became known for his charities. He distributed old clothes and Christmas turkeys to the poor and persuaded his brother-in-law to support missions in the coal-mining camps on his lands. One of Elliott's many admirers was so taken by him that in 1900 she urged her friends to vote for the Republican ticket simply because Teddy Roosevelt, the vice-presidential candidate, was Elliott's brother.

Elliott Roosevelt was probably never more respected and loved than during his stay in Abingdon. But he was privately tormented by the absence of his wife and children. Surely he had shown himself worthy to be forgiven. If only he might return some day to his apartment and find Anna waiting for him, her beautiful face glowing with love and understanding, her arms ready to enclose him in an embrace of reconciliation.

She did not come to him, however, and she would not receive him in New York. He had triumphed over his weaknesses, but he was condemned to prove himself month after month as if he were still the drunkard Anna had left in Paris. Would he ever be forgiven?

While Elliott struggled in Virginia, Anna faced her own ordeal in New York. She had not wanted to give up Elliott, but once she and her husband were separated, Anna became more conscious of having been wronged. She was now a woman alone in a society where almost all her peers were married. How should she behave? Could she give dinner parties without Elliott? Should she accept invitations to go driving with men? She had once been a social leader; now she was a social anomaly. She felt "desperately lonely and wildly furious" at the circumstances that robbed her of the fun of youth.

In 1892 while Elliott was seeking to redeem himself in the South, Anna sought to rebuild her own life in New York. A friend who visited Anna one chilly October afternoon in her new home on Sixty-First Street described a peculiarly feminine household, a place where a woman's purity and grace were secure from a man's abrasive presence. Anna had seemingly resolved the contradiction between man and woman by banishing man.

Anna was seated by the tea table in a cozy upstairs room. The sun had just set, and the curtains were drawn. A wood fire burned brightly on the hearth, the gas lamps were lighted, and the silver teakettle steamed. Anna wore a pink silk wrapper with white lace at the throat and wrists; she was pale from a recent illness, and to her friend her large blue eyes seemed "tender, even pathetic." The two women sat in armchairs near the fire with the tea table between them. "A sense of rest, of womanly refinement, of sympathetic intelligence, pervaded the room," the guest later recalled, "and the heart-to-heart talk that followed."

They had met to discuss a course of studies for the winter. Anna was determined to improve her knowledge, especially in natural sciences, so that she could help Eleanor, now almost eight, in her own studies. "Why, we must know about the moon, and all the recent discoveries in the planets!" Anna exclaimed. "I *must* know all this for my children's sake at least." A lecture on the moon was scheduled at Carnegie Hall for the next week; the two women would be there.

Anna wanted Eleanor and her brothers to know astronomy, but even more she wanted them to know religion. Every morning the children, even baby Hall, came into Anna's room for prayers before breakfast. Their father had lacked the moral fiber to stay on the path of righteousness; Anna hoped through religious training she could fortify her children against temptation. She told her friend that a love for Sunday and for the church could not be "awakened" too early. Looking across the tea table she said earnestly, "Is there anything else in life that can so anchor them to the right?"

While Anna and her friend were talking, the children ran in for a visit with their mother. Anna kissed her three-year-old, Ellie, and placed young Hall, now a year and a half old, in her lap; she brought a footstool for Eleanor and gave each child a biscuit. This was the hour that she wanted the children to remember as "mother's hour," and normally she would have read to them or gotten down on the floor to play horse or tag. Tonight, however, she was tired and did not want to interrupt her discussion with her friend. And so after a while she sent Ellie and Hall off to bed, allowing Eleanor to sit and listen.

Eleanor sat on the stool near the warm fire, listening to the adults. Her mother had needed her help in recent months: she often had headaches and called Eleanor to rub her head. Eleanor liked to feel useful, and sometimes her mother even let her sleep with her. Eleanor listened as Anna and her friend began to talk about French history, a subject the child had just begun to study. The women began a playful competition to remember key events, such as the time of Charlemagne's accession. When in doubt Anna "would spring lightly up" and pull down a volume from the bookcase to check the facts.

The visitor remembered Anna that evening as "sweet and loving and playful." As she left, she turned to see Anna at the top of the stairs, framed in the soft light of the sitting room. Eleanor stood shyly behind her mother in the door-way. "It was a home picture," the friend recalled, "with an earnest, sweet mother, rarely to be equalled, never to be excelled." Before she left, she had given Anna a copy of Horace Bushnell's *Christian Nurture,* a highly respected book on education, to give her ideas on child rearing. Anna was moved to tears. That night she lay in bed reading for a long time—she often read in bed now that Elliott was gone.

Bushnell's words fortified Anna in her belief that she could direct her children to a virtuous life. He argued that a child begins life as "a mere passive lump in the arms." It grows in response to the life around it: "A smile wakens a smile, . . . irritation irritates, a frown withers, love expands a look congenial to itself, and why not holy love?" Holy love: Anna's love of God had been awakened early in her childhood by her own parents, and she hoped to pass on that same Christian spirit to her children. Bushnell assured her that "the Christian life and spirit of the parents, which are in and by the Spirit of God, shall flow into the mind of the child."

When Elliott had lived with her, the children had received other impressions than the Christian spirit advocated by Bushnell. They had seen their father's drunkenness, rage, and depression. Anna now read in *Christian Nurture*: "The wickedness of the parents propagates itself in the character and condition of their children." In the Victorian household the woman must uphold virtue and purity, even if the man failed to set a proper example. Anna had eliminated Elliott's bad influence by exiling him. It had hurt her, but as she read *Christian Nurture* late into the night, she believed that her suffering and Elliott's would be justified if she could raise the children to respect "the right." Before going to sleep she wrote her friend a note thanking her for lending "that blessed book." Anna told her, "It has helped me to better resolutions, which only God will know how I keep."

Anna would do her best to raise her children, but she remained deeply disturbed by her situation. She refused to see Elliott, but she still missed him. And yet she could not call him back because he had wronged her and the children. In November she went into a hospital for an operation. While she was under ether she said things she had never revealed before: Elliott had made her utterly miserable . . . she had nothing to live for . . . she wanted to die.

Following her operation Anna contracted diphtheria. Elliott received vague reports from Anna's mother about her condition and wanted all the more to be with her. He felt "a great yearning," he told Anna's mother, "to be where I could *show* my love and help my beloved." He suspected that Mary Hall was hiding Anna's true condition. "If anything happens to Anna, and I was not with her," he warned her, "it will be a *lifelong sorrow* to any of us who remain."

Elliott fervently believed that his married life need not end in sorrow. During her illness Anna had dictated a note to him that closed, "Affectionately and suffering." These simple words told him that Anna needed him. She was lying in bed, probably pale and thin, only a few hundred miles away. If only he could be at her side. Elliott wrote letters to Mary urging her to support a reunion. He told her, "My nature is really starved for love, Mother." She must believe that he was "honestly worthy" of Anna's "trust and love."

Early in December Elliott received good news from New York: Anna was improving. He was so confident of his position in Abingdon that he wrote Mary, suggesting that Anna and the children should join him there. "I believe that Anna and I understand each other," he wrote, "better than we have ever done since the beginning of this awful episode." The past was now an "episode"—not an unalterable condition. "Anna understands and knows me now," he told his mother-in-law, and "I believe I also do know her. I *love her* more than I ever did in my life."

Elliott continued his work in Abingdon, sang in the church choir, and visited friends. Thanksgiving had passed, and Christmas was only a few weeks away. Perhaps he would soon be reunited with his family. After months of lonely exile, how proud he would be to show off his children in Abingdon; how wonderful it would be to fall asleep once more beside his wife. Elliott thus dreamed of holding Anna in his arms. But on December 7 his hopes came abruptly to an end. He received a brief, inexorable message from New York: Anna was dead.

Eleanor had been sent to stay with her godmother during Anna's illness. She was curiously unaffected by the news of her mother's death. Once her world had been whole: she had loved everyone and everyone had loved her. But then her father had gone off to live in Virginia, and Eleanor had begun to feel a strange barrier between her mother and herself. Anna had tried to be nice to her daughter, letting her read and recite poetry and stay up after the boys went to bed, but Eleanor felt like an outsider. She would watch tiny Hall sitting on her mother's lap while little Ellie played on the floor; sometimes she stood in the doorway with her fingers in her mouth, looking at the three of them, until her mother said to her, "Come in, Granny." Her mother called her that because she was so serious. The name made her feel even more ill at ease.

After her mother's death Eleanor and the boys went to live with their Grandmother Hall on Thirty-Seventh Street. Elliott wanted the children with him in Virginia, but in her will Anna requested that they be raised by Mary Hall, and none of their relatives would encourage Elliott to assume custody. He returned alone to Abingdon after the funeral, but Mary, moved by compassion, invited him to spend Christmas with the children.

The house on Thirty-Seventh Street, which had been filled with roses and lilies nine years before for Anna and Elliott's wedding, now held a beautifully decorated Christmas tree illuminated by candles. In the late afternoon on the day before Christmas Eleanor and her father, along with her brothers, aunts, uncles, and grandmother, sat down to their dinner of roast turkey. In the evening they sang carols. Anna's sister Pussie played the piano while Elliott led the singing with his good strong voice. Eleanor particularly remembered:

> Silent night, holy night,
> All is calm, all is bright. . . .

That night two stockings hung at the foot of Eleanor's bed, one from Grandmother Hall and one from her father. The next morning she found grandmother's stocking full of "utilitarian gifts"—a toothbrush, soap, a washcloth, pencils, and a pencil sharpener. In the other stocking her father had "put in little things a girl could wear—a pair of white gloves, a pretty handkerchief, several hair ribbons, and a little gold pin." Beneath the Christmas tree was another present, a fox terrier puppy bred by her father in Virginia. He gave it, she believed, "because he knew I would love to have something to care for and call my own." She, in turn, had made her father a handkerchief case and a tobacco pouch.

After breakfast the servants came into the living room and received their presents. Then the family went to a Christmas service at Calvary Church, where Elliott and Anna had been married. Eleanor nestled beside her father, and he held his prayer book so that she could read it with him. Anna had stood with Elliott long ago at the front of this church; now she was gone, but their daughter was with him.

Elliott would soon leave again for Virginia. He could not take Eleanor with him, but he painted a picture for her of a brighter future. In the library at Mary's house he told Eleanor that someday they would live together again. In the meantime she must be a good girl, write him often, and "grow up into a woman he could be proud of."

Eleanor had always loved her father, but never more than now. All dressed in black, sad and yet encouraging, he was wonderfully confiding. "There started that day," she later wrote, "a feeling which never left me, that he and I were very close and someday would have a life of our own together."

Elliott returned to Abingdon in January 1893 and resumed work for Douglas Robinson. Anna's death increased his burden of remorse, but Elliott could still look forward to further business successes and the chance to regain his children. As he worked, however, the prizes he sought were taken from him. In December he had lost Anna. In May Ellie and Hall came down with scarlet fever. Hall recovered, but the three-year-old Ellie was gravely ill. When the doctor told Elliott that his feverish child would probably not survive, he wrote Eleanor, who had been sent off to avoid contagion, telling her Ellie "may go to join dear Mother in Heaven." The danger to the boys increased his affection for Eleanor. "Dear little daughter," he told her, "you are father's love and joy."

Eleanor had been well coached in accepting death as God's will. She wrote her father, "We must remember Ellie is going to be safe in heaven and to be with mother. She is waiting there, and our Lord wants Ellie boy with him now." A few days later the child was dead. His tiny body was buried at Tivoli next to Anna's. Elliott wrote Eleanor telling her Ellie was "happy in Heaven" with his mother. She would have to be a "doubly" good daughter and sister now. "I know you will my own little heart," he wrote. Then sorrow welled up in him. "I cannot write more," he said, "because I am not feeling very well and my heart is too full."

Elliott resumed his work in Virginia, but now came another crisis. He had built a stable economic base in Abingdon through private investments and managing Douglas Robinson's interests. These enterprises had allowed him to experience, for the first time in his life, a sense of vocational self-worth. But in 1893 his and many other American fortunes were reversed by a financial panic and the beginnings of one of the country's worst depressions. The bank that Elliott helped establish went under, and the Robinson mines had to fire seventy-five percent of their workers. Elliott was distraught at both his own and the miners' difficulties. In August he wrote Eleanor, "I have had a very trying time of it down here and am now trying to quiet the poor miners in the coal field who will listen to no one but me, and who are absolutely, for lack of employment, *starving*." A month later he told Mary, "I have lost heavily, dear lady, and am in great distress and sorrow, for I was doing so well."

Only recently Elliott had believed his Virginia exile might end in personal triumph and reunion with his family. But even as he sought to conquer his own weaknesses, the world had shifted beneath his feet. He could not bring Anna or Ellie back, nor could he change the economic conditions that damaged his businesses. Fifteen years before, when Elliott's father had fallen to cancer, he had embraced Elliott, as if to pass his life on to his son. Now Elliott, beset with problems he could not conquer, reached out to Eleanor.

When Elliott was watching over the pathetic figure of his dying son, his mind had turned to Eleanor as if to the one rock in a world of sand. "You were never out of my thoughts and prayers for one instant all that time," he told her. He thought of her often in Virginia. In the spring he kept his room filled with violets because they reminded him of her. "They smell so sweet," he wrote Eleanor, "just like your sweet little self when I pick you up in my arms and bury my face in those soft baby cheeks."

Elliott found some comfort in his companionship with other children, who treated his rooms "as if they owned them for a nursery." In his closeness to the children of Abingdon, he could almost touch his own children. Eleanor's great aunt Ellie Bulloch told her many years later about one of those incidents in Virginia: "He was spending the evening with some friends, and a little fair-haired girl climbed into his lap and nestled close in his tender clasp and fell asleep there. They wanted to take her from him then, but he begged she might stay: '*they* did not know,' he said, 'that to me it was *another fair little head* I held, and it comforted me to feel her in my arms.'"

Although Elliott could not live with Eleanor, he showered her with attention. When he was in New York, he took her on walks and rides along Fifth Avenue and in Central Park. He gave her a cart and pony and encouraged Mary Hall to see that she learned to ride and drive. In the spring he ordered her flowers at Easter and was pleased to hear she wore them to church. "I thought of *you all day long*," he wrote, "and blessed you and prayed for your happiness." He even sent her instructions on grooming. "I am glad you are taking such good care of those cunning wee hands that Father loves so to be petted by"; he wrote, "all those *little* things will make my dear girl so much more attractive if she attends to them."

At home on Thirty-Seventh Street Eleanor tried to imagine that she and her father were together. Sometimes there was a knock at the front door and her father was really there. Eleanor would run from her room and slide down the banister into his arms. They might spend an afternoon together; then he would be gone again.

Eleanor missed her father, but in his absence she found other things to interest her, such as a summer trip to Bar Harbor, where she visited an Indian encampment and climbed Kebo Mountain. She wrote her father from Maine, telling him, "The names of the things we get to eat are too funny. Washington pie and blanket of veal are mild to some other things we get." She went fishing and caught six fish. "Don't you think I did well for the first time?" she asked her father.

Elliott was glad Eleanor was learning to ride and hike and fish. He wanted her to love the outdoors as he did. He also wanted to communicate to her the qualities of spirit he most valued. He reached into himself for what was best and sought to pass it on, distilled and purified for Eleanor. Elliott was a gentle man. He hoped his daughter would be tender too. He told her she should think of her mind as an "education house" and said, "You surely always wish to live in a beautiful house not an ugly one." He urged her to attend to the "big" virtues: "unselfishness, generosity, loving tenderness, and cheerfulness."

Eleanor was Elliott's greatest treasure. She was his "pretty companionable little daughter." But most of his days and nights were spent far from Eleanor and her little brother Hall. Elliott had once hoped to live with them again, but after Anna's and Ellie's deaths and the economic crisis of 1893 that hope often seemed illusory. Elliott's newly won self-confidence slipped away. He began to drink and fell once more into a cycle of depression and alcoholic oblivion. He took Eleanor out one afternoon and left her with the doorman at the Knickerbocker Club while he went in for a drink. After a long wait Eleanor saw her father carried out of the club, unconscious.

Mary Hall began to fear Elliott's visits and tried to shield the children from him. He sank deeper and deeper into despair. One of his notes to his mother-in-law said simply, "I have a desolate feeling that I cannot overcome—but I do not care to see anyone." During the summer of 1894 Elliott avoided his brother and two sisters and went to live incognito with his former mistress, Mrs. Evans, in an apartment on 102nd Street. He drank several bottles of liquor a day, beginning as soon as he got up. The apartment, even the bedroom he shared with Mrs. Evans, was cluttered with pictures of Anna.

In July 1894 he left New York briefly to visit a friend from his Paris days, Florence Sherman, who was living with her children by the seashore in Annisquam, Massachusetts. Elliott was so sick that Mrs. Sherman called in a physician, who told her he needed quiet and the attention of loved ones. His mind wandered and he talked in his sleep about his sister, Corinne Robinson, saying she "alone had given him the love he needed." During his stay in Annisquam he chatted with Florence Sherman, played with her children, went sailing. He seemed to recover and was much stronger when he returned to New York.

But in the city of his failures, Elliott returned to drink. Finally in August he fell into a coma and died—a victim of illness, alcohol, and despair. When Teddy, who had given up Elliott for lost, saw the body, he wept bitterly. The years seemed to dissolve, and he saw a younger Elliott—at dancing class, in European hotels, sailing on the Sound. Teddy, however, would not forget Elliott's disgrace. Having proposed his brother's exile, he now insisted that Elliott lie in the Roosevelt family plot rather than at Tivoli beside the wife he had mistreated. Mary Hall was more forgiving. She admitted that in recent years she had been afraid of Elliott, because she "never knew what he would do." "But still," she said, "he was the dearest man I ever knew, so gentle and kind-hearted." She had hoped that Elliott and Anna could be buried together. A few years later her wishes prevailed, and Elliott was reinterred beside his wife.

An Abingdon newspaper summarized local feeling for Elliott by saying, "His name was a byword among the needy." Florence Sherman wrote his sister, lamenting his loss. "He was so strong," she said, "and had such a gay, sweet nature." Even the boatman, who had met Elliott only once when he had taken him with Mrs. Sherman for a sail, had been drawn to him. A year after Elliott's death, the man asked after him. When Florence Sherman said he was dead, the boatman replied simply, "That's wrong."

It was wrong for Elliott to have died, Mrs. Sherman thought. Elliott had been exiled for reasons that made sense to Victorian moralists, but she viewed the situation differently, seeing Elliott as a tender man who missed his family. He loved his children "and ought to have been with them," she said. Elliott was dead, but something in him deserved to live. "See to it that he does not lose the place he deserves in his children's lives," she urged. A year later she wrote again. "I have been sadly wondering about his children," she said, "if they are well and strong and inherit anything of his charm."

Eleanor had begun to adjust to her father's death. She was accustomed to change, having lost her mother, father, and brother in less than two years. Only recently everything the world could offer had been hers: loving parents, houses in the city and country, pets and toys. One by one the pillars of that world had fallen. She adjusted, making do with less while dreaming of more. On learning of her father's death she pressed her regret into one pathetic sentence. "I did want," she said, "to see my father once more."

# 3

# Growing Up

*Mlle. Souvestre shocked me into thinking, and that on the whole was very beneficial.*

Eleanor Roosevelt, *This Is My Story*

Elliott was dead, but Eleanor continued to dream of him—not only while she slept but in daydreams as well. She invented scenes in which he was the hero and she the heroine. She dreamed of him when she awakened in the morning, when she went to bed in the evening, and whenever she was alone. When a conversation bored her or she could outwalk her chattering nurse, she withdrew into secret thought and was alone with her adoring father. Even while she clung to Elliott in her dreams, however, Eleanor came to know Thirty-Seventh Street, where she was raised by her grandmother and her uncles and aunts.

Among them she grew up in a world within a world. The people she knew had five-story town houses in New York and country estates along the Hudson River. She and her friends had their own maids and went to private schools. In front of her Thirty-Seventh Street house and on nearby Fifth Avenue Eleanor could watch a constant parade of well-dressed men and women, just like her relatives, driving by in smart carriages pulled by beautiful horses.

She realized, of course, that not everyone was wealthy. In her idyllic realm, however, even the poor seemed content to respect and serve the rich. They were the friendly servants in her grandmother's kitchen, a nice colored peddler who sold his wares on the train, and the slum children who were so appreciative when she and her aunts and uncles gave them Christmas presents and sang them carols. Eleanor probably never stopped to wonder whether these people ever longed for smart carriages and country estates of their own or why she had received such treasures and they had not. She knew only the world as it was.

One day when she was about twelve she glimpsed another world, where people were poor and desperate. She was riding in a horse-drawn stage with her governess. Suddenly a wretched-looking man jumped on the car and tried to snatch a purse from a woman nearby. Failing, he jumped back to the street and ran through the crowd followed by shouts of "Stop thief!" Eleanor was so shocked she jumped out of the moving stage and stood dumbfounded in the street until her maid came running and scolding after her. She got back on the car and went on to her French lesson, but all that day and for months to come she was disturbed by "the face of that poor, haunted man."

That face had no place in Eleanor's childhood domain. She would not really understand the man's desperation until two decades later when her own world collapsed around her. In the 1890s the world she knew—despite her personal sorrows—was a comfortable place. There was "a quality of tranquility in people," she later wrote, "which you rarely meet today." That tranquility was most apparent among the eastern aristocrats. Untroubled by income tax, labor unions, or civil rights legislation, the well-to-do were secure in their prejudices: laborers should be grateful for the wages they received, immigrants and dark-skinned people were inferior, the rich deserved to be rich, the poor deserved to be poor, the Protestant nations should rule the world. In 1895 who would disabuse them of these comfortable thoughts? Samuel Gompers had just begun his career with the fledgling American Federation of Labor, Vladimir Lenin was in prison in Siberia, Mahatma Gandhi was an obscure lawyer in South Africa, and Martin Luther King Jr. had not been born.

Eleanor's childhood world was tranquil in its absence of pressing social discord. It was also tranquil in its spiritual quality. On Sundays Eleanor could not play games and must read only the books that her grandmother considered appropriate. In the morning she recited biblical passages and hymns in French that she had memorized during the previous week. Her elders took her on afternoon walks, and in the winter the family sat by the open fire and read books aloud. On Sunday evenings they sang hymns around the piano. Eleanor later wrote, "This religious training was not just an affair of Sundays—there were family prayers every morning, and you grew up with the feeling that you had a share in some great spiritual existence beyond the everyday round of happenings."

Wealth and religion gave an aura of calm to Eleanor Roosevelt's adolescence. But even so she began to understand life's ambiguity and complexity, and she came to develop a character of her own. The ten-year-old orphan found herself in a peculiar household, among jarring personalities. The nominal leader of the Hall family was Eleanor's grandmother, Mary, barely fifty years old but made elderly by the early death of her husband and the burden of raising a large family. Next were two uncles and two aunts: Vallie and Eddie, both in their mid-twenties; Pussie, barely twenty; and Maude, in her late teens. Then there were the servants: a laundress, a butler, a cook, and a housemaid.

Each had a personal territory. Grandmother Hall spent much of the day alone in her room or with guests in a formal drawing room filled with massive gilded furniture.

Aunts Pussie and Maude occupied the library, entertaining themselves with piano, books, and guests. Uncles Vallie and Eddie were out much of the time socializing or playing tennis—each was a national champion. And the servants bustled about dusting, cooking, washing, and ironing, then retired to tiny bedrooms in a remote corner of the house. In all this rush of activity no one seemed able to draw the household into an orderly community.

Eleanor, her brother Hall, and a nurse, Madeleine, added other pieces to the family mosaic. Eleanor slept in a tiny room of her own, and her brother shared a bedroom with Madeleine. Years later Eleanor came to realize how the arrival of two children and a nurse must have upset the Hall household, and she praised her relatives for their consideration. "I marvel at the sweetness of my two uncles and the two aunts who were still at home," she wrote, "for never by word or deed did any of them make us feel that we were not in our own house." It was natural, however, for Eleanor to feel out of place. Among her relatives none was anything like a real mother or father. Grandmother Hall was preoccupied with her children; the aunts and uncles were absorbed in their own lives; and Madeleine, the nurse, terrorized Eleanor, scolding her viciously and pulling her hair for any misdemeanor. Always a timorous child, Eleanor became even more fearful of authority and began nervously chewing her fingernails.

Eleanor had once been able to take love for granted. And in her dream world she could still find comfort with the father who had once been near her. But she yearned also for acceptance in her new home. The depth of this longing was apparent one dark night when Aunt Pussie, ill with a sore throat, asked Eleanor to get her some ice. Her room was on the third floor, and the gas lights in the hallway had been turned off for the night. Eleanor had to tread down three flights of stairs to the dingy basement and find her way through the gloom to the icehouse in the back yard. Her legs shaking with fear, she returned safely with the ice, wonderfully pleased to have been needed.

Even while Eleanor was struggling to make a place for herself on Thirty-Seventh Street she faced the further challenge of finding acceptance with children her own age. She went out into the social world with a morbid sense of personal ugliness. Her mother and grandmother had both been great beauties and had carelessly let Eleanor know that she did not measure up; her teeth were too prominent, and her chin was too small. No one could possibly love her for her appearance, it seemed. She had taken these comments too seriously, perhaps gazing at herself critically in the mirror or touching forlornly the chin that refused to stand out. She wore an almost apologetic air when she met people, as if expecting them to be displeased with her.

Her grandmother's choice of clothes for Eleanor increased the child's awkwardness. The ten-year-old grew into a tall teenager, but Mary Hall seemed to want Eleanor to stay a little girl. She made Eleanor wear short dresses with nursery frills when other girls were wearing longer, more formal dresses. The child's only consolation was that she was hardly ever allowed to play with other children anyway. She seldom had guests or visited friends and almost never saw boys. A girlfriend's parents invited her to join them on a tour of the West when Eleanor was twelve. What a wonderful journey for a girl who had never been beyond the Catskills— but Grandmother would not let her go adventuring. When she occasionally attended dances, she was so unaccustomed to socializing and so self-conscious about her looks that she was acutely embarrassed.

Her only regular contact with children came at a small school she attended with half a dozen other girls in a nearby mansion. The class was taught by Frederic Roser, a pompous man with thick side-whiskers and a loyal following among prominent New York families. Eleanor did well in school, learning to recite long poems and to write fine compositions. But she had trouble making friends and seemed a grind and a prude to her classmates—she refused to join in their student pranks and scolded them when they talked furtively about sex.

In her early teens Eleanor Roosevelt was awkward and introspective, troubled by her own looks, undernourished in relations with adults and children. And yet, surprisingly, she was not morose and withdrawn. She grew up in a fragmented world, but she lived in a vital relationship to that world, and she fashioned from her experience—even from her sorrows—a sensitive awareness of herself and those around her.

Because Eleanor had no parents, her relationships with other people acquired special importance. Her little brother Hall, six years younger than she, was often the only playmate in the house. She might boss him—when they played Robinson Crusoe, he was always her servant Friday—but she recognized that he needed her attention. When they were separated, she wrote him daily letters, explaining to a friend, "I want him to feel he belongs to somebody."

Then there were her aunts and uncles. Vallie's main preoccupation was alcohol, and his drinking bouts became so frightful that Grandmother Hall hesitated to have guests to the house, fearing that they would see him at his worst. Yet the same Vallie taught her to jump her horse and was her companion at picnics and campfires in the country. Eleanor probably enjoyed Aunt Pussie most. She was a temperamental young woman who could scandalize her mother by inviting men to tea and smoking cigarettes with them. She was on top of the world when one of her romances went well but despondent when they turned sour. At her worst she would lock herself in her room for days at a time, refusing to speak to anyone. In her better moments, however, she enchanted Eleanor. Pussie loved music and the theater and once took her niece to meet a famous Italian actress. She was a fine pianist, and Eleanor loved to listen to her play in the library with the big bow window, filling with beautiful music the room where her father had told Eleanor about the life they would share.

Grandmother Hall was also a puzzling woman. Sometimes in her effort to raise Eleanor and Hall with a firm hand she seemed to deny them all pleasures. "No" came so readily to her lips that Eleanor took to phrasing her requests in the negative, hoping to persuade her grandmother to approve projects she might otherwise quash. Mary Hall made her granddaughter wear scratchy flannel underwear from early November to the end of March, whatever the weather, and required her to wear hot black stockings even on muggy summer days when Eleanor's fingers stuck to the piano keys. But her grandmother could suddenly surprise Eleanor with unexpected sensitivity. One day she and Eleanor were walking in the woods, and Eleanor hesitatingly told her how much she feared the nurse, Madeleine. She had borne her mistreatment for years without speaking, but now she burst into tears and admitted her suffering. She may have expected Grandmother Hall to be angry, but instead the stern old woman comforted her: it was all right to be upset; she should have told her sooner; she would be taken out of Madeleine's care.

In such ways Eleanor sometimes found friendship and support from her relatives. She also found companions among the servants. At Thirty-Seventh Street she would slip into the pantry after meals, and there Victor, the butler, chatted with her and taught her to dry dishes. When Eleanor was punished by being sent to bed without supper,

Victor and Kitty, the chambermaid, secretly carried food up to her room.

During the summers when the family went to the country, Eleanor spent many hours with Mrs. Overhalse, a laundress, whose domain was a room at the back of the house with a washboard, three tubs, and a wringer. Mrs. Overhalse was a cheerful woman who worked all day for the Halls and then returned to her own farm and children. As she worked, she and Eleanor talked by the hour. On a small stove in the laundry, fueled by coal or wood, sat an assortment of irons. Mrs. Overhalse showed Eleanor how to iron the simpler items, the handkerchiefs, towels, and napkins.

Eleanor had one other set of friends, the Roosevelt relatives. Her grandmother seldom let her visit Uncle Teddy, finding him too boisterous. But occasionally she relented, and on one fine weekend Eleanor spent two exhausting days at Sagamore Hill, a rambling house atop a grassy hill on Long Island Sound. Her uncle greeted her with a bruising hug and led her with her cousins on a trail of adventures. They climbed a high sand dune along the shore, linked hands, and tumbled down to the bottom. They went to the barn and jumped in the hay. Normally Eleanor would have worried about an adult catching them in their antics, but there was Uncle Teddy leading the pack. When it began to rain, he took them to the attic and recited poetry.

From such encounters Eleanor became aware of the tremendous variety of human types. There were not simply adults and children. There were many kinds of adults, each with unexpected qualities: an overworked washerwoman who was unfailingly cheerful; an artistic aunt who was by degrees animated and despondent; a boisterous, athletic uncle who loved poetry; an overbearing grandmother with an unanticipated capacity for sympathy. She had no father or mother, but she had people—strange and various and marvelously complex.

As the years passed Eleanor learned that she too could be a person, that she could shape her world. She was most happy in the family's large summer home at Tivoli on the Hudson River about a hundred miles above New York City. The house, called Oak Terrace, was of painted brick. A tree-shaded lawn sloped down through the woods to the banks of the river. Tivoli was a place for campfires and picnics, catching tadpoles in a stream, and playing in the woods with Hall.

Eleanor was enchanted with the beauty of Oak Terrace. She loved best the cool, early hours of the day when she could persuade an aunt to rise with her at dawn and walk in the gray light through the woods to the river. They would climb into a boat and row along the flat broad Hudson as the first rays of sunlight warmed the Catskill Mountains to the west. At Tivoli village they pulled the boat onto the shore and picked up the day's mail. Rowing back in full daylight, they reached Oak Terrace just in time for breakfast.

At Oak Terrace Eleanor indulged her love of books. Her aunts and uncles had filled the library—which had once been devoted to theological tomes—with lighter modern literature, works by Sir Walter Scott, Charles Dickens, and other authors whom Eleanor enjoyed. She filled her days with reading: she awoke at dawn and read books in bed before her morning sponge bath and breakfast; at midday she read while sitting in the trees or on the grass outside the house.

Out of the experience of growing up at Oak Terrace and Thirty-Seventh Street Eleanor developed a rudimentary philosophy of life. Many of her ideas were set forth in compositions she wrote for Mr. Roser's classes. She had seen her friends and relations try to win favor, and so she wrote an essay on pride. It took the form of a fable about some flowers in a greenhouse. Each flower claimed it was more beautiful than the rest and should therefore rule. The rose, the lily, and the orchid all made their claims: the one was brightest, the next more graceful, the last more colorful. Finally, the violet—the flower that had reminded Elliott of Eleanor—made its speech. "Why none of us excel," it said. "We are all beautiful in our own way. Some are beautifully colored. Others smell sweetly, and again others are graceful. We are all made well. From this day we are all equal." All the flowers agreed, but Eleanor added, "I always have and always will love the violet best."

Eleanor's allegory was based on limited knowledge of the world, but it reflects her youthful wrestling with a perception that would influence her later thinking on life: that people are both marvelously varied and fundamentally similar. In finding her own place in the world of her youth Eleanor was struggling to take part in a community of friends and relatives and still develop a character of her own. This challenge would vex her for years to come.

Eleanor was still an awkward child, but some who knew her recognized her qualities. Her Aunt Edith, Uncle Ted's wife, said after one visit, "Poor little soul, she is very plain, . . . but the ugly duckling may turn out to be a swan." At a party where Eleanor was occupying her accustomed position along a wall, her cousin Franklin Roosevelt asked her to dance. He enjoyed talking to her and wrote his mother a report. "Cousin Eleanor," he said, "has a very good mind."

Eleanor did not see her cousin Franklin again for several years because in the fall of 1899 she boarded a ship with her Aunt Tissie and sailed to England, where she was to attend school. It was a strange passage, for her aunt customarily spent Atlantic crossings in bed, and Eleanor supposed that she should too. On another journey two years later she had the good sense to go on deck even when the ship pitched and rolled over enormous waves and you "felt you were walking up a mountain or down one." But in 1899 she stayed below, and at journey's end she took her first steps in England on wobbly legs.

Aunt Tissie delivered Eleanor to Allenswood, near Wimbledon Common, a short distance from London. Everything was unfamiliar. The girls, fifty-five of them, wore a curious uniform: straw boaters; white blouses with bold, diagonally striped neckties; and dark ankle-length skirts. Most were English, but they spoke French in all their classes. They lived in a rambling brick schoolhouse ruled by a large, silver-haired Frenchwoman, Marie Souvestre. Gone were Eleanor's familiar rooms at Thirty-Seventh Street and Oak Terrace; gone were the faces of home. As her aunt drove away, Eleanor—a tall, willowy fifteen-year-old—felt "lost and very lonely." Among her possessions she clutched a packet of letters that she carried as a talisman against sorrow: her father's notes to her as a child.

At Allenswood Eleanor might easily have felt once more like an orphan. She might have found herself governed by a petty tyrannical headmistress and been taunted by mean classmates. Eleanor had adjusted before to life's disappointments—to parents' deaths and nursemaids' scoldings. She must have prepared herself to accept philosophically the hardships of a new environment. But she soon found that Allenswood suited her better than any home she had known since early childhood. The pleasures of the previous five years had been scattered moments salvaged from a fragmented life: the intermittent attention of aunts and uncles, the solitary hours spent reading, the school papers that won Mr. Roser's approval. These pleasures had been garnered from an environment that was often indifferent and some-times hostile. Pussie's sulkiness, Vallie's drunkenness, Madeleine's cruelty, Grandmother's preoccupation, and her schoolmates' coolness were all part of life in New York.

But Allenswood was different. The whole school seemed designed to encourage and draw out a girl like Eleanor. She had to speak French at all times. That was all right; she had learned French from her nursemaids as a child and had studied the language ever since. She must please Marie Souvestre, the proud matron of the school, who tore up students' papers when she thought their work was shabby. That was fine, for in Mlle. Souvestre Eleanor discovered a kindred spirit.

School life at Allenswood was carefully planned from rising to curfew. Each morning the girls stripped their beds to air, then remade them. After breakfast they went for a brisk walk on the common, no matter how cold the weather. The rest of the day was divided into class time, study periods, and sports. During the cold, damp months that extend in England from mid-fall to mid-spring the girls warmed themselves as best they could on lukewarm radiators. When they entered the dining room, they crowded like a flock of geese into the warmest corner of the room. Three times a week they were allowed a bath— ten minutes and no more.

The environment was austere, but Eleanor positively thrived. She enjoyed her new friends and new studies. In sports she, the most unathletic of girls till now, made first team in the rough game of field hockey. In the classroom she enjoyed studying German, Latin, Italian, Shakespeare, and history. She especially liked the history class taught by Mlle. Souvestre in the school library, a large carpeted room with tall wood bookcases, a huge elaborately framed mirror, and a high arched window looking out on a broad expanse of lawn. Marie Souvestre was short and stocky, her snow-white hair gathered in a bun. Her intelligent, kindly face shone with dedication as she walked up and down in front of the girls, telling them about the great events of the past.

Within a few weeks Eleanor felt at home in the new school. Rereading her father's letters, she felt his support and advice. She ran across a passage where he urged her to be careful of her appearance, especially of her "cunning wee hands." For years she had chewed her nails; now she allowed them to grow. Eleanor would try to be the kind of girl her father wanted her to be, especially in the company of Mlle. Souvestre, who had also lost her father when young and had known Elliott and Anna. She had met Eleanor's parents in Paris in 1891 and had instructed Aunty Bye, Elliott's sister. When Grandmother Hall arranged for Eleanor's admission to Allenswood, she had recommended Eleanor for "her purity of heart" and "nobleness of thought." No doubt these family connections helped the relationship between teacher and pupil. But Mlle. Souvestre was soon attracted to Eleanor's own personality and sat her in a privileged position opposite her at the dinner table. The headmistress saw in Eleanor not merely a good pupil but an attractive human being; Eleanor was equally drawn to Marie Souvestre and soon came to feel closer to her teacher than she had felt to anyone since her father's death.

Through Mlle. Souvestre Eleanor became aware, for the first time in her life, of a public world beyond the narrow sphere of her own family and friends. In the evenings the headmistress sometimes invited her favorite girls to her study. Often she read them French plays, poems, and stories. But she also talked to them about public affairs. Between 1899 and 1902 England was engaged in a bloody war in South Africa against the Boers, Dutch settlers in the Transvaal and Natal.

Many Englishmen believed that God fought on the side of the English army, and of necessity Mlle. Souvestre allowed the English girls to celebrate the army's victories in the gymnasium. But in her study she shared her real feelings with some of her favorite students. Might, she told them, did not make right; the big nations of the world ought to allow the small countries to run their own affairs; the Boers ought to have been left to govern themselves.

Grandmother Hall or Mr. Roser would have been scandalized. Surely God expected that the great Christian nations of the world, especially England and the United States, would "take up the white man's burden" and rule the more backward nations—for their own good, of course. Eleanor's own uncle, Theodore Roosevelt, had recently won national acclaim for his role in the Spanish-American War. As President he would soon wage a war in the Philippines to suppress a native insurrection and establish American rule over the "little brown brothers" of the Pacific. Marie Souvestre considered the allegedly benevolent colonialism of the great nations pure hypocrisy. The fine words of the colonizers simply disguised their greed.

Eleanor must have been shocked but excited by Mlle. Souvestre's pronouncements. She had always taken the public world for granted. Now it turned out that political life could be talked about, even criticized. People were not simply caught in the stream of history, hopeless observers of the great events around them. They could evaluate, criticize, even influence public affairs.

When Eleanor was not at school, she vacationed with friends in England and on the Continent. She was in London in 1901 when a long, solemn funeral procession bearing the body of Queen Victoria passed on the street below as Eleanor watched from a window. Carriage after carriage clattered through the crowd-lined streets. A sudden hush fell over the people as a gun carriage with its tiny coffin came into view, bearing the petite monarch who had reigned for sixty-four years and had set the tone for social life in the English-speaking world. Eleanor sensed "great emotional forces that seemed to stir all about us."

On other journeys she came to know new cultures. In 1901 she joined Mlle. Souvestre for a tour of France and Italy. As was customary, Eleanor always traveled with a chaperone. Sometimes this seemed an empty formality— as when Grandmother Hall hired a woman to accompany Eleanor on one transatlantic passage and the woman was so ill she stayed below decks during the whole journey. But in theory someone had always been there to look out for Eleanor. With her headmistress, however, she was a traveling companion, a young adult. She packed and unpacked bags, purchased tickets, and checked train schedules. Mlle. Souvestre even let her go exploring on her own in Paris and Florence. Her mentor taught Eleanor that "the way to make young people responsible is to throw real responsibility on them."

Mlle. Souvestre also showed Eleanor the pleasure available to the traveler who opened herself to her environment. She believed you should immerse yourself in the experience of another country, not only seeing local sights but also eating indigenous foods and speaking native tongues. In Marseilles they ate bouillabaisse and drank wine in a cafe overlooking the Mediterranean and watched fishing boats with red sails dart across the harbor.

On the train to Pisa Mlle. Souvestre suddenly decided to get off in Alassio, a small town on the Mediterranean. She grabbed her carrying bags and leaped onto the platform, followed by the startled Eleanor. Standing beside her puffing headmistress as their train vanished down the tracks, Eleanor was shocked. She had barely managed to get her bags from an overhead rack, and the trunks were in the baggage car. It was the early evening and their hotel reservations were in Pisa, not Alassio. But Marie Souvestre assured her that they would manage. The Mediterranean, she said, was a lovely blue here in the night with the stars shining overhead. She wanted to stand on the beach and watch it. And watch they did; on that soft Mediterranean shore Eleanor scolded herself and swore she would never again be a "rigid little person."

With Marie Souvestre Eleanor felt the constraints of life give way. The world was a larger place than she could have imagined while living on Thirty-Seventh Street and associating with Grandmother Hall's closed circle of friends. If Grandmother had taken Eleanor to Florence, they probably would have stayed in a reputable hotel where they would associate with other well-to-do Americans and Englishmen. In her headmistress's company Eleanor stayed with an artist friend of hers in his villa overlooking Florence. He was painting an enormous canvas of the Last Supper, and Eleanor spent hours studying the painting and the interesting-looking models who came by to pose. She could speak enough Italian to go out into the city alone to explore its little shops, where she admired the gold and silver filigree work, and the museums, where she was enchanted with paintings like Botticelli's graceful "Spring." She was sixteen, and years later she thought she had never been "keener" and "more alive to beauty."

In 1902 Eleanor and her headmistress made two more trips to the Continent. They visited Rome in the winter and stayed in a large palace room heated by a tiny portable charcoal stove. Marie Souvestre took Eleanor to the Colosseum and filled its stony ruins with images of ancient Romans in togas. They went in the spring to France and Belgium. Eleanor particularly remembered a visit to a school where girls were taught "practical" skills—cooking and housekeeping.

Eleanor's years at Allenswood and her travels on the Continent nourished her confidence in herself and changed her from a shy, awkward child into a confident, graceful young woman. Like the ugly duckling in the fable, she had lived for years among people who were different from her. In New York she had always felt inadequate. At Allenswood her fears dissolved: she did not have to strain to win attention; she simply had to be herself. It was easy because she found there other people like her—more interested in ideas than social conventions, less conscious of physical than intellectual beauty.

But someday she must leave Allenswood and return to America. The contrast between her two worlds was painfully apparent in the summer of 1901 when Aunt Pussie came to England to take Eleanor home for the school break. While in London Pussie, predictably, had fallen in love. As their ship steamed away from England, she kept her niece awake with her lamentations: she would never see her beloved again, her heart was broken, she would throw herself into the ocean.

Eleanor was afraid her aunt might actually attempt suicide and stayed awake to watch her. But Pussie survived the trip and her sorrows, and a few weeks later she was in love again. Eleanor was accustomed to her aunt's unsteady affections, but this was more than she could comprehend. Incautiously, she reminded her aunt that she had been wildly in love with another man only a few weeks before.

Pussie was outraged at any suggestion of her fickleness. Cornered, she turned on her niece. What did Eleanor know about men? Didn't she know she was the ugly duckling of the family? She would never even have a beau of her own. Who would want her? Eleanor probably bore these familiar slights stoically. But then Pussie attacked Elliott, revealing to Eleanor all the facts she had never before known about her father's drunkenness and adultery. Not only was Eleanor ugly, but her father had been a disgrace to the family.

Eleanor could have borne Aunt Pussie's comments on her looks, but the attack on her father reduced her to tears. He had been her friend and her ideal. For years she had tried to live up to his expectations. Surely Pussie was lying. Eleanor asked her grandmother, hoping for a repudiation of Pussie's claims. Reluctantly, Mary Hall admitted the truth. The revelation of Elliott's failings, however, failed to shake Eleanor's love for her father. Perhaps it even strengthened her feeling that they needed one another, that he was as vulnerable as she. She would continue to carry his letters and think of him as a warm, caring father. But she longed to be back with her new mentor and friend, Marie Souvestre. She persuaded her grandmother to send her back to Allenswood for one more year. That was in the summer of 1901; however, she could not remain abroad forever. In the spring of 1902, when she was seventeen, she asked for yet another year at Allenswood, but this time her grandmother was adamant. She must return to New York.

Under the best of circumstances she would have feared the return to Thirty-Seventh Street. But now she was not merely going home, she was coming out. This was the year Eleanor must make her debut in New York society. She would be expected to attend dances, make light conversation, and look as attractive as possible. Many girls would be enchanted by the prospect, but Eleanor was at best ambivalent. After several years as a young adult in a stimulating environment, she must narrow her vision once more and accept her place in New York society.

# Illustrations

Elliott Roosevelt with his children, Hall, Elliott Jr., and Eleanor in 1892. Soon he would return to his "exile" in Virginia. Elliott Jr. died a few months later, and Elliott, himself, in 1894.

Eleanor with Sara Roosevelt at Campobello in 1904. A year later she would marry Franklin, and live for many years in the shadow of her domineering mother-in-law.

Eleanor Roosevelt in 1900, a student at Allenswood in England. Bright and alert, she was Mlle. Souvestre's favorite pupil.

Eleanor with baby Franklin in 1914. When the first Franklin Jr. died a few months after birth, Eleanor blamed herself for failing to care enough for the infant. Though she often felt inadequate as a mother, this photo suggests the great tenderness Eleanor often felt toward her children.

Eleanor and Franklin in 1907, boarding a train for Campobello. Now in their early twenties, he was a promising young attorney, and she was becoming a conventional society matron.

Eleanor in 1914 with Elliott, James, Franklin Jr., and Anna. "For years," she wrote in her *Autobiography*, "I was always just getting over having a baby or about to have one.

Franklin, John, and Eleanor in 1930. Franklin was governor of New York, and John was a student at Groton. When Eleanor became First Lady of New York State, a reporter had predicted, "she will be the busiest woman in official life today." As a teacher, writer, lecturer, and Franklin's "eyes and ears" she was living up to that forecast.

Eleanor Roosevelt and Malvina Thompson at the Democratic National Headquarters in 1936. "Tommy" was Eleanor Roosevelt's private secretary for 31
years; she was, Eleanor said, "the person who made life possible for me."

Eleanor and Lorena Hickok (on her left with long tie) visiting a Puerto Rican
slum in 1934. For many years "Hick" was one of Eleanor's closest friends and
shared her interest in liberal reform.

Eleanor with Elinor Morgenthau and Jane Adams, 1929. Eleanor's personal growth in the 1920s was facilitated by her friendship with women like these who were active in public life.

Eleanor Roosevelt inspecting a subsistence homestead in 1936. Eleanor was one of the foremost supporters of the homestead program, especially of Arthurdale, her pet project.

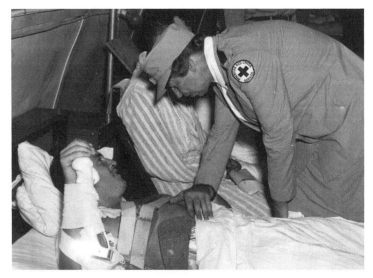

Eleanor visiting a hospital in the South Pacific in 1943. "Every time she grasps a new hand," a reporter said, "her face lights up with a resolute effort to feel sincere, not to leave this a mere empty gesture."

Eleanor at Val-Kill with Wiltwyck School children, 1954. For Eleanor the picnic was an instrument of public policy. By entertaining she sought to promote good will among black children, U.N. diplomats, and many other groups.

Eleanor inspecting a WPA project to convert a city dump into a waterfront park, Des Moines, Iowa, 1936. She traveled tens of thousands of miles each year to learn at first hand about conditions around the country, acquiring the nickname "Eleanor Everywhere."

Eleanor and Fala at Val-Kill in 1947. She enjoyed the peace of her country home, but in her mid-sixties she was as active as ever and chaired the U.N. Human Rights Commission.

On her way to Israel in 1955 Eleanor visits with children at a Jewish camp in France. Like many other Americans Eleanor had disparaged the Jews during her early years, but she grew into a staunch supporter of Israel and a friend of Jewish refugees in Europe.

# Eleanor and Franklin

*How your father would have loved to see you in your little house.*
*The word 'Home' meant everything to him! . . . He would have loved*
*to see you developing into a famous little housewife.*

Anna Bulloch, *letter to Eleanor Roosevelt*

"I miss you every day of my life," Mlle. Souvestre wrote Eleanor. When the fall term began at Allenswood the school seemed different, less friendly, without Eleanor. Some of the new students were lonely and ill-at-ease, and none of the English girls knew how to help them. Marie Souvestre could imagine Eleanor taking the situation in hand and making the shy girls feel "rapidly at ease."

She realized that Eleanor belonged in America. "You fulfill your destiny more where you are," she said, "than you would near me." But she worried about Eleanor's future. Could the young girl preserve her unique sensitivity in a life that would be "entirely new and entirely different"? Marie Souvestre hoped that Eleanor would not allow New York's "social dissipations"—"evenings out, pleasures, flirtations"—to undermine her character. There are "more quiet and enviable joys," she told her, than to be the most sought-after debutante.

What were those "enviable joys" and what was the "destiny" the English schoolmistress imagined for her star pupil? Probably she hoped that Eleanor would enter some field of public service. Marie Souvestre was one of comparatively few women in 1900 to have a career. In England and America a small number of women were lawyers, doctors, journalists, social workers, or college professors. Most professional women were unmarried because conventional wisdom held that one could not be a good wife and mother while holding a job. But the headmistress regarded the sacrifice of husband and children as a small price to pay for the chance to enter public service. She hoped that Eleanor would not be limited to a brief term as a debutante and a routine life as wife and mother.

She would have been proud of her young friend if she could have seen her on the evening of January 20, 1905. Eleanor had spent the afternoon teaching dance and calisthenics at the Rivington Street Settlement House on the Lower East Side. The streets, crowded with "foreign-looking people," filled Eleanor with "a certain amount of terror." Nonetheless she sought full exposure to immigrant life. Her friend Jean Reid, who played the piano while Eleanor taught dance, came and went in her carriage. Eleanor, more daring, took the streetcar, even though she trembled as she walked past rough-looking men who mingled around dingy saloons on the narrow streets. She also visited tenement homes, walking up filthy stairways to dark apartments where families of eight or ten crowded together in one or two rooms.

As a settlement house volunteer Eleanor had entered a field that attracted some of the most talented women in America. Following the example of Toynbee Hall in London, American philanthropists, many of them women, had established settlement houses to combat poverty and ignorance in the immigrant ghettos in New York, Chicago, and elsewhere. These reformers sponsored the study of music, art, literature, and crafts, and they provided practical assistance through visiting nurses, cooking classes, and employment bureaus. Two women, Lillian Wald and Jane Addams, were in the forefront of settlement house work. They were pioneers not only in social work but also in showing that women could have vital roles in public affairs.

In New York City upper-class women joined together in an effort to make their own modest contribution to urban reform. Unwilling to become full-time social workers but eager to help immigrants and other poor people, a number of these women formed the Junior League, the organization that brought Eleanor to Rivington Street. The League consisted of young socialites who, Eleanor said, "were anxious to do something helpful in the city in which we lived."

It was fashionable to lament the condition of the poor, and some of the girls appeared more interested in the League's social prestige than in its work. But Eleanor enjoyed her contact with immigrant children. On the chilly night of January 20, 1905, two girls accompanied her to the trolley. They liked their teacher and had come along to chat. In the snow-covered streets men and women in tattered clothes walked carefully around puddles, and horses pulling wagons slipped on wet cobblestones. As dusk fell, women in apartments above prepared meals on coal stoves. The girls arrived at the tracks, where a streetcar came clanking and hissing to a stop. Eleanor said goodbye and boarded the car.

If Eleanor had wanted to enter a career in social work, her instinct for charity would have served her well, and her mentor, Marie Souvestre, would have approved. When she climbed aboard the trolley, however, she left the Lower East Side for another world, where women with careers were regarded as anomalies. Mlle. Souvestre had warned Eleanor that this other world—the world of debutante parties and social convention—would "take you and drag you into its turmoil." But despite this warning and despite Eleanor's own misgivings about parties, she had become a debutante. Her grandmother, mother, and aunts had all made debuts, and as Eleanor later admitted, she was "haunted" by her upbringing and believed society was "really important."

Her first social season, however, had been a trial, and the major event of the year, the Assembly Ball, had been "utter agony." A few boys invited her to dance, but for long intervals she sat awkwardly at the side of the room while other girls, pretty and smiling, waltzed by with attentive partners. Years later she recalled her mortification. "I knew I was the first girl in my mother's family who was not a belle," she wrote, "and though I acknowledged it to any of them at the time, I was deeply ashamed."

Eleanor's sense of failure as a debutante might have driven her to take social work more seriously as an avenue for her talents; on the Lower East Side she was clearly needed and appreciated. She did join a second philanthropic organization, the Consumer's League, and took part in its investigation of working conditions for women in the city's garment factories. She felt twinges of sympathy for the girls who had to stand all day at machines. Eleanor remained, however, a kind of upper-class tourist among them, and she later admitted, "By spring I was quite ready to drop all this good work and go up to the country and spend the summer in idleness and recreation."

Eleanor could look favorably upon social recreation in part because her "failure" as a debutante was not as complete as she had feared. Among the young men and women who attended parties and balls there were some who recognized her grace and intelligence. Nor was Eleanor as unattractive as she sometimes thought. If one looked at her small chin and large teeth, she did seem homely. But look again at her glowing complexion, her alert eyes, and her supple figure, and she was, in her way, a lovely girl. One of the most handsome and popular young men of the day, Franklin Roosevelt, had the good sense to recognize that loveliness.

They met by chance on a train during the summer of 1902 after Eleanor's return from England. They were fifth cousins, and Eleanor's father had been Franklin's godfather. Over the years they had met occasionally at parties, and so they immediately recognized each other. Eleanor was on her way to her grandmother's at Tivoli, and Franklin was traveling with his mother, Sara, to their country estate at Hyde Park. Sara was an imposing woman with fine patrician features. She wore a black dress in mourning for her husband, James, who had died two years before; a heavy dark veil fell from her hat to the seat. She was cordial to the young cousin just returned from England; Franklin, less restrained, was positively delighted to see her.

During the ensuing months Eleanor and Franklin often ran into one another at debutante parties, at first by chance and later by design. He began to ask her to lunch and to tea in the city. Then he invited her to Hyde Park, where they went on long walks and carriage rides through the forests and meadows that surrounded the house. Franklin, a student at Harvard, was a handsome young man with an oval face, dark eyebrows, and hair cut short over his ears. His eyes were by turns serious and playful. He seemed constantly alert, and his intelligent animation captivated Eleanor.

She told Franklin about her tragic family life, her parents' deaths, her adolescence with Grandmother Hall, the years in England. Life with Mary Hall had become more difficult because of Uncle Vallie's drinking. On his sprees at Tivoli he had taken to sitting in his window with a gun and shooting at people on the lawn. He never hit anyone, but his antics were so embarrassing that the Halls no longer invited guests to the house. Eleanor had to worry also about her brother Hall, whom she cared for as though he were her own son. Franklin's affection for Eleanor must have grown in part from his realization that she had so little: her parents were gone; her guardian's life was a shambles; and yet she, who had no mother of her own, was playing mother to her orphaned younger brother.

In the fall of 1903 Franklin invited Eleanor to the Harvard-Yale game. The football season had been one of the most exciting in the school's history. Harvard had just replaced the wooden bleachers at Soldier's Field with a modern stadium of steel and concrete; seating forty thousand, it was the largest in the country. The stadium had been given a memorable christening a few weeks before when "Pop" Warner's Carlisle Indians delighted the fans by hiding the ball beneath a player's jersey and scoring a touchdown against a befuddled Crimson defense—the famous "hidden-ball trick."

Franklin, as editor of the student newspaper, the *Harvard Crimson,* became part of the season's fun when he wrote an editorial criticizing the team for lackluster play and calling for a spirit of "aggressive, vigorous determination—a spirit that will begin when the game begins and will not vanish until the game ends." Thirty years later during the Great Depression he would try to inculcate a "winning spirit" in the nation at large when he told the people, "We have nothing to fear but fear itself." Then he would be inaugurated President of the United States. In 1903 his patriotism brought a more prosaic reward: he was made cheerleader.

Thus it was that on November 21, 1903, Eleanor sat in the stands at Soldier's Field while Franklin, all arms and legs, encouraged the crowd to cheer. On the bright green turf the burly players in leather helmets hammered at one another. The multicolored crowd swayed and sang and shouted. Three times Harvard came within Yale's ten-yard line, and three times the Crimson failed to score. Franklin led the cheering at each approach to the goal and was crestfallen each time Harvard lost the ball on downs or a fumble. When the game was over, and he rejoined Eleanor, Harvard had lost 16–0. Franklin was probably somewhat downcast at that moment, inclined to be self-consciously stoic. But Eleanor could comfort him, knowing better than he that it was just a game.

The next morning Eleanor and Franklin sat side by side at a church service at Groton School, a few miles from Cambridge. Although he was only twenty-one and she was nineteen, it was one of those moments when young people feel themselves magically transformed into adults. They had come here alone without a cluster of relatives, and they were acting as parents, visiting Hall, whom Eleanor had recently enrolled in the school. They knelt together, sang together, recited the creed together. After the service they visited with Hall. Then they went off alone for a walk.

Franklin knew the countryside well because he too had attended Groton. As they strolled along, he may have talked about his years at prep school, the Harvard-Yale game, or Eleanor's brother. But in his mind was another subject: Eleanor herself. He had never even kissed the lively girl who was walking by his side, and she would have been shocked at so forward a gesture from him. But during the past year they must often have held hands and looked into one another's eyes, acknowledging the bond that had grown between them. In those autumn woods Franklin gave words to his feelings and asked Eleanor to marry him. She must have been expecting the question, for she immediately accepted.

By agreeing to marry Franklin she was turning her back on a career, but in that moment the most important thing in her life was the chance to be Franklin's wife. She still admired Mlle. Souvestre, certainly, but all the women she associated with in New York were married or planned to marry and have children. "I felt the urge to be part of the stream of life," she later wrote. She had "a great curiosity about life and a desire to participate in every experience that might be the lot of woman."

"The lot of woman . . ." That destiny seemed wonderful when Franklin, so earnest and so handsome, proposed. Eleanor's mother had been disappointed in marriage and had died in sorrow. Now Eleanor had a chance to be a wife and mother herself; surely she would be more fortunate than her parents and would find happiness in a family of her own. After she accepted Franklin's proposal, she tried to recite a poem to tell him how important this moment was for her. She could not remember all the words, but these she uttered:

> Unless you can swear, *"For life, for death!"*
> Oh, fear to call it loving!

She had wondered whether Franklin could love her "for life, for death." Could one as lighthearted as he make such a commitment? But with his proposal she forgot her doubts. He was hers, and surely they would be lovers for life.

After an interval of a year and a half Eleanor and Franklin were married. They spent the summer of 1905 honeymooning in Europe. On a hot July afternoon they found themselves traveling by carriage through northern Italy toward Cortina, a lovely pastoral village in the heart of the Dolomites, the most hauntingly beautiful mountains in Europe. The carriage climbed slowly beside the swift, clear Ampezzo River. Eleanor and Franklin looked out on meadows speckled with wildflowers and saw bare-footed farm women with bright handkerchiefs around their heads working in the fields beside their men.

The carriage drove out of the meadows into Cortina, a cluster of buildings with balconies and shutters and a yellow stone church whose steeple rose to a point far above the village streets. The Faloria, an inn where the Roosevelts would stay, stood on a steep hill outside Cortina. It was a "queer little hotel," according to Eleanor, but everything was clean and fresh, and the servant women, dressed in traditional peasant costumes, were charming. Eleanor and Franklin went to their room and began to unpack.

During the months since their agreement to marry they had grown accustomed to life together. First they had had to handle Franklin's mother, Sara. She had married his father when she was twenty-six and he was fifty-two. Franklin had an older half-brother by his father's first marriage, but their age difference was so great that Franklin was virtually an only child. Since his father's death Sara had devoted herself to her son, even moving to Cambridge to be near him while he attended Harvard.

When Sara first heard of Eleanor and Franklin's engagement, she declared that they were too young to marry and took Franklin on a cruise in the West Indies, hoping he would reconsider. Eleanor resented Sara's doubts, but Franklin's love survived the voyage, and subsequently mother and daughter-in-law formed a close relationship. The wedding took place on March 17, 1905, with Uncle Ted—now President Theodore Roosevelt—in attendance to give away his niece. It was often said that the extroverted Teddy had to be "the bridegroom at every wedding and the corpse at every funeral," and true to form, he had stolen attention away from Eleanor and Franklin at their own reception. But they were more amused than annoyed when they found themselves alone in one room while their guests thronged around the President in another.

They had moved into a hotel while Franklin completed his studies at Columbia Law School. Their honeymoon was their first chance to be together for any length of time without the constant pressure of law school, and now they were learning more about each other. The character of their relationship and the difference in their temperaments—their ability to bring each other both happiness and sorrow—was apparent in Cortina.

During the past month Franklin had been delightfully attentive. He "has been a wonderful maid," Eleanor wrote Sara during the Atlantic crossing, "and I've never been so well looked after." His letters to his mother, full of banter about places and prices, reflected his good mood. Their suite in London had cost "$1,000 a day." In Paris they had ordered "thousands of dollars worth of linen, 8 doz. tablecloths, 6 napkins, 1/2 pillow case and a handkerchief, all very attractive and full of holes." Seeking to draw his mother into his facetious mood, he told her of a bargain in Venice: "The furniture and woodwork, also mosaic floors of one of the old palaces can be got for about $60,000. If you care to have it, cable me."

In their room at the Faloria Eleanor and Franklin put away their clothes. Late that afternoon they may have strolled along a path fringed with pine forests and looked at the beautiful mountains. The Dolomites loom high above lush green valleys; their fantastic limestone peaks look more like ruined castles or enchanted mesas than ordinary mountains. Some are pink as roses, others white as chalk, and at sunrise and sunset they seem to dance like flames. On clear evenings Eleanor and Franklin could watch the shadows lengthen over the Ampezzo Valley and light play on limestone peaks. Ten miles down the valley the huge mountain Antelao, rising two miles above sea level, would glow against the sky, every point and crag standing out clearly in the pure air. From the village at sunset they could hear a band playing light classical music.

One afternoon Eleanor and Franklin hiked along a forest path to the Belvedere, a place where tourists took tea and enjoyed a famous view of the valley. They must have enjoyed being together like this—their solitude was still new to them, still special. As an older woman Eleanor would question whether she had really been in love during her early married life: "It was years later," she said, "before I understood what being in love was or what loving really meant." But Eleanor's letters to Franklin during their engagement belie her later doubts. If love is a soulful yearning of one human being for another, Eleanor loved Franklin. "I am hungry for you every moment," she told him; "you are never out of my thoughts, Dear." If love is a sense of joy in one's relationship to another, Eleanor loved Franklin. "I have never known before what it was to be absolutely happy," she wrote. And if love is a tender regard for the happiness of another, Eleanor loved Franklin: "I love you *so* dearly," she declared, "and I hope that you, too, Dearest, are very very happy." Nor did Franklin fail to return Eleanor's love. After their engagement he said of their relationship: "You can imagine how completely happy I am—it gives a stimulus to everything I do."

After an hour or so Eleanor and Franklin walked out onto the Belvedere, a high promontory, jutting like the bow of a ship into the clear air of the valley. Here at an inn they sat at a table and drank tea. Then as the distant peaks glowed in the late afternoon sun, they walked back down the mountain. Eleanor cherished long hikes like this with Franklin: he was her husband, her companion, her friend.

But there were times when Franklin was less companionable: not that he was ever deliberately cruel, but sometimes the difference in their temperaments hurt Eleanor. He was buoyant and gregarious; she was shy and subdued. In her adolescence one of her aunts told her that if she was stuck for something to say, she should take the alphabet and work through it: "A—Apple. Do you like apples, Mr. Smith? B—Bears. Are you afraid of bears, Mr. Jones? C—Cats. Do you have the usual feeling, Mrs. Jellyfish, about cats?" Eleanor had progressed as a conversationalist beyond apples, bears, and cats, but she was still a recluse in comparison to her husband.

Franklin was self-assured, and many women admired his good looks. A woman in Paris had said repeatedly, *"Qu'il est beau, qu'il est charmant"*—"My, he's handsome; my, he's charming." It was wonderful to be the bride of such a handsome man, but Eleanor continually worried about pleasing him. The day after they were married she tore a page in one of Franklin's books. She was so upset that "cold shivers went up and down" her spine, and she dreaded telling Franklin. She need not have worried, for he was eager to console her. "If you had not done it, I probably would," he said. "A book is made to be read, not to be held." That incident had ended pleasantly, but Eleanor remained an insecure bride. When they sailed from New York she was full of "qualms" about being seasick and disgracing herself with her husband, who loved the ocean. They wanted children, but Eleanor was "seriously" worried that she might be infertile. This fear and her native shyness made sex more an ordeal than a pleasure. She accepted Franklin's embraces, of course; that was her duty. But to her, as she later admitted to her daughter, the linking of their bodies was uncouth and embarrassing.

Eleanor needed reassurance. Not only was she eager for Franklin's approval, but she was also eager for Sara's acceptance. After resisting her mother-in-law's initial efforts to cool Franklin's ardor, Eleanor had come to regard Sara as a surrogate parent: someone to treat with love and deference. Sara was now "Dearest Mama," and Eleanor had barely left New York on her honeymoon when she wrote her mother-in-law, "I shall look forward to our next long evening together, when I shall want to be kissed all the time."

If the price of being kissed was a submissive regard for Franklin and his mother, Eleanor was more than willing to pay the price, and even to belittle herself in so doing. She and Franklin took turns writing Sara from Europe. Eleanor's letters were more colorful, Franklin's more humorous. He might entertain his mother with accounts of thousand-dollar hotel rooms, but Eleanor could evoke the Venetian atmosphere by writing, "It isn't so much what we see, though everything is interesting, but it's the life and color of the place which makes you feel that nothing could be quite so lovely." Eleanor's letters were charming, and yet she apologized to Sara, telling her, "I can't write like Franklin, and I'm really quite ashamed to send you such stupid epistles after his amusing ones." Sara might have written Eleanor to tell her her letters were as appealing as Franklin's, but she probably did not. There was something gratifying in her daughter-in-law's doting humility.

The person who had most respected Eleanor's intellect and character had been Marie Souvestre, but the headmistress was dead—that source of inspiration and comfort was gone. Eleanor had gone to visit Allenswood while she and Franklin were in London, hoping perhaps to recapture the enthusiasm she had felt there. But the excursion made Eleanor feel "dreadful." Seeing the school without being able to visit with her white-haired mentor proved how much Eleanor missed Marie Souvestre's support.

Franklin seemed to be blessedly free of the anxieties and self-doubt that troubled Eleanor. Wherever he was, he mixed easily with others. Franklin liked people: he liked talking to them, learning about them, laughing with them. On shipboard had been six Asians who barely spoke English. Franklin discovered that they were officers in the Japanese navy on their way to England to take charge of two new warships. He was continually with them, trying to learn about their navy, then at war with Russia, and telling them about the American fleet. In Venice they had visited an old publishing house, and Franklin, the erstwhile editor of the *Harvard Crimson,* engaged a monk in a long conversation about printing.

In Cortina he made friends with Kitty Gandy, with whom he and Eleanor played bridge one evening. Kitty was young and vivacious and, for her time, a liberated woman—not at all like the young bride Eleanor. Kitty ran her own hat shop in New York City, and as it turned out, she was a good mountain climber. This talent pleased Franklin, for he wanted to climb the Faloria Alp, an eight-thousand-foot peak overlooking Cortina, and he assumed that the strain would be too much for Eleanor. Over cards, he and Kitty agreed to go up the mountain together.

Eleanor was stunned. She was not habitually jealous, but something was disturbing about Kitty Gandy. Surely she had never begun a conversation by asking someone whether they were afraid of bears. She ran her own business. Why, she even smoked Franklin's cigarettes!

The next morning Franklin arose promptly at seven, an unusually early hour for him. He shaved, ate breakfast, and at eight Eleanor watched him start up the mountain with this other woman. Kitty wore a big, bright hat that seemed to proclaim her sprightly independence, and Eleanor was "jealous beyond description." Eager for Franklin's return, she spent the morning climbing a rocky slope at the base of the Faloria Alp, where her husband and Kitty would descend. The wait seemed interminable: where was Franklin in all that silent mass of rock?

Eleanor would later say that during her early married years she was "an entirely dependent person." She was willing to suppress her own desires, even to deny her own achievements in order to win favor as a "conventional, quiet young society matron." She gave up even her few hours of settlement house work when she married Franklin, which may have made her all the more resentful of the businesswoman, Kitty Gandy. On that Thursday morning it was only natural that Franklin should be high up the Faloria while Eleanor waited below. Men did more things than women. What seemed unnatural, however, was this other kind of woman, this Kitty Gandy, who was climbing high above with her Franklin.

"B—Bears. Are you afraid of bears, Miss Gandy?"

"Why, no, Mrs. Roosevelt, are you?"

"Oh, yes, Miss Gandy. Oh, yes, I am afraid of bears."

Several thousand feet up the mountain the two climbers were nearing the summit. They could now see mile after mile of Dolomites—"pink and yellow rocks, and white slopes of pure limestone." Great white clouds, "magnificent" in their forms, moved silently over the peaks. Franklin had no idea of the turmoil Eleanor was feeling in his absence. He was not "serious" about Kitty. He probably considered her somewhat eccentric—more a tomboy chum than a rival to his wife. During the climb she smoked all his cigarettes.

After four hours Franklin and Kitty reached the summit. They came back quickly, but by now Eleanor had given up waiting and returned to the inn. When she saw Franklin, she was probably both happy and resentful. Here he was, pleased with his adventure and oblivious to her suffering. Nothing remarkable had happened; he was the same man he had been in the morning. Had he been thoughtless, or had she been oversensitive?

That evening the hotel proprietress, Mme. Menardi, gave a dance in the dining room. The hotel maids, the cook, and some villagers did the *Schuhplattler,* a native dance. The hotel that evening was like a "house party," with no social barriers between guests and the help. Franklin spent the evening dancing with Mme. Menardi, talking with the cook, and smoking with a porter. He told his mother he "had the time of my life."

Eleanor had nothing like the time of her life. That evening she probably wished Franklin were just a little less frisky: first the hike with Kitty Gandy and then his absorption in the hotel party, all in one day. Certainly she did not expect him to devote every moment to her, but she needed to be comforted and reassured, and that day she felt more like a wallflower than a bride. The next morning when Franklin paid the bill and they drove away from Cortina, Eleanor was "perfectly delighted." Now she could have Franklin all to herself.

As the young couple traveled by carriage farther into the Alps, Franklin was as lighthearted as ever. He told his mother, "It was very dusty, and the horse flies were so bad that I had to get out my revolver and shoot several brace. I only skinned the horse once and shot one fly off the end of the driver's nose without scratching him."

The next day they went up Stelvio Pass high in the Alps in a coach pulled by six large horses. Franklin walked in front along the switchbacks and through the tunnels that took them up into the snow. At the side of the road he picked wildflowers; then he walked back to the carriage and handed them to Eleanor. She buried her face in the bouquet. The wild jasmine was the sweetest thing she had ever smelled.

After their honeymoon Eleanor and Franklin moved into a small town house at 125 East Thirty-Sixth Street.

Sara had located the house for her "children" while they were in Europe and after consulting with them had arranged to have the kitchen and basement whitewashed, new wallpaper hung, and the master bedroom—a third-floor room with a small dressing room and a bath—painted white. She also suggested that the house be wired for electric lights, to replace the gas lights, which were still common. The house was narrow but elegant, and Franklin called it their "fourteen-foot mansion."

During the next two years Franklin finished law school at Columbia, and in the fall of 1907 he became a clerk in the firm of Carter, Ledyard, and Milburn at 54 Wall Street. As was customary, Franklin received no salary during his first year of work. But his trust fund of one hundred thousand dollars brought in five thousand a year, and Eleanor had an annual income of seventy-five hundred. In an age when a dollar fifty would hire a house-cleaner for a day, the Roosevelts were prosperous.

As a beginning attorney Franklin spent much of his time in municipal court work. He enjoyed the sharp give-and-take of legal battles and liked the human contact with ordinary men and women. He later wrote, "I often think my Municipal Court work laid the foundation for politics better than any other factor in my life."

While Franklin was busy in his new career, Eleanor was learning to manage a household. Her chief adviser and constant companion was Sara, who came by every day in her carriage to drive up Fifth Avenue and around Central Park with her daughter-in-law. Sara loved the coziness of family relationships and believed that no other friendship could be on the same plane. She had grown up with ten brothers and sisters. At their estate at Algonac on the Hudson her family would gather by a fire in the den on rainy days and take turns reading aloud. Sara would embroider or sew as she listened, snug and close in her large family.

Now with her husband dead and only one child of her own, Sara indulged her love of family in the willing company of Eleanor and Franklin. Having been motherless for so many years, Eleanor welcomed Sara's attention. During her honeymoon she had written Sara from Europe, "We will have such long arrears of kisses and cuddly times to make up when we get home!" Her mother-in-law taught her how to direct servants, plan formal dinners, buy clothes, and furnish the house. Eleanor was deferential to a fault: "Yes, Mama" came almost automatically to her lips. Side by side in the carriage on their daily rides, they looked like a distinguished teacher and her favorite pupil. Sara was dignified, self-assured, matriarchal. Eleanor was attentive, earnest, and eager to please.

The loving companionship between Eleanor and Sara may have been intensified by a certain loneliness in the lives of each: the motherless Eleanor and the daughterless Sara craved one another's devotion. But their association reflects also the intensity in women's friendships that was common at the turn of the century. Living much of their lives in a purely female world, women formed emotional bonds with other women and helped one another face their common experiences as daughters, wives, mothers. The ties between Eleanor and Sara, like the domestic ties between many other women at the time, were both practical and sentimental.

Both women were pleased when they learned after Eleanor's return from Europe that she was pregnant. Eleanor was worried, however, because childbirth was reputedly the most painful experience a woman could undergo. A girlhood friend encouraged her by telling her: "When I am a little afraid of the future I look around and see all the people there are and think they had to be born, and so nothing very extraordinary is happening to me." Eleanor took courage from this practical suggestion, but she was often ill during her pregnancy.

On the afternoon of May 2, 1906, the long wait ended, and Eleanor gave birth to her first child, a girl named Anna. Like most newborn infants Anna must have been wrinkled and frail, unable to focus her eyes and barely able to move. The child was just a "helpless bundle" to Eleanor, but in its weakness it wound itself "inextricably" around her heart. Anna was the first of six babies Eleanor would deliver. She would later say of herself: "For ten years I was always just getting over having a baby or about to have one." Most of her pregnancies made her sick, and she developed the habit of suffering in silence, lest she trouble Franklin or Sara with her problems. She later wondered if this stoicism did not have a bad effect on her personality, killing in her "a certain amount of the power of enjoyment" and making her "draw away from other people."

Although bearing children was a major preoccupation for Eleanor during the early years of her marriage, caring for them was less so. A succession of nurses changed diapers, served food, administered discipline, and provided entertainment for the Roosevelt children. Eleanor did not even nurse the infants; the first children were fed by bottle, and when they proved sickly, Eleanor paid wet nurses to care for them. With Anna and her other children Eleanor felt both love and awkwardness. She was drawn to her daughter, but she was uncertain how to care for her.

Eleanor's relationship to Anna and to her husband after two years of marriage is revealed in a group of letters she wrote Sara during the summer of 1907 while vacationing on Campobello, a Canadian island off the coast of Maine. Before boarding the train that would carry them north from New York City, Eleanor and Franklin posed for a picture. Dressed in a dark three-piece suit, a stiff white collar, and a dark bowler hat, Franklin looked more like an established business executive than a young man just out of law school. Eleanor too looked mature for her years. Wearing a long black dress and a wide white collar, she was positively matronly. At twenty-two she already looked the part of conventional wife and mother.

They traveled by Pullman through the night. Before dawn the baby Anna awoke. She seemed pleased with the strange surroundings and babbled happily to her nurse and Eleanor, whom she awakened with the prattle. The women watched dawn break over the Maine countryside while Franklin, undisturbed by his daughter's chatter, slept on through the night.

The Roosevelts disembarked at Eastport on the Maine coast near the Canadian border and went to a boat that would take them to Campobello. The island consisted of a few square miles of woods, bogs, and beaches set in the cold waters of the Bay of Fundy. Franklin's parents had discovered Campobello during the summer of 1883. They liked the sea air, the rustic lodge with open fires, and the intelligent society of summer visitors. Almost every year after that Franklin went with his parents to Campobello, where he learned to fish, swim, canoe, and sail. He introduced Eleanor to the island in 1904 during their engagement. Normally Sara was in charge on the family estate, issuing commands to the household servants and to the crew of the *Half Moon,* the family yacht, but this summer in her absence Eleanor and Franklin were in charge.

The boat carrying them to Campobello came to rest in Welshpool, a cove on the western side of the island. The Roosevelts transferred their luggage to a carriage and drove to a large rambling house they called "Granny's Cottage." It was newly painted, and Eleanor thought it looked "grand." She and Franklin unpacked, greeted the servants, and set up Anna's crib. The beach house with its many rooms contrasted with the house at 125 East Thirty-Sixth Street. Instead of urban sounds outside their door, Eleanor and Franklin could hear the call of seabirds and the surge of waves on the beach. They would spend the summer hiking, canoeing, and sailing around the island and on the open waters of the Bay of Fundy.

On clear days Eleanor and Franklin often picnicked with Anna aboard the *Half Moon.* They usually took along Blanche Spring, a trained nurse, who was one of Eleanor's closest companions. She was a big, muscular woman with a square jaw and a seemingly endless reserve of energy. She loved children and helped Eleanor learn to care for her own. Although Sara did not approve of her daughter-in-law's friendship with someone as menial as a nurse, Eleanor was "deeply attached" to Miss Spring. Since her childhood, when two of her closest friends had been the butler Victor and the laundress Mrs. Overhalse, Eleanor had enjoyed the company of unaffected working people.

With a crew of three to help with the sailing, the Roosevelts picnicked on the *Half Moon* or on deserted shores. Eleanor and Blanche would sit in comfortable wicker chairs in the spacious cockpit, with Anna playing on the deck between them and Franklin confident at the helm. One afternoon the boat was caught in a strong east wind blowing before a storm. Undaunted, Eleanor could tell Sara, "The day was delightful and the wind made our sail home more interesting and exciting."

The summer was full of amusements for the young couple. Franklin took Eleanor out in his birchbark canoe, built for him when he was a boy by the chief of a local Indian tribe. Paddling the craft in his sleeveless shirt, he looked like a real woodsman: sinewy and deeply tanned. The Roosevelts had their own tennis court, and Franklin spent many hours rolling the sand and clay surface. He often played doubles with friends, while Eleanor looked on or saw to the preparation of tea. She felt awkward on the court and was more in her element on walks along the beach.

When storm clouds blew in off the North Atlantic, Eleanor and Franklin were driven inside to other activities. Franklin and a neighbor, George Clymer, spent hours working together on their stamp collections. He and Eleanor often read aloud to each other in the parlor. The books were probably chosen by Franklin, for they dealt with military and naval history. But Eleanor listened contentedly. Bertram L. Simpson's *Indiscreet Letters from Peking,* for example, was full of "gruesome details," but Eleanor found it "most interesting."

The summer of 1907 was above all a time when Eleanor and Franklin came to know themselves as parents. Franklin, who was slowly growing accustomed to being a father, liked to roll up his trousers, place Anna on his back, and wade into the water. Eleanor wrote Sara, "The Baby is too sweet and makes us shriek with laughter when she puts her whole hand into my cup of tea." Anna was a year old and growing more interesting by the day. During the summer Anna said her first words. Franklin was "Gaga," and the paid skipper of the *Half Moon* became "Cap." Anna grew tan and chubby; Eleanor carried her to the market periodically to weigh her on a produce scale and reported proudly that her daughter had reached twenty-five pounds. The child began the summer as a crawler; then one day she tried to walk, fell, cried, and tried again. Within a few days she was walking so expertly that she chased Duffy, the Roosevelts' scottie dog, all over the house. "Duffy's life is becoming daily more trying," Eleanor told Sara.

In New York City Anna spent most of her time with servants while Eleanor was busy with other activities. But in Campobello mother and daughter were often together. Anna still had a nurse, but in midsummer this helper was called away for a few days and Eleanor and Blanche Spring cared for Anna. Blanche was as unaccustomed to daily child care as Eleanor—she was more a medical adviser and a companion than a babysitter. But at first the task seemed easy. Eleanor reported, the baby "has her crib in our room and is too good and sweet." A few days later, however, the novelty of responsibility wore off, and Eleanor complained, "My lady Anna is the mischief itself, and I will be glad when Nurse returns to manage her, as Nurse Spring and I, not being used to her, have had some quite hard struggles with little tempers and wildest animal spirits which break out at inopportune moments!" The nurse came back. "Anna is very happy to have her back," Eleanor wrote, "but I am glad to say I think she missed me a little last night." Eleanor's pleasure in Anna's affection suggests a furtive desire to be closer to her daughter. But convention and convenience kept her from attending to the children's daily needs.

During the summer of 1907 in Campobello Eleanor seemed wholly contented with her life. She saw Anna just enough to enjoy her antics without being bothered by her needs. She was frequently with her husband; and because Sara was far away, Eleanor and Franklin were in complete control of their household. In September, however, the Campobello idyll came to an end, and Eleanor returned to a world in which she was becoming anxious and discontented.

On the surface Eleanor's life was pleasant enough. She bore children in rapid succession—four during her first five years of marriage. She served on charity boards, helping to direct assistance to the poor. She embroidered and knitted; took lessons in French, German, and Italian; and attended courses on art, music, literature, and the Bible at friends' houses. And she read so much current literature that there was seldom a work of history or fiction that she missed. Eleanor was also growing adept at managing the household. She seemed in command of the details, such as preparing the house for the family's return from a trip to Campobello: she wrote home instructing her servants that first the chimneys should be swept; then two "*honest* Cleaners" should be employed to begin at the top floor and work their way down; the children's mattresses should be beaten on the roof; every book in the library should be removed, dusted, and reshelved. At home Eleanor sent thank-you notes, bought presents, and saw that bills were paid on time.

Although she pursued many kinds of domestic and cultural activities, Eleanor was profoundly discontented with her life. She later concluded that she had become too dependent on her mother-in-law and was too reticent about expressing her own opinions and declaring her own needs. She was, Eleanor wrote, "simply absorbing the personalities of those about me and letting their tastes and interests dominate me." She was "not developing any individual taste or initiative." Eleanor wrote these words when she was fifty-two. As a young girl in her twenties, however, she could not identify her problem so clearly. She simply knew that many things upset her: she wanted to be more in control of her life than seemed possible, and she wanted more love than was given her.

Despite her domestic efficiency, she was unhappy with her role in the household. She felt that she did not know enough about cooking or raising children. Servants usually did these things, but Eleanor did not like being so dependent on their help. The children's nurses actually bossed her around; and when the cooks were occasionally absent, she was helpless. One winter Eleanor took cooking lessons at Columbia University, but she "got little good out of it" because they used modern gas ranges and prepared gourmet meals. What she needed was to be able to use an old-fashioned coal range and cook simple meals for her family.

Eleanor felt even more helpless on the nurse's day out. On one nurseless evening Eleanor had to care for her baby while hostessing a dinner party. Instead of falling asleep conveniently at six-thirty, when her parents were dressing, Anna began to howl in her crib. Distraught, Eleanor called the doctor for a quick course in child care. Had she burped Anna after her last bottle, he asked. That precaution—so obvious to mothers and liberated fathers of three generations later—Eleanor had completely overlooked. The doctor told her how to calm Anna by rubbing her back, and with some effort Eleanor quieted the child. By now the guests had arrived, but Eleanor was "so wrought up" she had to leave them continually to check on Anna. That night Eleanor "registered a vow" that she would never again "have a dinner on the nurse's day out."

In various ways Eleanor's efforts to manage her own children often ended disastrously. She read that children need fresh air, and so she ordered a box with wire sides to be hung from Anna's window for her to sleep in during her morning nap. The arrangement worked for a time, but Anna sometimes cried in her curious perch, and hearing her, one of the neighbors threatened to call the Society for the Prevention of Cruelty to Children. That ended the baby-cage experiment, but Eleanor continued reading about child rearing—and discovered that she had hung Anna on the wrong side of the house anyway. Sunshine, she learned, is more important than fresh air; Anna's cage had been in the shade.

Each of Eleanor's efforts to enlarge her sphere of competence seemed to end in frustration. In 1908 the Roosevelts acquired a car for their use at a summer home in Seabright, New Jersey. It came with a hand crank, no windshield, and frequent blowouts, but Eleanor was determined to drive it and did—into a gatepost. That ended for a decade her efforts to master the automobile. She was interested in doing volunteer work in the slums: sitting on charity boards with other socialites seemed too far from the real issue of poverty, the poor people themselves. But she was dissuaded from returning to the Lower East Side by Sara and other friends who told her that such activities would be irresponsible—she would come home with germs and contaminate her own children.

Eleanor was frustrated at not being able to find new outlets for her talents. She was even more frustrated by a sense of detachment from the very houses she lived in. Sara had chosen the young couple's first house, and then in a seemingly extravagant burst of generosity, she built her children a house on Sixty-Fifth Street. It was larger and more elegant than their rented house, but Eleanor never felt that it was truly hers. Sara and Franklin planned it, and although Franklin consulted with Eleanor, he and his mother made most of the important decisions about it. Eleanor might have adjusted to that and still made the house her own except that Sara had built not one house but two. The second was right next to Eleanor and Franklin's, had a common wall and adjoining doors—and was occupied by Sara.

One evening shortly after moving into the new house, Eleanor sat at her dressing table and wept. Franklin asked her what was wrong. She did not like, she cried, to live in a house that was "not in any way" hers. Franklin, like many other men in his generation, tended to see his wife's display of emotions as an irrational outburst rather than a valid complaint. He told her gently but firmly that she was "quite mad" and that she would be better in a "little while." Then he left Eleanor alone until she "should become calmer."

In such ways Franklin failed to understand Eleanor's needs. The differences in their temperaments, so apparent at Cortina during their honeymoon, continued to create problems. Eleanor later decided that during the early years of her marriage she had had "painfully high ideals."

She expected Franklin to behave in specific ways—to attend church every Sunday, for example—and he did not always meet her expectations. Unfortunately, she often neglected to tell him what she expected and became morose and withdrawn when he did not please her.

Franklin had little sympathy or understanding for his wife's unhappiness. He was, on the whole, quite satisfied with life. He enjoyed his legal practice and his friends. He spent many evenings with Eleanor and also went out with male companions, going on sprees until three or four in the morning. He sometimes went to church with Eleanor, but if the sun were shining brightly on Sunday morning, Franklin was as likely to play golf. Eleanor tried to become involved in Franklin's recreations. She secretly practiced golf, hoping to play with her husband. Then she accompanied him for a few rounds. Her shots must have sliced into the woods or dribbled off the tee, for after only a few holes Franklin told her she might as well give it up. A disappointed Eleanor turned in her clubs.

In this matter and many others life did not work out for Eleanor as she might have wished. She had abandoned the chance for a career in the hopes of finding happiness in marriage. But as a bride she felt out of touch with life's most elemental activities: running a household, raising children, and caring for her husband. Servants and Sara prevented Eleanor from feeling in control of her domestic life, and Franklin often failed to give her the love and reassurance she craved.

While Eleanor was struggling to find both love and autonomy, she was bringing new life into the world. She bore her first son, James, a year and a half after Anna. Among Eleanor's fears had been that she would not be able to give Franklin a boy; lovely as Anna was, the Roosevelts shared the common prejudice that a mother's greatest achievement was to bear a son. Years afterward

Eleanor's prose was lyrical when she recalled her "relief and joy" at her son's birth: "My heart sang when James was safely in the world."

Fourteen months later she gave birth to another boy, Franklin Jr. This second son was "the biggest and most beautiful" of Eleanor's children. Within a few months of his birth, however, he brought Eleanor more sorrow. In October 1908, when the infant was seven months old, he caught a flu. Within a few days he was dead.

Sara had watched over the baby with Eleanor and Franklin. She wrote in her journal, "Poor Eleanor's mother heart is well nigh broken. She so hoped and cannot believe her baby is gone from her." The day after the infant's death Sara sat beside its casket. "It is hard to give him up," she wrote, "and my heart aches for Eleanor." They took the body to Hyde Park, to a small graveyard behind the stone church where they worshiped. The air was cold; a small group of friends gathered for the burial service.

"Ashes to ashes, dust to dust . . ." The time-honored formulas for adjusting to death ran through Eleanor's mind. But it was hard to accept this death: if only she had been a better mother, she thought; if only she had cared enough. Before her she saw a tiny casket, earth cascading onto a lifeless child, the unalterable end of something.

Eleanor could not accept Franklin Jr.'s death. Her father had left her a Bible that she would carry with her all her life; in it she placed three poems on the death of children. Eleanor mourned for the baby all fall and scolded herself for leaving so much of his care to nurses. She scolded Franklin too for not having done more, for caring less than she did, for being someone other than her ideal husband. Franklin, ever rational, tried to make Eleanor see how "idiotically" she was behaving. But he too grieved, and ten months after the baby's death, a new Roosevelt, named Elliott, was born.

# 5

# A Politician's Wife

*I looked at everything from the point of view of what I ought to
do, rarely from the standpoint of what I wanted to do. . . . So I took
an interest in politics. It was a wife's duty to be interested in
whatever interested her husband, whether it was politics, books, or a
particular dish for dinner.*

Eleanor Roosevelt, *This Is My Story*

On an autumn day in 1910 Eleanor Roosevelt stood in
front of Nelson House, a five-story red brick hotel in
Poughkeepsie, New York, listening to Franklin address a
crowd. He was nearing the end of a spirited race for the state
senate, but this was the first time Eleanor had heard him
deliver a campaign speech. She had been at home that fall
with the baby Elliott, who seemed especially vulnerable
because Eleanor had just recently lost a child. Perhaps
Franklin Jr. would have survived, she was told, if he had
been breast-fed rather than bottle-fed. Poor women could be
hired to feed the sons and daughters of the wealthy, and so
Eleanor found an immigrant woman to nurse baby Elliott.

Although Eleanor had not accompanied Franklin on his
campaign tour, she supported his plans. She alone of
Franklin's close friends encouraged him to enter politics.
His boss, Lewis Cass Ledyard, objected that Franklin was
jeopardizing a brilliant legal career by running for office.
His mother complained that politicians must mingle with
the masses. But neither Franklin's legal career nor Sara's
patrician scruples could keep him from public life. He

**105**

dreamed of following Theodore Roosevelt's course, becoming, in succession, a state legislator, Assistant Secretary of the Navy, Governor of New York, and then President. In 1907 he told his fellow law clerks that some day he would occupy the White House; one of them later remembered, "It seemed proper and sincere; and moreover, as he put it, entirely reasonable."

Franklin's political career began in 1910 when John Mack, the District Attorney of Dutchess County, suggested that he run for the legislature. Franklin gave a speech at a Democratic Party picnic—a sauerkraut-and-beer affair—and so impressed local party leaders that they agreed to nominate him for the state senate. In his acceptance speech on October 6 he promised "a very strenuous month" of campaigning.

If he were to win, Franklin would need to be both energetic and lucky. The district, which consisted of three rural counties, had elected only one Democrat to the state Senate since 1856. Moreover, the incumbent, Senator John F. Schlosser, was solidly backed by the state's strong Republican machine.

During the campaign of 1910 Senator Schlosser had his incumbency, but Franklin had his ambition—and a rented red Maxwell touring car. No one before had campaigned by car in that region. The automobile was still in its infancy, and "horseless carriages" ventured at some risk onto roads designed for horse-drawn vehicles. Most cars had no windshield, no roof, and no doors. Drivers and their passengers wore goggles, raincoats with collars that turned up to the ears, and, in colder weather, fur coats that covered them to their ankles. Breakdowns and blowouts were so common that an eighteen-pound tool kit offered by Hammacher, Schlemmer was practically a necessity. An advertisement published in 1908 suggests the resourcefulness demanded of early drivers. "Here we are—stuck!" it reads. "Did it ever occur to you that the Damascus hatchet would be a mighty convenient and dependable acquisition to the auto tool chest? When the wheel drops out of sight in the mud, get out the Damascus, cut a pole for a lever, right things up, and then on your way again."

Franklin may not have carried a Damascus hatchet, but roads in his district were often primitive. Putnam, Dutchess, and Columbia Counties stretch a hundred miles along the Hudson and twenty miles east to the Connecticut and Massachusetts borders. Scores of country roads cut between the region's steep forested hills and rolling farmland. Maps gave little indication of the condition or even the location of the roads. Franklin was so disoriented once during the campaign that he gave a speech in Connecticut without realizing that he had crossed out of his district.

Franklin had a traveling companion, Richard Connell, who helped with the inevitable repairs and taught Franklin about politics. Connell was campaigning for Congress. In a month the two men covered two thousand miles, carrying the campaign up and down the lower Hudson River counties, to little towns like Fish Kill, Rhinebeck, Pine Plains, Red Hook, and Chatham. They talked to farmers husking corn or sitting in country stores, they bought drinks for all the people in local saloons and hotels, and they delivered as many as ten speeches a day. Dick Connell was a flamboyant speaker who concluded each address by pulling an American flag from his coat and declaring, "The same old flag that waved at Lexington, the same old flag that Sherman carried on the march to the sea . . ." Franklin carried no flag, but he did learn from Connell to remove the pince-nez glasses that made him look too formal and to address his audiences as "my friends."

When he spoke in front of Eleanor in Poughkeepsie he was already a veteran of dozens of political rallies. But at twenty-eight he was hardly the seasoned politician he would later become. To Eleanor he seemed "high-strung, and at times nervous." His ideas were appealing: he spoke against the influence of political bosses and special interests in the legislature, and he wanted honest and efficient government. He paused so long between points, however, that Eleanor sometimes worried that he had lost his train of thought and might not be able to go on. She must have wondered whether her husband was in over his head. Even his mentor, John Mack, warned him that the odds were five to one against his being elected.

A few days before the election the *New York Times* announced that it would use beacons on the roof of the *Times* building to signal the outcome of the state and national elections. On election night lights swept over the city from atop the two-hundred-foot edifice. A shaft of light moving back and forth to the north indicated that Democratic candidate John A. Dix had won the governorship. A steady light to the west heralded Woodrow Wilson's victory as New Jersey governor. And another shaft of light pointing steadily north indicated that Democrats had won the state legislature. Franklin was elected to his first public office by a margin of 1,140 votes, roughly twice the victory margin enjoyed in Franklin's district by Governor-elect Dix.

Franklin's victory changed his life—and Eleanor's. She believed that "it was a wife's duty to be interested in whatever interested her husband." Franklin was interested in politics and, more fundamentally, in people. He was drawn not so much to a particular political philosophy or program as to the *process* of politics. Eleanor later wrote, "He probably could not have formulated his political philosophy at that time as he could later, but the science of government was interesting—and people, the ability to understand them, the play of his own personality on theirs, was a fascinating study to him."

Eleanor too was interested in people. She made new friends in Albany after she and Franklin moved there for his first term, and once she knew the town she began to feel "responsible" for the wives of other new assembly-men and newspapermen, just as she had cared for lonely new girls at school in England. In Albany she broadened her social contacts beyond the aristocratic friends she had known in New York City. "I was not a snob," she later wrote, "largely because I never really thought about why you asked people to your house or claimed them as friends. Anyone who came was grist to my mill, because I was beginning to get interested in human beings, and I found that almost everyone had something interesting to contribute to my education."

Watching the legislature was also part of Eleanor's edu-cation. She went often to the capitol gallery and listened to the debates. Soon she came to recognize and appreciate individual speakers. Tom Grady she considered one of the greatest speakers she had ever heard. She liked Bob Wagner, "Big Tim" Sullivan, and old Senator Brackett, who she said "looked like a church deacon and was prob-ably as wily a politician as ever paced the Senate floor." And she caught her first glimpse of a man whose career would greatly affect her husband's—Al Smith.

Eleanor also met Louis Howe in Albany, a man who would have a vital role in her own life as well as Franklin's. He was a newspaperman with an instinct for politics and believed Franklin had a great political future. But Eleanor was at first put off by Howe, a small gnomelike man who smoked "a great many cigarettes." During the fall of 1912 Franklin was sick with typhoid fever; Louis came to New York to manage his campaign. He sat at Franklin's bedside, puffing cigarettes and talking strategy. Without Louis's help Franklin would "probably have lost the election," but Eleanor saw him only as an obnoxious intruder and made a "nuisance" of herself over the visits.

The young matron was willing to meet new people, but there were limits to her liberality. In Howe she saw an ugly, uncouth man—missing his real strength of character. Like her mother and Sara and most of the women she knew, she still believed that some people were "socially acceptable" and that others, due to manners or breeding or race, were not. But still Eleanor was learning, slowly, to appreciate the variety of human types and the complexity of social relationships by her exposure to legislative contests. Franklin was one of a group of insurgent state senators who sought to prevent the legislature from sending a Tammany Hall candidate to the U.S. Senate. Franklin was both daring and precocious to take on the most powerful political group in the state so early in his career. The insurgent legislators met at the Roosevelt house; Eleanor provided them with refreshments and listened quietly to their discussions far into the night.

Franklin survived the Senate struggle, but Eleanor found out how difficult life can be for the losers in a political fight. One of the insurgents ran a small country newspaper that depended on a contract for printing government notices. In the next year the Tammany Democrats punished him for his opposition by withdrawing the government business, and the paper failed. Eleanor was outraged. Apparently politics was not a free competition among ideas. If a person was not independently wealthy, he might be forced to compromise his principles. Then he "might be a slave and not a public servant."

Although Eleanor was intrigued, and sometimes disturbed, as the lessons of politics were revealed to her, she could not lose herself in Franklin's career. She began to realize that something within her "craved to be an individual." And what did it mean to be an individual? Eleanor probably did not know. By her own later admission she was not "a feminist in those early days." She did not expect to enter a profession or earn her own living. She did not even expect to be able to vote, and she was "shocked" when Franklin came out for woman suffrage. Eleanor had simply assumed "that men were superior creatures and knew more about politics than women did." She became a supporter of woman suffrage for the ironic reason that Franklin was for woman suffrage so she "probably must be too."

Eleanor did not expect to achieve a sense of selfhood by assuming a man's role in the world of men. But how, then, could she become an individual? What were her choices? At first her desire for personal growth centered on the orthodox desire to have her own home. She was delighted when Sara gave her and Franklin a cottage at Campobello; for the first time in her life she had a house she considered her own, and it became "a source of great joy" to her. She was pleased also to move to Albany, where Sara would not be "within call." It was not simply that Sara dominated Eleanor, but Eleanor contributed to her own loss of independence by going to Sara, deferring to her, depending on her. In Albany she would have to manage the house and plan entertainments without the assistance of her mother-in-law. "I had to stand on my own feet now," she later wrote, "and I wanted to be independent." This was a very limited sort of independence, well within the confines of a traditional "woman's role," but for Eleanor it was nonetheless a form of growth.

Although Eleanor's self-confidence as the mistress of her house grew with the years, she preferred the companionship of her adult friends to her children, who saw more of their nurses than of their mother. Eleanor moved to

Albany with three children, Anna, James, and Elliott. Anna and James and the younger nurse had a room over the library at the back of the house. Elliott and his nurse were in a room next to Eleanor and Franklin. Eleanor had tea "every afternoon" with the children and read to them or played with them until they went to bed, but she had little patience with their childish foibles. When she allowed Anna to have lunch with Franklin and her and Anna spent "a solid hour over the meal" in the first attempt, Eleanor sent the child back to the nursery.

Eleanor and Franklin were able to cooperate effectively in fostering his political career, but differences in temperament still kept tensions between them. Franklin's choice of friends and social activities often varied from Eleanor's. She was more comfortable with older people— even with her mother-in-law—than with young people, whom she felt "inadequate" to meet "on their own light, gay terms." Her cousin Theodore Douglas Robinson was in the legislature with Franklin; he and his wife, Helen, loved a good time and once went to a party dressed in baby clothes. We can imagine Franklin laughing boisterously at their antics, but Eleanor . . . Eleanor would be nonplussed. She might try to fit into the spirit of frivolity, but her aloofness would be all too apparent. She later confessed that she "must have spoiled a good deal of fun for Franklin because of this inability to feel at ease."

Eleanor did not insist that Franklin stay at home all the time and associate only with people she enjoyed: if he wanted to be with companions she disliked or to go somewhere she wanted to avoid, Eleanor encouraged him to go out by himself. But Franklin could be as hurt by Eleanor's desire to stay at home as she could be upset by his choice of entertainments. He was as eager that she fit in with his moods as she was that he accommodate hers.

Franklin's own vulnerability was apparent in April 1912 when he wrote Eleanor from a passenger freighter, the *Carrillo*, bound for Panama. Eleanor's brother Hall had come along, and so had Franklin's friend Matthew Wainwright. They enjoyed talking, drinking, and playing cards together, but despite this good company Franklin also wanted Eleanor to join them. Eleanor, however, chose to stay in New York with the children, claiming that her seasickness would spoil the trip. Franklin was annoyed. Surely Sara and the nurses could have cared for the children, and as for the seasickness, the ocean all the way down to Cape Hatteras and into the Caribbean was as flat calm as the Hudson River. Missing his wife, he decided to "record all the minutest details" of what he saw, hoping to make her more willing to join him on his next trip.

The ship steamed south through beautiful warm days. When darkness fell, Franklin stood at the rail under a starry sky and watched for lights on nearby islands. On the second night out he spotted a light on San Salvador, where Columbus first touched land in the New World. A student of naval history and an avid sailor, Franklin was so excited that he immediately wrote Eleanor. If only she were with him. . . . "I am becoming more cross every day at the thought of your missing this trip," he wrote, "for it is really a wonderful opportunity thrown away."

They sailed on. More conversations and more games. Franklin beat Hall at cards, but Hall beat him at checkers. It was a fine trip, and yet without Eleanor—Eleanor who would have talked to him at day's end and might have held him while the ship rumbled on through the night—without her, Franklin's pleasure was incomplete. "I do wish you were here—" he wrote; "it is hard enough to be away from the chicks, but with you away from me too I feel very much alone and lost. I hereby solemnly declare that I *refuse* to go away the next time without you."

Although Eleanor must have missed Franklin, she was probably happier staying with the children in New York. The open ocean, games of shuffleboard and cards, chumming around with friends who liked to drink—all these were in Franklin's element rather than hers. Neither could become a different person solely for the sake of the other.

In June 1912 Eleanor and Franklin attended the Democratic National Convention in Baltimore. This was Eleanor's first presidential convention, and she was startled by the delegates' cavorting. Politics, she believed, should be the meeting ground of the nation's best minds and highest ideals. But the floor fight between Champ Clark and Woodrow Wilson for the presidential nomination seemed more like a circus than a chautauqua. The demonstrations appeared "senseless," and when Clark's daughter was carried around the auditorium in a procession—what could be less ladylike? Eleanor was frankly "appalled." Ill at ease, she left Baltimore for Campobello before the end of the convention.

Franklin stayed on and led New York's liberal Democrats in their support of Woodrow Wilson, who finally won the nomination. When he was elected President that November, Wilson, the Princeton University president turned reform governor of New Jersey, rewarded Franklin for his support by appointing him Assistant Secretary of the Navy, a post the young man had long coveted. Barely thirty-two years old, Franklin was now second only to Secretary Josephus Daniels in the naval chain of command. He was entitled to a seventeen-gun salute whenever he boarded a battleship—a gray-haired admiral received only thirteen.

Theodore Roosevelt, who had held the position a few years before, used it as a springboard to the Presidency. Franklin hoped to follow his example, but he was also delighted in the office for its own sake. Ships and the sea fascinated him. He loved to sail and surrounded himself with nautical lore. He collected so many naval books, letters, models, and prints that Eleanor jokingly predicted that she and the children would have to abandon their home to make room for Franklin's collections. As Assistant Secretary of the Navy he could indulge a boy's love of the sea as well as a man's ambition for the Presidency.

On March 17, 1913, Franklin moved into his new office. Seated at Theodore Roosevelt's old desk, he wrote Eleanor, telling her how pleased he was with his new position. "The delightful significance of it all," he wrote, "is just beginning to dawn on me." He assured his wife, "I am thinking of you a great deal and sending you 'wireless' messages." But in his excitement he had nearly forgotten their anniversary. "I didn't know til I sat down at this desk," he confessed, that this is the day "of happy memory." On this day and many others to come Eleanor would often have to be content with "wireless messages" from a husband too busy to lavish his affection on her.

But Eleanor knew her duty. It never occurred to her, she said, "to question where we were to go or what we were to do or how we were to do it." And so she took the children, four servants, a nurse, and a governess and moved into a red brick house at 1733 N Street near the Capitol. The house had served as a temporary "White House" for Theodore Roosevelt before he moved to 1600 Pennsylvania Avenue. Its bow windows looked out onto a lovely tree-lined street. The yard, though small, contained a rock garden and a rose arbor. During the warm days of spring and summer Eleanor and Franklin often ate breakfast with the children among the roses.

Louis Howe came to Washington as Franklin's personal secretary and moved into an apartment near the

Roosevelts. Every morning he came by the house and walked with Franklin to the State, War, and Navy Building. During Franklin's seven years in the Navy Department, Howe served as his political adviser, reminding him of ways in which his contacts with ship construction workers and dock workers could help Franklin's political career.

As Assistant Secretary, Franklin helped direct a naval force of 269 ships and sixty-five thousand men. He planned expenditures that used up one-fifth of the federal budget, oversaw naval procurement, and inspected ships and harbors. His boss, Naval Secretary Josephus Daniels, was twenty years older than he. In contrast to his young assistant, Daniels was a cautious, even plodding administrator. One afternoon the two men stood for a photograph on a portico overlooking the White House. Daniels looked directly into the sun, his hair shaggy, his face benign. Roosevelt stood behind him, half a head taller, grinning broadly. When Daniels, who came from North Carolina, saw the picture, he told Franklin: "We are both looking down on the White House, and you are saying to yourself, being a New Yorker, 'Some day I will be living in that house'—while I, being from the South, know I must be satisfied with no such ambition." A newsman said Franklin was as "friendly as an airedale pup and young enough to want to look older." Other men might have felt threatened by such a precocious subordinate, but Daniels genuinely liked Franklin. He and Franklin soon settled into a constructive partnership.

Franklin spent many days at his desk in Washington, but he particularly cherished the times that his work took him to sea. When an American submarine sank with all hands, Franklin went out in a similar ship to prove his confidence in its seaworthiness. He was probably never happier than when observing the world from a ship's bridge, and he must have been in heaven on October 26, 1913, when he delivered the official farewell to a fleet of battleships bound for the Mediterranean. He arrived at Hampton Roads aboard the naval yacht *Dolphin.* Nine battleships lay at anchor in a double line, accompanied by a hospital ship and supply ships. Under a driving rain, a swarm of launches and whaleboats darted between the vessels and the shore, carrying sailors returning from leave, women bidding their men farewell, and stores for a seven-month voyage. The *Dolphin* dropped anchor at the head of the column to the sound of a seventeen-gun salute from the flagship *Wyoming.*

Then began a series of visits and inspections. Fleet commander Charles J. Badger came on board the *Dolphin* with three other admirals and was saluted with trumpets and cannon. After lunch on the *Dolphin* the admirals returned to their ships and Franklin took a launch to the flagship *Wyoming.* He saw gunrooms, storerooms, the ship's bakery, and a bulletin board—which advertised a crew debate on the merits of woman suffrage.

The inspection tour completed, the *Dolphin* steamed down to the Virginia Capes ahead of the fleet to review the ships as they sailed out into the Atlantic. A school of dolphins played near the bow as Franklin watched the fleet approach. On each ship bands played and sailors manned the rail; each fired a parting salute as they crossed the *Dolphin*'s bow and steamed out into the Atlantic. Franklin was jubilant. "The big gray fellows were magnificent as they went past with all hands at the rail," he wrote Eleanor, "and I only wish a hundred thousand people could have seen them." During such moments Franklin could not imagine a better life: a distinguished job in Washington, the chance to mingle with sailors and ships. He wrote a friend, "I now find my vocation combined with my avocation in a delightful way."

In Washington Franklin found honor and pleasure. Eleanor too had a vocation in the nation's capital: she paid calls and gave dinners. Her work was neither as challenging nor as honorific as Franklin's, but she believed it was important nonetheless. Before moving to Washington Eleanor was told that her duty was "first, last, and all the time to look after the Navy itself." Many of the young officers' wives would have difficulty in Washington on their husbands' meager pay. By entertaining and visiting them, Eleanor could make their lives more "pleasant." Eleanor was also told she must make formal calls on the wives of congressmen and cabinet officials. Eleanor's "heart sank somewhat" at this news, but she ordered calling cards and practiced her introduction: "I am Mrs. Franklin D. Roosevelt. My husband has just come as Assistant Secretary of the Navy . . . ."

During her early years in Washington Eleanor spent weekday afternoons making calls. She followed a rigid schedule: Mondays the wives of Supreme Court justices, Tuesdays of congressmen, Wednesdays of Cabinet members, Thursdays of Senators, and Fridays of diplomats. The congressmen's wives were particularly elusive, for many lived in rooming houses or hotels and moved frequently, but Eleanor sought out all the New York congressional wives and visited with them or left her calling card. With the end of each day's round of calls she felt assured that she had assisted Franklin's career: a dozen or so prominent women would tell their husbands that the wife of the Assistant Secretary of the Navy had paid her respects that day. By social alchemy Eleanor would thus encourage people to accept Franklin himself. The Roosevelts would be insiders; they would belong.

While in Washington Eleanor gave birth to two more boys: John in 1914 and Franklin Jr. in 1916. The older children, Anna, James, and Elliott, were now in school. As in their earlier years, they were still raised by servants, who were given a free hand. An English governess, whom the children called "old Battleax," knelt on Anna's chest, locked Elliott in a closet for three hours, and forced Jimmy to walk up and down the sidewalk in front of the Washington house wearing his sister's dress and carrying a sign on his back that read, "I am a liar." Eleanor intervened and fired the woman only after finding her dresser full of liquor bottles.

The children were high-spirited, and Anna, who was growing into a tall, blond tomboy, often led them in playing Indian at Hyde Park, sliding down the roof at Campobello, and dropping waterbombs on their mother's tea guests in Washington. Franklin often joined the children in play. In the winter he rode sleds with them down the long slope behind Hyde Park and chased them back up the hill. On picnics outside of Washington he jumped from rock to rock in a creek with Anna on his shoulders. He organized family games of baseball and hare and hounds.

Eleanor was less relaxed with the children. "I was never really carefree," she later wrote. She breakfasted with the children, kissing each on the cheek before the meal, and she read them stories after tea. At bedtime she gathered them around her knees and heard their prayers. Despite these affectionate gestures, however, she often seemed remote. At her desk she often repulsed her children's pleas for attention with the cold greeting, "What do you want, dear?" Cherishing order, she was unable to show spontaneous goodwill in meeting the varied needs of five youngsters. She felt more at home, seemingly, in making her social rounds.

Eleanor tried to be home every afternoon by five to have time with the children, but often she had to dine out with Franklin or entertain guests at home. Because conversation in the Roosevelt dining room often turned to sensitive political or military topics, Eleanor required the servants to remain outside until she called them in by ringing a bell. The bell itself was an heirloom, an Old Mother Hubbard with a dog under its arm; it was made of silver and had belonged to her mother, who would have approved of her daughter's growing social finesse.

One of the leading ladies in Washington society, Frances Parkinson Keyes, grew to know the Roosevelts during these early Washington years. In a memoir written two decades later she recorded her impressions. Franklin was tall, wore tight collars, and was "immensely popular." Keyes thought he was "exceptionally handsome" and remembered that women referred to him as "Adonis." Eleanor was "far less striking" but was "cordial and charming," and her eyes were kind. She was meticulous in observing "days at home" to receive guests. The only exception occurred one Wednesday when two Senators' wives arrived and were told that Eleanor might not be able to receive them. The wives were ushered into an empty drawing room, "where there were no signs of preparations for tea; they looked at each other in astonishment." Soon the maid returned and said that Eleanor would be glad to see them. She led them upstairs, and there was Eleanor in bed with a newborn child. Nothing less would have prevented her from serving tea.

The Roosevelts entertained often, and they always seemed to have room for one more person at their table. In the evenings they hosted many "parlor meetings" where friends came to discuss public affairs. Eleanor attended these meetings, usually sitting near the fire, busily knitting "as she glanced from the speaker to the audience, keenly alive to all that was being said and the impression that it was making."

Eleanor grew to know a much wider world while she was in Washington than she had known in New York City or Albany. Simply by making calls on scores of women whom she did not know, Eleanor forced herself to overcome the shyness that had so often limited her communication with other men and women. In Washington's diplomatic community Eleanor actually had an advantage over Franklin: she could speak three foreign languages to his two.

She and Franklin met a wonderful assortment of people. Eleanor came to admire M. Jusserand, the French ambassador, an expert climber who had grown up in the French mountains. He had belonged to Theodore Roosevelt's "walking cabinet," a group of outdoorsmen who accompanied the President on strenuous point-to-point hikes in the countryside around Washington. Once Teddy and his colleagues had to strip naked to swim a stream; Jusserand kept on his gloves—in case they should meet any ladies, he said.

The Roosevelts dined often with a friend of Uncle Ted's, Sir Cecil Spring-Rice, the British ambassador. Spring-Rice was so interested in the study of American history that his wife sometimes had to coax him to put aside his book to keep a diplomatic appointment. He scolded Eleanor for her unfamiliarity with her nation's history—she had learned mainly British history in her schooldays—and "remarked how strange it seemed that we citizens of the United States read so little of our own history."

Eleanor also came to know Henry Adams, then an old man and one of the most astute observers of Washington's political scene. He lived in a fine house on Lafayette Square, opposite the White House, and told Franklin that he had seen many Presidents come and go and that none had greatly affected the country. From such statements Adams gained a reputation as a cynic, but Eleanor remembered him best for parking his victoria in front of the house and watching contentedly while the Roosevelt children and their Scottish terrier played in the carriage.

Jusserand, Spring-Rice, and Adams were only a few of the public figures Eleanor met in Washington. Such contacts helped her grow as a person. But she expressed in many ways the narrow conventions of her aristocratic upbringing. She accepted the routine of Washington's social life and was shocked that her cousin Alice Roosevelt refused to make the endless round of afternoon calls. Making calls was something every decent woman did. There were rules that one must observe, she believed, to earn one's place in society.

There were also people with whom one should not associate. Like most other Protestant aristocrats in the early twentieth century, Eleanor disdained Jews. In 1913 she could write Sara, "I've got to go to the Harris party which I'd rather be hung than be seen at. Mostly Jews." Two days later she reported, "I went to a Jew party . . . for the Baruchs on Monday night. It was appalling. I never wish to hear money, jewels, and labels mentioned again!" When Franklin brought home the great jurist Felix Frankfurter for lunch, Eleanor told Sara he was "an interesting little man, but very Jew."

Eleanor could be equally condescending toward some of the people she and Franklin met on their official travels. In November 1913 she and Laura Delano, one of Franklin's cousins, accompanied Franklin on a naval inspection tour to New Orleans. They spent a boring two hours with him at a navy yard, where according to Eleanor, a meticulous Franklin "counted every rivet." Eleanor reported to Sara snobbishly that they spent their first day with "prominent political (not social) citizens." During the next two days they encountered many individuals they considered gauche. At a supper party Eleanor ran into "an awful man called Cunningham, a power politician but very common." The next morning they took a boat to Biloxi, on which the "very common"

Cunningham aggravated Eleanor's sensibilities by providing champagne for breakfast. Laura came in to dinner that evening with a man who wore high patent-leather shoes, unbuttoned so that the leather flapped as he walked. At the table the two women encountered more strange behavior: all the husbands and wives sat side by side instead of being distributed gracefully around the table, and contrary to polite convention, the salad course followed the soup. When Laura and Eleanor went to their room after the day's gaucheries, they giggled uncontrollably for fifteen minutes. What strange people they had seen!

In such attitudes Eleanor still viewed the world through the blinders of an elite New York background. She had overcome some of her anxieties of early married life, becoming more efficient in running her household and more confident of her usefulness to Franklin, but she was following the example of her mother and of other socially prominent women she had known into the charming but largely ornamental life of a prominent society dame. She seemed destined to bask in the reflected glory of her husband's prominence.

# Grief

*The bottom dropped out of my own particular world, and I faced myself, my surroundings, my world, honestly for the first time.*

Eleanor Roosevelt, *letter to Joseph Lash*

On an October day in 1916 the naval yacht *Dolphin* anchored off the coast of Campobello Island. Using his power as Assistant Secretary of the Navy, Franklin had ordered the ship to collect his wife and five children and deliver them to Hyde Park. On board the *Dolphin* Eleanor was taken from the scenic calm of Campobello into contact with a world at war. The United States had not yet been drawn into the European conflict, but at sea, amid uniforms and steel, the war seemed suddenly close. In these same waters the navies of Germany and England had been blasting one another's ships—and sinking many American vessels as well—during the past two years. As the *Dolphin* cruised southward through the Atlantic, Eleanor heard rumors of German submarine sightings along the coast, and in one port she was told that the Germans had just landed a party of officers.

From the open ocean the ship steamed into New York harbor and up the tree-fringed waters of the Hudson River to the Roosevelt dock at Hyde Park. On the familiar country estate the war was again remote. Back in

Washington, however, the conflict was the major topic of conversation in Congress, in executive offices, and at dinner parties. The war would eventually draw forty million men into battle and claim twelve million casualties. Men had already died by the hundreds of thousands. For the first time in history they were killing one another with bombs dropped from airplanes. In the Dolomites, where Eleanor and Franklin had honeymooned, armies were fighting in the passes, and the mountainsides bristled with heavy artillery.

For a time it seemed that America might remain neutral. Woodrow Wilson was reelected President in 1916 using the slogan "He kept us out of war." His pacifist Secretary of State, William Jennings Bryan, gave out miniature plowshares made from old guns—a gesture Eleanor Roosevelt admired. But the country found it difficult to isolate itself from the outside world. The health of the American economy depended on continued trade with the belligerents, and it proved impossible to trade with the Allies without drawing Germany into submarine warfare against American commerce. Most Americans believed too that the Germans were responsible for the war and were fighting with inhuman ferocity. The Germans were characterized as "Huns," and many Americans, including Eleanor Roosevelt, believed that they bayoneted Belgian babies for sport.

In April 1917 Woodrow Wilson decided to address a joint session of Congress, asking for a declaration of war. Eleanor urged Franklin to get her a seat in the crowded gallery and listened "breathlessly" as the somber President, wearing an American flag in his lapel, urged the nation to go to war to vindicate "human right" against "autocratic governments backed by organized force." Americans should fight for "the things which we have always carried nearest our hearts," he said, "for democracy, for the right of those who submit to authority to have a voice in their own Governments, for the rights and liberties of small nations." Wilson's idealism stirred Eleanor: perhaps through bloodshed the world could be made a better place. But she realized that the price would be high. Eleanor went home that night "half dazed by the sense of impending doom."

Most Americans had opposed the country's entry into World War I, but once war was declared, the nation was afire with patriotism. Within a year three and a half million Americans were drawn into the armed services and two million of them shipped abroad. The American flag appeared everywhere on houses, offices, and stores. At thousands of induction centers pretty girls pinned badges on men who registered to fight, and many states outlawed the teaching of German in their schools. Men who had heard about the glory of battle from grandfathers who fought in the Civil War were suddenly given the opportunity to participate in what they had been taught to think of as one of life's solemn adventures. A young engineer, Russell Strong, went to enlist in New York City; he was so eager to go that he took special care at each streetcorner to avoid an accident, lest he lose the chance to fight for democracy. Theodore Roosevelt, twenty years after his exploits on San Juan Hill, begged President Wilson to let him lead a division to Europe. Wilson said no, and Teddy languished; Eleanor thought it was "a bitter blow from which he never quite recovered."

The war quickly changed the very face of the nation. In Washington, D.C., the population rose by 130,000 with the influx of administrators, stenographers, and soldiers. Many worked and slept in "tempos," makeshift buildings that sprang up on parklands throughout the city and lined the Mall from the Capitol to the Washington Monument. Thousands of uniformed men crowded the streets, continually saluting one another. The war filled the city with trucks moving men and matériel, and then as gasoline supplies ran low, it brought back the horse and buggy. In summer 1918 gasless Sundays were legislated in the capital, and even President Wilson went for his Sunday afternoon drives in a horse-drawn carriage.

Franklin was infected by the patriotic fervor. As Assistant Secretary of the Navy he held one of the key positions in the war machine, but he wanted to be involved in the actual fighting. A desk, no matter how important a desk, seemed a pitiful station now that real men were risking their lives on ships and in the trenches. He considered resigning his post and enlisting but was persuaded he could do more for the cause by staying where he was. As if to make amends for his cerebral contribution to a war requiring other men's muscles and nerves, he and fellow bureaucrats met each morning to exercise. Dressed in their office clothes and standing in precise rows, they did calisthenics in the parks near their offices. Franklin fought the war with brisk jumping jacks, and he fought with ideas: ordering supplies, posting ships, discussing strategy. He suggested one of the most effective tactics of the war, mining the North Sea to restrict German naval operations.

Eleanor too was caught up in the spirit of the war, sensing that she must somehow contribute to a movement that seemed the great event of her lifetime. The reality of the war impressed itself upon her when she met men in the French and British diplomatic corps who had been wounded, including a French colonel who was in constant pain. In subtle ways she began to assert herself. Eleanor could not enlist to fight, of course, but she was proud of her brother Hall when he did. Grandmother Hall was shocked to learn that Hall had enlisted. Why, she asked Eleanor, had he not hired a substitute to fight in his place as many gentlemen had done during the Civil War? Eleanor would normally have deferred to her grandmother, but her sense of the war's importance gave her courage. She replied hotly, "A gentleman is no different from any other kind of citizen in the United States, and it would be a disgrace to pay anyone to risk his life for you." Eleanor may have been surprised at her own forthrightness, for she later described this argument as the first time she had ever stood up against the conventions of her family.

The war drew millions of women into unaccustomed roles. Some entered work that had traditionally been carried on by men, becoming wireless operators, mechanics, and mail carriers. More carried the traditional woman's role as nurturer into the outside world, becoming nurses, canteen workers, and hospital aides. As the war strained the country's agricultural resources, even home economics became a form of patriotism. Under the direction of Herbert Hoover the Food Administration urged Americans to plant "victory gardens" in their own yards and to conserve food to increase supplies for overseas shipment.

For organizing her family and servants effectively Eleanor was selected as a model for large households by the Food Administration. She held daily meetings with her ten servants to determine ways to cut waste. The laundress reduced soap consumption by half; the cook made certain that no food was wasted. Bacon was removed from the family diet and meat served only once daily. The *New York Times* reported that in the Roosevelt household "each servant had a watchful eye for evidence of shortcomings in the others, and all are encouraged to make helpful suggestions in the use of 'left overs.'"

In such ways Eleanor was taking control of her own household, no longer the young bride who was frightened of her own servants and dominated by her mother-in-law. But her work was not restricted to the house. For the first time since her social-work days on Rivington Street,

Eleanor went to work in the outside world. Like many other women, she volunteered several days a week to work at the local canteen. The 781 canteens in the United States were staffed by seventy thousand women. Usually in railway stations, they were places where soldiers lined up for coffee, sandwiches, newspapers, postcards, and stamps.

Eleanor arose each morning at five in order to oversee the household before leaving for the canteen. At the station she worked in a little corrugated tin shack where a cookfire burned in an old iron stove. Eleanor wore a gray poplin uniform with white collar and cuffs. When the trains arrived she dished out food to the uniformed men, some boisterous, some shy, as they crowded around the counter. During the summer of 1918 when the children were at Hyde Park, Eleanor worked compulsively, arriving at the hot canteen at nine or ten in the morning and working straight through until the middle of the following night. The work was a kind of therapy, a rite of passage for her into a world more common, more elemental, and seemingly more substantial than the aristocratic world of her upbringing. She gloried in the democracy of the canteen and felt elation in turning her blueblood hands to swishing a mop over the canteen floor.

With each month of work Eleanor's self-confidence grew. For years she had been afraid of learning to drive a car—ever since damaging the family auto while taking lessons in her mid-twenties. Now ten years later she finally learned to drive. At the same time she learned to use the family chauffeur more efficiently, giving him a complicated list of instructions every day for moving the five children around the city to their various activities. Even Sara had to admire Eleanor's executive ability; she said she had never seen anyone organize her help so efficiently.

Eleanor's talents were soon put to work in another area: the domestic manufacture of clothes for the armed forces. Across the nation millions of women volunteered time to make hospital bedsheets, operating gowns and caps, sweaters, mufflers, and dozens of other items for the soldiers. One of the most popular was the "comfort box," containing cigarettes, shoelaces, a toothbrush, a razor, matches, cards, chocolate, chewing gum—and a self-addressed postcard on which the recipient could thank the donor. Eleanor was active on the Navy League's Comforts Committee, which supervised the knitting of sweaters, socks, washrags, and aviators' helmets. The committee provided volunteers with knitting instructions and a supply of gray and khaki wool. Within a few weeks the Comforts Committee produced sweaters for the first twenty-seven hundred marines shipped abroad. By the end of the war they would supply articles for 133 destroyers and fifty-six battleships. Wherever women appeared on buses and trains and other public places they could be seen working with steel needles on gray wool. "No one, " wrote Eleanor, "moved without her knitting."

By helping to organize the knitting program and working in the canteen Eleanor made contact with vital forces that were shaping history. In the canteen she helped soldiers who would be fighting in France within a few weeks. When she knit an aviator's helmet, she was helping some young man who must fly a mile above Germany in an open cockpit. Recalling the months of hard labor, she wrote some years later: "The winter of 1917–18 wore away and remains to me a kaleidoscope of work and entertaining and home duties, so crowded that sometimes I wondered if I could live that way another day. Strength came, however, with the thought of Europe and a little sleep, and you could sleep, and you could always begin a new day."

As active as she was, Eleanor felt at times dissatisfied with her part in the war—she was so remote from the actual fighting. When she was finally offered the chance to go abroad with the Red Cross, the prospect thrilled her, but she could not justify leaving the children. Franklin, more fortunate, did go overseas in 1918 aboard the destroyer *Dyer*, a journey he undertook with childlike enthusiasm. He went to inspect naval installations rather than to fight, but the trip put him in closer contact with the war. Crossing the ocean, Franklin could stand on the bridge of a fighting ship. In France he insisted on being driven to the front lines and actually fired a cannon.

While Franklin was away Eleanor spent a month alone in Washington, leaving the children with Sara at Hyde Park. With no domestic chores to occupy her, she worked all the harder at the Navy League and the canteen. Washington was so hot and humid that she found she could sleep only when she was exhausted. In September Franklin returned from France. He was ill from pneumonia and had to be moved into Sara's house in New York. Eleanor came north to nurse him back to health.

During the long hours at his bedside she learned about his adventures abroad and he heard about her work in Washington. Solitary moments like these were rare because both were now working so hard. It must have pleased Eleanor to be useful to Franklin. The last two years had marked a major change in their relationship. In 1914 and 1916 Eleanor bore their last two children. Like many other women in that age, she then practiced birth control by abstinence, moving into a separate bedroom. Because she had never enjoyed sex, the change was probably welcome. Franklin was still her mate, her friend. They were partners in raising children and now in fighting the war. And it was still pleasant to be with him, to be able to help him. While he lay asleep she could bustle around his room, arranging his things.

One day as Franklin slept Eleanor came across a packet of letters addressed to him in a familiar hand. They were from Lucy Mercer, Eleanor's friend and personal secretary. During the past few years Lucy had become almost a member of the family, sitting casually on the floor beside Eleanor sorting out invitations, helping her plan her schedule. She often ate with the Roosevelts and sometimes was Franklin's dinner companion when Eleanor was away. Lucy was bright and vivacious, a perfect counterpart for Eleanor.

Eleanor began to look furtively through Lucy's letters, perhaps hoping they were simply the formal notes of a family friend. But the words before her eyes were not formal: Lucy Mercer was writing to someone she loved and who evidently loved her in return. Eleanor was stunned. Franklin had loved her and promised always to love her. Then he had done this—he, the father of their children. How could he make love to Lucy, to her own secretary? How could he betray his wife?

And why did Franklin "betray" Eleanor? During their years together they had been in many ways a loving couple; but Eleanor had often refused Franklin the lighthearted companionship he sometimes craved. If he had tried to explain himself, he might have mentioned the lonely cruise on the *Carrillo,* when she had refused to accompany him. She, in turn, might have mentioned his hike up the Faloria with Kitty Gandy, when she had been left alone in Cortina during their honeymoon. At various times during their married life both Eleanor and Franklin had left the other "alone." More damaging than these isolated moments of separation were the psychological gaps in their friendship, where the differences in their personalities diminished the range of their association. Other friends would find in Eleanor a lighter side that was too seldom revealed in her relationship with Franklin. But Eleanor and Franklin were unable to give each other the sort of companionship each most needed: Franklin had difficulty being sufficiently serious for Eleanor, and she was unable to be sufficiently lighthearted for him.

Franklin's affair with Lucy Mercer was but one thread in the complex fabric of his relationship with Eleanor. But in 1918 when Eleanor read Lucy's love letters, the whole structure of her bond with Franklin seemed to collapse. He was a scoundrel, and she was his victim. What should she do and to whom could she turn in her despair? She might have confided in some friend: Franklin need never know that she had seen the letters. But she must talk with a real confidant, and she had no closer intimate than her husband. Her sorrow was all the worse because the one person close enough to hear of her grief was its cause. And so she must confront Franklin.

Caught off guard, weakened by his pneumonia, Franklin must have tried hard to find words to explain himself and to comfort his sad and angry wife. But what could he say? She had the evidence: he had broken his marriage vows; he had loved and been loved by his wife's own secretary and friend. He must have been mortified by his wife's discovery and at the same time torn between his attachment to the companionable Lucy and his connection to Eleanor, his wife and friend.

Within a few weeks Eleanor and Franklin worked out an agreement to preserve their marriage: Eleanor would stay with her husband, but he must never see Lucy Mercer again. It seemed the only solution. They had children to raise, and Lucy, a Catholic, would not be able to marry a divorced Franklin anyway. Then too, Franklin's political career would be destroyed by the stigma of separation, for divorce was rare during the first part of the twentieth century. Sara Roosevelt came to Eleanor's assistance, bringing her considerable influence to bear on the side of reconciliation.

For a time Franklin was contrite. He revealed to no one the inner pangs he must have suffered at the loss of so pleasant a friend as Lucy. That part of his life, the happiness she had brought him and the joyful contact they had shared, was relegated to the past. He saw no more of Lucy and did his best to be a better companion to his wife. He even abandoned for a time his Sunday morning golf games to accompany Eleanor to church.

Their correspondence during the next summer suggests that on the surface, at least, their reconciliation was complete. From the Connecticut shore, where she had taken the children on vacation, Eleanor wrote Franklin an account of the family's adventures. "I wish you could have seen John in the water," she said. "He got knocked over and over, but he didn't mind, just spluttered and gasped and came right back to be 'brought in' by a wave!" Along with such details on the life of their three-year-old son, she reminded him continually of her love. "I miss you dreadfully," she wrote, "and wish you could always be here." During that summer race riots broke out in Washington, and Eleanor worried for her husband's safety: "Do be careful not to be hit by stray bullets," she wrote him. After a lapse in his correspondence, she received two letters and a telegram in one day. She told him, "I had begun to picture you with all kinds of illnesses as is your wont when left alone!" As if to cement her bond to Franklin, Eleanor became for a time even more solicitous of Sara's love, writing her that she missed her "more and more." She continued, "Instead of becoming more independent, I am growing into a really clinging vine."

In such ways Eleanor went on with the life she had known before the war and before Franklin's infidelity. But in times of personal crisis the course of a human life can seldom be charted with a straight line. Even while Eleanor was following an accustomed role, her mind was full of turmoil. Her life had changed and so too, seemingly, had the world itself. She began to spend solitary hours in Washington's Rock Creek Cemetery. On a hillside near the city stood scores of elegant monuments, but one statue constantly drew Eleanor to it. In a circular grove stands the figure of a woman draped in a long robe. The woman's eyes are curiously arresting, filled with sorrow and yet serene in their triumph over sorrow. The two elements are in perfect balance: her sadness does not diminish her strength, nor does her composure belie her sorrow. Eleanor stared at that face by the hour, seeing her own in the bronze features. The statue was placed there by Eleanor's friend Henry Adams in honor of his wife, who died by suicide. The woman is called "Grief."

During 1918 and 1919 Eleanor knew grief. She had been disappointed before in life, of course. She had lost her parents while young, lost a brother, and lost a son. She had overcome those sorrows, but this new sorrow seemed to go deeper, to be rooted in the very nature of life. The world itself seemed to echo Eleanor's personal despair—to be at times a grim, purposeless place. Even as Eleanor learned about the Lucy Mercer affair, a deadly epidemic of influenza found its way from Europe to the United States. In less than a year half a million Americans would die of the Spanish flu—ten times as many as lost their lives on the battlefields of the Great War. The disease struck the capital in September, and within a month all the schools and theaters were closed. Men and women, fearing for their lives, walked the streets with faces covered with gauze masks. Franklin, the five children, and three Roosevelt servants all came down with the disease. Eleanor worked so hard tending her family and carrying food to flu victims in temporary Red Cross hospitals that there was "little difference between day and night" for several weeks. The Roosevelts and their servants recovered, but in Washington the disease killed thirty-five hundred people.

Early in 1919 Eleanor had encountered another form of sorrow when she went to Europe with Franklin. In Paris it seemed to her that "practically every Frenchwoman was dressed in black." The authorities had outlawed long black veils, a traditional sign of mourning, but women who had lost husbands, fathers, and sons could not be restrained from showing their grief. Eleanor and Franklin went out into the countryside on a battlefield tour. They stopped at Saint Quentin Canal near Amiens, where only recently men had fought with bullets, missiles, and bayonets. Eleanor felt sick that day. Troubled by illness and personal distress, she tried to imagine "the way the soldiers felt on the cold, gray, foggy morning when they, with full packs on their backs and rifles in their hands, plunged down one side of the canal and climbed up the other."

At the beginning of the war Eleanor had sought to take part in a glorious cause. She had tried to participate by helping out soldiers who would give their lives in battle. With her work she had gained new confidence in herself, but that confidence had been shattered by Franklin's infidelity. It was hard for her, a woman, to imagine life without the support of a loyal man. Feeling betrayed by her husband but uncertain how to forge an identity of her own, she had at first become more of a "clinging vine," hoping to regain the sense of domestic security she had lost. Now, however, her unhappiness began to draw her out in new ways, teaching her that the world needed something more than women to knit aviators' helmets and to scrub canteen floors. Out of her own grief she attained greater sympathy for other sufferers. During 1919 she spent many hours visiting wounded men in Washington. At St. Elizabeth's Hospital she saw the war's most pathetic sacrifices, men who had lost their minds after seeing too many comrades slain, spending too many nights in trenches with artillery shells falling nearby, or drifting for too many hours in the ocean after the loss of a ship. A doctor took her into a long ward where the men were assembled during the day; he locked the door carefully behind them after they entered. Slowly they walked through the room, talking as casually as possible with the inmates.

Eleanor saw at the far end of the ward a fairhaired boy. He was standing in a shaft of sunlight that came from a window high above, touching his head "almost like a halo." He muttered incessantly. What was he saying, Eleanor asked. The doctor told her the boy had been in Dunkirk when German planes bombed the town. In his mind he was still there repeating orders he had heard while the bombs fell. Eleanor and the doctor finished the visit and went out, locking the door behind them. She asked the doctor what the chances were that the Dunkirk victim would recover. "Fifty-fifty," he told her.

Eleanor was distressed by St. Elizabeth's. She realized that many of the patients could never recover, even with the best of help, but the hospital was understaffed and overcrowded. Perhaps Eleanor could do something about it. When the war began she had thought of service as personal acts of domestic work.

Through her administrative ability she had come to achieve greater influence as one of the organizers of the canteen and the knitting program. Now she discovered that she had additional power as the wife of a government official. Over the years she had met many men in Washington who influenced policy. One of the most important was Franklin K. Lane, the Secretary of the Interior and a close friend of the Roosevelts. After seeing the squalor of St. Elizabeth's she went to Lane and told him that something should be done. He conducted an investigation that verified Eleanor's observations and persuaded Congress to increase the hospital's appropriation. Thus Eleanor discovered that the exercise of power—the shaping of public policy—was possible not only through holding office but also by judicious use of personal contacts.

In the turmoil of her life following the Lucy Mercer affair Eleanor also discovered in herself another kind of power, less tangible and much rarer than political power: in her contacts with the war wounded she began to exercise a saintlike capacity for love. The politician shapes the external conditions of human life; the saint touches the wellsprings of human emotion. By helping to reform St. Elizabeth's Eleanor acted as a politician. During her hospital visits she also exercised an influence that was more personal. One observer who saw Eleanor give emotional support to a patient was Elenor Androvette, a woman from Staten Island whose son was in the hospital from April to July 1919. Badly wounded, he lay in a bed by the wall in a long ward. Eleanor learned that he had lost his appetite, and she tried to restore his interest in food by bringing him cold lemon jelly and cakes.

"He always loved to see you come in," Mrs. Androvette wrote Eleanor. "You always brought a ray of sunshine with you, always had something to say to him." Her son came home in July and died before summer's end; he was twenty-one. "When he went, he took part of my life with him . . . ," she said. "Only a mother knows. He was such a good boy. His home and family was his one thought." After expressing her grief, Mrs. Androvette thanked Eleanor for her help. "I know when you go to the hospital it is in a spirit of love," she wrote.

"A spirit of love." Within the past year Eleanor had been bitterly disappointed in love. She had given herself to Franklin, and he had betrayed her by falling in love with another woman. In her grief over disappointed love, however, Eleanor found her capacity for love strangely enlarged. She had sought contact with other men and women by passing out canteen sandwiches; she found a deeper affinity for her fellows in her appreciation of their sorrow, their vulnerability. And she discovered ways to act that not only pulled her up from despair but also helped alleviate the sorrows of others.

In 1920 the Roosevelts left Washington. Franklin resigned his position in the Navy Department before his term expired in order to run for the Vice Presidency of the United States on the Democratic ticket. Nineteen-twenty was clearly a Republican year, and so Franklin did not expect to be elected. But the nomination gave him the opportunity to extend his political contacts and gain political experience. The high point of the campaign was a long journey by train across the country. Eleanor came along and developed new appreciation for the size and diversity of the nation. "I was thrilled by the new scenery," she later wrote, "and the size of my own country, with its potential power, was gradually dawning upon me." Franklin often left her alone while he plotted campaign strategy or drank and played cards with aides and newsmen on the train. Often during the trip Louis Howe sat with her. He had seemed so strange once, but he was now becoming one of her closest friends. Howe, who had picked Franklin as a political winner in the Albany days, also recognized Eleanor's talents. He spent long hours talking with her and coached her on politics.

In November Warren Harding was elected President, and for the first time in a decade Franklin was out of public life. The Roosevelts moved to New York, where Franklin once more entered the law. Eleanor did not simply retire to her domestic roles of ten years before; the lessons of Washington, particularly of the past two years, stayed with her. She worked for the newly formed League of Women Voters and sought other outlets for her talents. She believed she was "thinking things out for myself and becoming an individual."

During the summer of 1921 the Roosevelts were again in Campobello. Franklin was almost forty now but was as active as a boy. One afternoon as the family was sailing, they sighted a brushfire on the shore and put it out. Later that afternoon Franklin went swimming in the cold waters of the Bay of Fundy. After all this exercise he felt curiously tired. He went to bed, and the next day he was still low. He found that he could not move his legs—he was paralyzed from the waist down. For a time he and Eleanor hoped that he was suffering from some temporary malady. But at last a doctor confirmed the worst: Franklin had polio.

Eleanor moved a cot into Franklin's bedroom to nurse him through the long nights. We can imagine him lying in bed with Eleanor nearby, both of them awake but silent. Franklin may have recalled his athletic youth: as a boy he had sailed an iceboat over the frozen Hudson River in front of Hyde Park—steel runners hissing over silver ice on crisp winter days. Now he could not even walk. Unable to sleep, he might have spoken with his wife, lying nearby.

What could she say to comfort him? Franklin was so helpless. He could not even urinate unless Eleanor assisted him with a catheter. What did she see when she looked at his wasted flesh? Here was the man who had betrayed her, suffering his own grief. He had hurt her more than any other human being, and yet his life and hers were inextricable. His infidelity was everything, and it was nothing. It destroyed a dream of idealized love. It left her with a man, flaws and all, who needed her, and whom, perhaps, she too needed.

# 7

# **Public Service**

*I suppose if I were asked what is the best thing one can expect in life, I would say—the privilege of being useful.*

Eleanor Roosevelt, *Success Magazine, 1927*

They carried Franklin on a stretcher from the house at Campobello to the beach. Seeing the children on the porch, their faces full of fear, he smiled bravely and sang out, "I'll be seeing you chicks soon." He was loaded onto a motorboat and began the two-mile passage to Eastport. Only thirty-nine, he would never again carry a child on his shoulders into the surf or row his canoe beside the shore or hike along the beach. His future had collapsed into the needs of the moment: a stretcher, a private railway car, an appointment in a New York hospital.

After weeks of therapy Franklin was allowed to go home to the Sixty-Fifth Street house shortly before Christmas in 1921. He was still paralyzed from the waist down. In Washington the energetic young naval administrator had climbed the steps to his office three at a time; now he could not walk a single pace. Casts were placed on his legs and wedges driven between the plaster and his flesh to prevent Franklin's muscles from drawing too tight and twisting his legs under him. While bearing the pain of this treatment, he tried daily to flex muscles that refused to answer his command.

Eleanor oversaw Franklin's therapy and supervised a house full of people, each demanding her attention. Louis Howe moved in to provide companionship for Franklin and to keep him in touch with public life. Eleanor had to make room for him. Anna, tall, blonde, and attractive at age fifteen, had trouble in school and adopted a devil-may-care attitude that annoyed her mother. Eleanor must learn to deal with her first teenager.

Sara was living next door again and saw in her son's broken body an excuse to mother him for the rest of his life. Surely, she reasoned, he would never recover the use of his legs, and so he must come home to Hyde Park and live with her. For the first time in her life Eleanor stood up to Sara: Franklin must not be sheltered by well-meaning relatives from the demands of the world. With the family's help he should make every effort to regain the use of his limbs and to stay involved in politics and the law. Eleanor's disagreements with her mother-in-law were often acrimonious. Gone were the days when she would ride through the streets of New York in a carriage with the imposing Sara and defer to her every comment with a dutiful "Yes, Mama."

Eleanor was eager to help Franklin, but at the same time she was disturbed by her own apparent loss. She had learned during the past four years to give part of her life to a world outside her family. Now she must spend her attention almost exclusively on a handicapped husband and five bewildered children. During the winter of 1922 Eleanor slept on a cot in one of her children's rooms and used Franklin's bathroom as a dressing room. It was, she later wrote, "the most trying winter" of her entire life.

Anna, who had a room of her own, upset Eleanor by complaining that Louis Howe had a larger room. Like most adolescents, Anna worried whether her parents loved and understood her. Eleanor wanted sympathy too: she could not spend her whole life serving Franklin and the children. One afternoon she was reading to her two youngest boys when she suddenly began sobbing. Elliott, just home from school, fled at the unaccustomed sight. Louis tried to comfort her but failed. Eventually the two boys went off to bed, leaving their mother still crying. Finally Eleanor found an empty room, poured cold water on a towel, and mopped her face. The incident proved to be a catharsis. Many trials lay ahead, but Eleanor began to adjust to her new circumstances.

For the next five years much of Franklin's energy went into his efforts to regain mobility. His arms as well as his legs had been affected by polio, but the arm muscles came back to life quickly, and he was soon able to move himself around on a makeshift wheelchair. Control of his legs was more difficult. The weeks of therapy turned into months, the months into years. Franklin bought a houseboat so that he could spend the winter motoring up and down the Florida Keys fishing, sunbathing, and swimming. He purchased an old resort at Warm Springs, Georgia, where mineral waters flowed from the rocks into a pool. Franklin turned Warm Springs into a sanatorium and spent hours at a time in the waters exercising his muscles. After many visits he could walk along the bottom of the pool buoyed up by shoulder-deep water.

Franklin learned to walk with crutches, then braces and a cane, then with braces alone, using the muscles in his hips to swing his legs forward. Anna remembered him struggling down the tree-lined driveway that leads from the Roosevelt mansion at Hyde Park to the old New York–Albany post road. Looking down the long tunnel made by overhanging branches, he inched along, painful step by painful step. He wanted to walk to the end of the drive and back, but the distance was too great and his recovery too limited. As Anna watched, he shuffled along resolutely, but "oh, so slowly."

For the Roosevelt children the change in their father was frightening. From being their mentor in every outdoor sport—sailing, riding, swimming, hiking—he was suddenly more helpless than the youngest of them. Franklin did his best to reassure the children. He showed them his legs and named each of the muscles, telling them which ones he was working on. Whenever he managed the slightest movement in a dormant muscle, he would shout with glee, making his battle into "a spirited game." But for months at a time when Franklin was in Georgia and Florida the children had no father. Years later James, who was fourteen when his father was paralyzed, reflected: "Only now do I realize how sorely we missed him during that period. But when we saw him, he was so—well, so damned gallant that he made you want to cry and laugh and cling to him and carry him in your arms and lean on him for support all at the same time."

Through his therapy Franklin came into contact with scores of men and women from all walks of life who had suffered like him from polio. In subtle ways these contacts and his disease changed him. Prior to 1921 he had sometimes been impulsive, frivolous, and snobbish. Now he became more serious and compassionate, more understanding of common people and their needs. Francis Perkins, who would work for Franklin in Albany and Washington, believed polio made him "completely warmhearted, with humility of spirit and a deeper philosophy."

Eleanor's life was changed too by Franklin's illness. In some ways she was drawn closer to her husband, first as his nurse and later as his surrogate in parenthood and politics. When Franklin's energy for therapeutic exercises waned, Eleanor encouraged and even goaded him on.

When he sometimes tried to neglect his strenuous work-outs, Eleanor would talk to him like "an old master sergeant," one doctor recalled.

"Franklin," she would say, "there are certain things that we have to do to get you better."

"Oh, damn!" Franklin would reply. But he did his exercises.

Franklin's paralysis changed Eleanor's relationship to her children, requiring her to become, in some ways, their father as well as their mother. He would have taught the children to swim—now Eleanor must teach them. She had never learned to swim and had been afraid of the water ever since Uncle Ted had pushed her off a dock to encourage her to learn. And so she took lessons in a YMCA pool in New York City. She even attempted to master the art of diving—a difficult task for a forty-year-old. She usually struck the water with awkwardly bent knees and a loud "thwack." But she persisted.

Franklin's paralysis also required Eleanor to improve her driving. She had learned to drive in Washington, but she had no confidence at the wheel and had two minor accidents shortly after Franklin was paralyzed. Once she turned too fast into the entrance to Hyde Park and slammed into the stone gatepost. Another time she lost control of the car as she was driving through the woods taking the family to a picnic; it dropped backward over a steep bank, plunged down a hill, and came to rest against a tree. No one was injured, but from then on Eleanor tried to improve her driving by "sheer determination."

While drawing her into new domestic responsibilities, Franklin's handicap also provided Eleanor with an excuse for broadening her role in the outside world. With luck and determination Franklin would be able to reenter politics, but in the meantime he could not travel or make the necessary political contacts. Eleanor, however, could involve herself in the affairs of the Democratic Party and so keep the Roosevelt name in the public eye.

Within a year of Franklin's contracting polio, Eleanor joined the Women's Division of the Democratic State Committee. The leaders of the Women's Division were interested in Eleanor because they had heard of her husband: the state senator, Assistant Secretary of the Navy, and vice-presidential candidate. They knew little about Eleanor herself. During the previous decade, when Lillian Wald was helping immigrants on the Lower East Side, Eleanor was pouring tea in Washington. When suffragette Alice Paul was arrested in 1917 for picketing the White House, Eleanor was still ambivalent about votes for women. Eleanor's experience during the war had broadened her horizons, but she had not yet formed a consistent attitude toward social reform or women's rights.

Eleanor's refined upbringing was apparent as she began her work with the Women's Division. In spring 1922 she gave her first political speech, an appeal for funds at a Democratic luncheon. Still fundamentally shy, Eleanor had been reluctant to speak in public and was so self-conscious that she doubted whether she could be heard. While delivering this and other speeches, she felt awkward and often giggled, almost childishly, although there was nothing to laugh about. Such shyness was common among women trying to overcome an upbringing that taught them they had no place in a polling booth or on a podium.

Louis Howe helped Eleanor overcome her weaknesses as a public speaker. He sat at the back of the room when she spoke and studied her manner. No gentle critic, he told Eleanor her giggling was "inane" and encouraged her to speak directly and confidently. "Have something you want to say," he told her, "say it, and sit down." Eleanor listened and improved. She soon was able to show that she was not merely a society lady dabbling in politics. The

Women's Division published a monthly newspaper. Eleanor became its editor and with Louis's help learned about advertising, circulation, makeup, and headlines. The party wanted to establish local political organizations for women. Eleanor traveled throughout the state, and by 1924 all but five counties were organized. Through hard work Eleanor earned a place on the executive board of the Women's Division.

She discovered, moreover, that the Democratic philosophy corresponded with her own growing liberalism. Writing about Al Smith, the Governor of New York, she said, "The Democrats today trust in the people, the plain, ordinary, every-day citizen, neither superlatively rich nor distressingly poor, not one of the 'best minds' but the average mind." The passage echoed her essay on the flowers, written thirty years before: "From this day," said the violet, "we are all equal." In 1895 her humanity had extended to her family and her school friends. By 1925 she was becoming aware of the country as a whole and the great variety of Americans.

During her political apprenticeship she also associated herself with organizations devoted to social and political reform. In 1920 a group of women who had fought for suffrage formed the League of Women Voters; they intended to educate women in the use of the newly won ballot and to formulate a program of enlightened legislation. Eleanor had been impressed with the League when she heard a speech by Carrie Chapman Catt, a wonderful white-haired veteran of the suffrage fight. Eleanor went to work for the League before Franklin's paralysis and continued to be an active member. One of her assignments was to survey national legislation for the League. She compiled her report with the assistance of Elizabeth Read, a lawyer, who instilled in Eleanor the desire to be systematic and thorough in her work.

Eleanor acquired a further education—in American labor unionism—by contact with the Women's Trade Union League. Her teacher was Rose Schneiderman, president of the New York branch. Schneiderman was a small, red-haired needleworker who had never finished primary school. She had taught herself the theory of trade unionism and had organized women workers in New York. Eleanor joined the WTUL in 1922 and gave her presence at union meetings a personal touch by bringing along hot chocolate and cookies—and helped raise funds for a union headquarters in New York. At these meetings and through friendship with Rose Schneiderman, Eleanor grew interested in a legislative program for working women, including maximum-hour and minimum-wage laws.

Eleanor also began to consider what a "living wage" should be. For her parents a decent standard of living had included country estates, horses, and servants. For their servants it had meant a small room, food, and clothing. Eleanor now came to believe that every man and woman deserved more than a subsistence wage; a "living wage" should include provisions for education, recreation, and health. To bring about these conditions she favored widely varied social legislation: a forty-eight hour week for women, a child labor law, better treatment of blacks, and U.S. membership on the World Court. The memories of the war stayed with her, and in 1923 she agreed to serve on the jury to evaluate entries in a one-hundred-thousand-dollar competition among peace plans.

As she came to discover ways in which the United States might become a more just society, she became conscious that she herself, though a member of the American aristocracy, belonged to a disadvantaged class: womanhood. Although women had gained the right to vote in 1919, they had not yet been fully accepted into the political system. In New York the male leaders of the

Democratic Party were glad enough to allow women to form their own division of the party and to work for political candidates, but they were reluctant to let them participate in selecting nominees and determining policy.

Eleanor had begun thinking about the place of women in public life during World War I. In an interview conducted at her home in 1924 she gave a remarkably candid account of how her thought developed as she neared her fortieth birthday. The journalist, Rose Feld, devoted most of her article to Eleanor's political philosophy. Just by sitting with her subject for an hour or so, she could see how fully Eleanor had integrated her domestic and public roles. Early in the interview Eleanor's "flaxen-haired daughter" came into the room "to ask motherly advice about a coat, to discuss lessons and vacations, and to receive directions about tea." Later on a man came by to have tea and talk politics. Eleanor urged him to help her "organize" Dutchess County and gave him detailed suggestions as to how to begin. The reporter was impressed that Eleanor was able to be both a mother and a party worker. "Politics," she wrote, "has not made a masculine woman of her."

This stereotype—that a woman must lose her femininity to engage in public life—was the background against which Eleanor had developed her own views on women in politics. She now believed that the inferior position of women in America was the result of a philosophy that both sexes embraced. The typical American husband looked down on his wife and tried to keep her out of public life. He smiled "benignly on her" and established boundaries on her development: "My dear," he would say, "you're a very wonderful person. I love you and honor you. . . . Lead your own life, attend to your charities, cultivate yourself, arrange your teas and dinners, bring up the children, run the house, and be happy. One thing only I ask of you, and that is that you keep out of my business and keep out of politics. Leave those things to me. Don't bother your pretty head about them. It's a man's game, much too rough for a woman."

The "sheltered" condition of the American woman was "a national weakness fostered by men." But women were all too willing to accept their decorative role. As Eleanor spoke to the reporter, she grew exasperated at remembering conversations over tea with Senators' wives in Washington, when she was just beginning to take an interest in politics.

"What does your husband think of such and such a bill?" she would ask. "How does he stand on child welfare, on the minimum wage, on the eight-hour day?"

These things were "of interest to every human being in the country," but "in nine cases out of ten" the woman would "smile coyly" and reply: "Oh, you mustn't ask me political questions. Mr. So-and-So never discusses politics with me. I never ask him."

Eleanor was particularly bothered by the satisfaction the underdeveloped woman would take in admitting her own ignorance: "She says it with pride and admiration. Her great big noble adoring husband won't burden her precious little head with politics. No. She must be free to lead her own life." Perhaps as Eleanor remembered these conversations, she recalled her own limitations in those years, her subordination to Sara, and her acceptance of conventional thought about the social classes. Forcefully she added, "If it weren't so stupid, it would be funny."

When Eleanor first began to take a larger role in the world, she had thought mainly of what she could do as an individual. With her exposure to the political process, she came to realize that she and her friends in the League of Women Voters, the Women's Trade Union League, and the Women's Division—women who were deeply involved in public life—were all too rare in America. More typical were the housewives she met by the dozens every time she canvassed Dutchess County in the environs of Hyde Park. She would urge them to attend political meetings where they could learn about important social issues and find out what other women were doing.

The work was "heartbreaking," and often she and other speakers addressed nearly empty halls. For every woman who came, several stayed at home, fearing that their husbands would disapprove. "Many of the women there," Eleanor said, "believe first of all that it's not quite respectable to vote, anyway, and as for voting the Democratic ticket, that is equal to social ostracism." Eleanor spent two weeks working on one woman who finally agreed to attend a Democratic committee meeting. Eleanor said "a prayer of thanks" for this convert, but the woman called the next day to decline because she had just discovered Eleanor's committee was Democratic, and her husband would never approve. If the ladies would change their affiliation to the Republican Party, the caller suggested hopefully, she could join.

Eleanor must have reflected again, "If it weren't so stupid, it would be funny."

At times during the 1920s Eleanor questioned whether American women were prepared to assume public office. Most of them, she thought, were "backward" in political affairs. But they must be given a chance to learn. In 1924 she insisted that women be allowed to choose female delegates to the Democratic National Convention. The party leaders eventually conceded, and when the delegates met in New York City that August, the state was represented by several women.

Eleanor followed the convention closely. In some respects the Eleanor Roosevelt who attended the convention of 1924 was similar to the woman who had gone to the 1912 convention in Baltimore. She was a gracious

hostess, opening the house on Sixty-Fifth Street to entertain delegates. She sat in a box with other spectators and
knitted while the convention met. Will Rogers, seeing her
there, quipped, "Knitting in the names of the future victims of the guillotine?" Rogers's remark was more perceptive than he probably realized, for just as Madame La
Farge in *A Tale of Two Cities* looked innocuous while she
quietly influenced state policy, Eleanor Roosevelt had a
second role at the Democratic Convention.

Not merely the spectator this time, Eleanor was in
charge of a group of women who sought to present
reform proposals to the resolutions committee. Eleanor
soon discovered that the men on this and other committees had no interest in hearing from women. She and her
colleagues had to stand outside the door at important
meetings and had to wait all night before anyone would
even receive their resolutions. Even then, she never
learned whether the measures had been discussed: their
reception was "veiled in mystery behind closed doors." In
1924 Eleanor and the Democratic women met defeat. The
experience, however, was valuable in drawing the patrician
Eleanor into sympathy with other victims of injustice and
making her more aware of discrimination against
American women. A few years later she commented wryly
that the convention was "a new step in my education."

Eleanor's "education" during the 1920s was facilitated
by a new community of friends. Her associates during
early adult life—Franklin, Sara, her relatives, and her society confidants—had encouraged her to be a traditional
wife and mother. They asked her to raise children, care for
a husband, and attend to the parochial duties of a New
York socialite. Her reward had been affection, respect,
and the enveloping support of the society she knew. Now
as she grew more interested in the world outside her

household, she made friends with people whose ambitions were similar. She found herself "more and more interested in workers" and less in her old associates "who were busy doing a variety of things, but who were doing no job in a professional way."

Most of Eleanor's new friends were women—unmarried women with professions. They had no place in Eleanor's social world, but suddenly they were the most interesting people she knew. Elizabeth Read, Eleanor's mentor in the League of Women Voters, was an accomplished lawyer and student of international law. Elizabeth's apartment-mate, Esther Lapp, was also in the League; she taught at Barnard and wrote articles on women's rights and the plight of immigrants.

On the Democratic State Committee Eleanor's best friends were Nancy ("Nan") Cook and Marion Dickerman. Nan and Marion fought together for woman suffrage and abolition of child labor. During the war they went overseas as nursing orderlies and worked in a London hospital. In 1919 Marion ran for the New York Assembly, becoming the first woman to seek a legislative office in the state, and Nan served as her campaign manager. Marion lost, but she ran better than expected, and both women decided to stay active in Democratic politics.

These four women were not only Eleanor's mentors, helping her build confidence in herself, but also became her close friends. Once a week Eleanor spent an evening with Esther and Elizabeth in their Greenwich Village apartment, exchanging ideas and reading French literature together. She invited Nan and Marion to visit her at Hyde Park. Marion had recently toured a coal miners' camp in West Virginia, where the workers were on strike. She told Eleanor and Sara the lurid details of industrial poverty. Sara Roosevelt took an immediate dislike to Marion. A few years earlier Eleanor might have been equally ill at ease in Marion's company, but now her sympathies went to her new friend.

With her growing independence Eleanor came to crave her own home. The house at Hyde Park was Sara's domain, and the house in New York next to her mother-in-law's was not really her own. Nor were the places where she followed Franklin for his therapy. He loved spending the winters in Florida on a houseboat, but Eleanor was never comfortable there. The fish did not bite for her, the celebrated tropical moon and stars "only added to the strangeness of the dark waters," and when the wind blew in the night "it all seemed eerie and menacing."

Franklin had often been insensitive to Eleanor's needs, just as she had been to his. But he recognized the value of her new friends and her need for a place uniquely her own. He had his own circle of friends, people who enjoyed traveling on the houseboat and fishing off the Florida Keys. He had Warm Springs, Georgia, and started a model farm there. These were not places Eleanor enjoyed; nor was she content in the homes in New York and Hyde Park, where she could never seem to escape Sara's influence.

Franklin realized that Eleanor's friends gave her a companionship he could not; he also realized they were the sort of persons a politician should know. Choosing to support her new independence, he encouraged Eleanor to build a house for herself on the Hyde Park estate. They chose a site in the woods by Val-Kill Brook. Franklin designed a house modeled on old Dutch dwellings. It became a large, rambling structure they would call Val-Kill Cottage. After the house was completed in 1925 it became the place where Eleanor, Marion, and Nan lived at Hyde Park. They were so close that they thought of themselves as a kind of family and even ordered towels embroidered "EMN," the first letters of their names.

The three women helped one another develop new projects. They were troubled about the gap between city and country life and believed that small industries should be established in rural areas. And so they decided to set up a small factory at Val-Kill to manufacture good reproductions of early American furniture. Nan and Marion had experience as teachers and wanted to create a new kind of school. With Eleanor's help they undertook the purchase and administration of Todhunter School in New York City. Eleanor became part owner of the school and joined the faculty. She became a superb teacher in history, drama, and English and did her best to tie her lessons in to daily life.

Eleanor's new friends were not simply an alternative to her family life; they became intertwined, rather, with her husband and children. Franklin welcomed them to Hyde Park and encouraged the building of Val-Kill. They in turn helped Eleanor with the children. Eleanor was eager that young Franklin and John have the same kind of outdoor experiences that they would have had with their father if he were not paralyzed, and so one summer she set out on a camping trip to Canada, taking along Nan and Marion. With two tents, a few pots and pans, a Red Cross first aid kit, and a spirit of adventure they headed north. In the 1920s commercial campgrounds were rare, and early in the trip they found themselves camping beside the Ausable River in a farmer's field. Nothing could have been more attractive to four boys than a swim in the river, but Eleanor doubted she could swim well enough to help one of them if he got into trouble. Fortunately, another "gypsying" family was swimming in the river, and the father agreed to look after Eleanor's brood.

Were these strangers New York gentry? Did they have a town house in New York City and an estate on the Hudson? Eleanor might have wondered about such things twenty years before when she was honeymooning with

Franklin in Europe, but on a camping trip with her new friends and her new outlook on life it just did not matter.

The wanderers continued north through Montreal along the St. Lawrence River toward Quebec. Another night, another farmer's field. The boys collected wood for a fire, and Franklin whacked his leg with the hatchet. With no nurse or doctor to call upon, Eleanor patched up the nasty cut herself. They went on to Quebec City and then south again to New Hampshire's White Mountains, where they climbed a mountain by burro. Finally they came to Maine and to Campobello. Eleanor had not been here since Franklin's illness. "In spite of all our trials," she wrote, it "was still serene, beautiful, and enjoyable."

By 1928 Eleanor had achieved a kind of serenity herself. She was forty-four. During the past seven years she had helped Franklin, she had raised the children, and she had established a role for herself in public affairs. But 1928 would offer new challenges to her personal equilibrium. In the fall she took her youngest son, John, to Groton, unpacked his clothes, and helped him settle in. She had made this trip three times before when each of her sons reached twelve. Anna had married Curtis Dahl two years before, and with all the boys now in school or college, Eleanor came back to a childless house.

Busy as she had been during the past few years, she had spent many evenings reading and playing cards with Franklin Jr. and John. She had never liked sending the boys to school at such an early age, but Franklin had insisted: he had gone to Groton when he was fourteen and felt like an outsider because the other boys had already formed friendships. Eleanor might accept her husband's reasoning, but still she was depressed; she "resented" taking John to Groton "because there was then no child left at home."

The loss of her children to school, college, and marriage made Eleanor's working life and her friendship with other working women all the more important. It was fitting, then, that in 1928 she took on her most difficult job to date: she agreed to run the women's side of the Democratic national campaign. She and Franklin were both strong supporters of Alfred Smith's bid for the Presidency. Eleanor believed that Smith genuinely cared about "the welfare of the average man and woman."

Franklin expressed his feeling about Smith in a nominating speech at the Democratic Convention in Houston. Supported by leg braces, he grasped the podium and spoke in a strong voice that boomed over the convention hall. Alfred Smith, he said, has "that quality of soul which makes him a strong help to all those in sorrow or in trouble; that quality which makes him not merely admired but loved by all the people—the quality of sympathetic understanding of the human heart, of real interest in one's fellow men." Franklin attributed Smith's sensitivity to his having struggled "up to eminence from obscurity and low estate." Governor Smith, he said, "senses the popular need" because he has lived through "hardship."

Franklin was talking about Al Smith, but could as easily have been describing Eleanor's growth—or his own. They had not had to overcome poverty, but Eleanor's struggle to find a life for herself in the public world and Franklin's efforts to rebuild his life after being paralyzed had nourished in each of them a sympathy for the problems of other men and women.

After the convention Franklin headed the Businessmen's Division in the campaign and gave a few speeches, but he still hoped to regain the use of his legs and returned to Warm Springs for more therapy. The Democratic chances for winning the Presidency in 1928 were remote: the country had never been more prosperous than under the Republicans during the previous eight years, and the Republican presidential candidate, Herbert Hoover, had a national reputation as a brilliant administrator. Moreover, Al Smith was a Roman Catholic.

That should not have mattered, but it did. "If I needed anything to show me what prejudice can do to the intelligence of human beings," Eleanor wrote, "that campaign was the best lesson I could have had." A Catholic President, according to the bigots, would transform the country. A Georgian told Franklin he opposed Smith because, if elected, Smith would invalidate all non-Catholic marriages; the man worried that all his children would then be illegitimate. Franklin roared with laughter and said he considered himself "safely married" even though he lived in New York, where Smith was Governor. But the Georgian and millions like him were not persuaded.

Al Smith's campaign drew Eleanor into national politics as never before. She worked at party headquarters in New York City and traveled widely to give campaign speeches. But even as she broadened her experience in public affairs, events were taking shape that would limit her ability to engage in politics. Because Smith could not run for reelection as Governor of New York while seeking the Presidency, the party leaders wanted Franklin to be the Democratic gubernatorial candidate. He was ambivalent; if he were chief executive of the largest state, he would have to abandon the course of therapy that might still allow him to walk. Howe, too, was cautious; 1928 did not seem like a Democratic year.

On the day that the party leaders were to nominate a gubernatorial candidate Franklin knew that Smith wanted him to run, but he decided to play cat and mouse with the party leaders. He was in Georgia and refused to come to the phone. Knowing that Franklin would come to the phone for his wife, Smith persuaded Eleanor to put through a call. She needed to catch a train and had time only to say hello to her husband before turning the phone over to Smith, who "persuaded" him to run.

A few weeks later Hoover had beaten Smith, but in New York Franklin won handily, and Eleanor Roosevelt became First Lady of the state. A reporter visited her at the Sixty-Fifth Street house shortly after the election. They met in the library in the early afternoon, just after Eleanor had finished teaching at Todhunter. She came into the room with her arms full of books, pamphlets, and letters that cascaded onto the sofa and the floor as she sat down: "There appeared to be reading matter enough for months."

The reporter had already learned about Eleanor's many activities: teaching at Todhunter, editing a Democratic newspaper, running a furniture factory, serving on the boards of numerous civic organizations. People she interviewed told her about Eleanor's energy and efficiency. Her household staff was so well organized that she could easily expand lunch or dinner from five to twenty places. She carefully planned her lessons at Todhunter, organized the manufacturing schedule at Val-Kill, and prepared her remarks at board meetings. On her frequent train rides between New York and Hyde Park she read articles on foreign affairs, domestic policy, American history, and travel.

Eleanor planned to continue her busy schedule while in Albany. She would commute to the city every Sunday evening and return to the Governor's mansion on Wednesdays. The factory at Val-Kill would remain open under her direction. She would serve on civic, educational, and welfare committees in Albany. What about the burden of housekeeping in the Executive Mansion, the reporter asked. That was no formidable matter to Eleanor: "I rarely devote more than fifteen minutes a day to it," she said.

The interviewer was impressed by Eleanor's energy and competence. "Putting it mildly," she wrote, "if Mrs. Roosevelt continues with all her present activities after she moves to Albany, she will be the busiest woman in official life today." Eleanor's achievements were already so impressive in 1928 that most people saw her persona—her public image—and missed the complexity of her character.

Eleanor was not as confident as she may have seemed in the fall of 1928. She had achieved a great deal on her own and as Franklin's surrogate during the past seven years, keeping his name before the public. But the surrogate had also become an independent force with ideas of her own and a mission of her own. Fortunately, her political ideas were close to Franklin's and so most of the time they served the same interests. But Franklin's election to the governorship would force Eleanor to curtail her own political activities.

Eleanor did her best to find a rationale for her self-denial. She told the reporter that women in America were not yet ready to assume political positions. "Women," she said, "should go slow." They should recognize the superior political skill men had gained through generations of experience. "I do not think many women are ready for political office," she declared, "and the fewer women placed in office the better, for the present." Eleanor held that women should gain experience in public affairs, learn to lead other women, and then finally seek office. This slow, deliberate approach to achieving political equality was in part a realistic assessment of current conditions. Relatively few women were entering public life or the professions at any level; with so little experience, Eleanor thought, they could not expect to achieve equality overnight.

But Eleanor's hesitancy to declare that women were men's equals derived also from her own lack of self-confidence. Despite all her achievements, she still saw herself as subservient to her husband. In her autobiography Eleanor wrote: "I accepted his nomination and later his election as I had accepted most of the things that had happened in life thus far: one did whatever seemed necessary and adjusted one's personal life to the developments in other people's lives." Thus going to Albany was a "necessity" rather than a triumph. Eleanor hinted at her frustration in a revealing moment at the beginning of her postelection interview in the library. "I don't like public life," she said. "I thought when we came back from Washington, we were through with it."

On January 1, 1929, a reluctant Eleanor Roosevelt became First Lady of New York. As she had feared, Franklin's new position did seem at first to limit her. After his election she resigned from the Democratic State Committee and told Franklin she would no longer speak on political subjects. It soon became apparent, however, that Eleanor would not merely live in the shadow of her husband. Every Sunday evening she took the train from Albany down the Hudson River to New York to teach at Todhunter. She remained active in the Women's Trade Union League, delivered speeches, and published articles. People came to her with their political problems, and she communicated them to Franklin. By 1930 she had earned a reputation as a sympathetic and well-informed public figure, and people brought her their personal difficulties with the government.

Despite her decision to stay out of politics, Eleanor served as a consultant to the Women's Division. She also traveled to remote villages in upstate New York, met with farm women, and organized their districts. In 1930 Franklin was reelected Governor by a landslide and became the first Democrat to take upstate New York; his political adviser, James Farley, credited Eleanor and the Women's Division with this achievement.

Eleanor's public life brought her into contact with groups of people whom Franklin knew less well. Eleanor did her best to introduce Franklin to these groups. On the twenty-fifth anniversary of the Women's Trade Union League, she arranged for shopgirls and trade union leaders to travel by boat up the Hudson River to Hyde Park. While Eleanor stayed in the background, Franklin delivered a speech that won their admiration.

During the four years that Franklin was Governor of New York Eleanor and Franklin learned to help one another politically. Their partnership was apparent each summer when they made trips together in a state-owned barge to investigate public institutions. Franklin became the first Governor to visit every state hospital, asylum, and prison in New York. While he talked to the administrators, he often sent Eleanor to poke behind the scenes, and he taught her to be a good observer. When she returned from one of her tours and told him she approved of the menu, he asked her, "Did you look to see whether the inmates actually were getting that food?" She quickly learned to probe more deeply: checking cooking pots to see if their contents corresponded to the published menus; noticing whether beds in wards were too close together; and scrutinizing patients' attitudes toward staff. Through such inquiries Eleanor became her husband's "eyes and ears."

Franklin needed Eleanor's help and cared tremendously about her good opinion of him, but he sometimes needed to make political alliances that required him to compromise his principles. He particularly disappointed Eleanor with his stand on the World Court, the judicial equivalent of the League of Nations. Eleanor favored any measure that might increase understanding among nations. Franklin, however, wanted to win favor with American isolationists to improve his chances for the Presidency. He therefore issued a statement in 1932 opposing America's entry into the World Court. For several days Eleanor refused to speak to her husband.

In 1930 Eleanor was given a chance to review her marriage for a reporter doing an article on the subject "What Is a Wife's Job Today?" He met her in a large, high-ceilinged room on the second floor of the Executive Mansion in Albany. The room had "great charm" and was filled with artifacts reflecting both Eleanor's and Franklin's interests: "happy reproductions of early American history" and "spirited pictures of yachts, cutters, and full-rigged ships." The reporter told Eleanor that four other women had suggested he interview her as "the ideal type of a modern wife."

To provide her description of a "wife's job" Eleanor compressed twenty-five years of marital experience into a conversation that must not have taken more than an hour. A wife, she declared, has three major roles: partner, mother, and housekeeper. Of these the first was most important. "Today," she said, "we understand that everything else depends upon the success of the wife and husband in their personal partnership relation." In some marriages there were "vampire husbands" who dominated their wives "ruthlessly"; in others "vampire wives" took from their mates and gave "little or nothing in return." Eleanor argued that mutual respect was an essential ingredient in a good marriage. A woman should "develop her own interests . . . so as not to lose the possibility of being a stimulating personality!"

How did a husband and wife come to be good partners? Eleanor did not talk about intimacy or romance—ingredients that had apparently gone out of her own marriage. Instead she argued that the presence of "some great common interest" was essential to partnership. "It is entirely through the interests that a man and woman share," she said, ". . . that the light of a true marriage shines!" By this definition she and Franklin had improved their marriage since the Lucy Mercer affair. Their political partnership was already one of the most impressive in America.

But Eleanor did not reveal to the reporter what she revealed to Nan and Marion and Anna: that there were painful gaps in her relationship with Franklin. The two had formed a creative alliance in public life and as parents, but they had neither made love nor shared the same bedroom for more than a decade. At Hyde Park they did not even occupy the same house: Eleanor slept at the big house only when Franklin had important guests and wanted to keep up appearances.

Eleanor and Franklin satisfied their needs for intimacy—for contact with people who shared their feelings, humor, and ambitions—mainly with other people. In Louis Howe Franklin had a friend who was both devoted and blunt: neither man hesitated to criticize as well as to praise the other. And in Missy Le Hand, Franklin's personal secretary, he found a lighthearted friend who provided a flirtatious companionship he seldom enjoyed with Eleanor. She had begun working for Franklin during his vice-presidential campaign in 1920. She accompanied him to the Florida Keys and Warm Springs. Some who knew them suspected they were having an affair: Missy was sometimes seen sitting on Franklin's lap in his office, and his paralysis should not have impaired his sexual potency. But there is no clear evidence—no equivalent of the Lucy Mercer letters—showing that Franklin and Missy were lovers. Their affair was conjectural; their intimacy was not. At the end of a day at Warm Springs Missy was usually Franklin's companion for cocktails. In the Executive Mansion in Albany she served as hostess in Eleanor's absence.

Similarly, Eleanor felt most relaxed, most herself, with her own friends. During the 1920s Nan Cook and Marion Dickerman were her closest companions. When she took a place of her own, they shared it with her. When she revealed her criticisms of Franklin, they listened to her.

When she wanted to teach and to run a furniture factory, they were her colleagues. Certainly these friendships and her relationship with Franklin overlapped. Eleanor was cordial to Missy Le Hand and was perhaps even relieved that Missy's presence in Warm Springs and Albany released Eleanor to pursue her own interests. Similarly, Franklin was pleased that Nan and Marion provided a companionship for Eleanor that he could not.

Although most of Eleanor's intimates in 1932 were women, the one exception was the most "manly" man in her life, her bodyguard, Earl Miller. Strong and handsome, he had been a boxer, horseman, and state trooper. Earl taught Eleanor to ride and shoot and accompanied her on her travels. He was much younger than she—and his fellow troopers at first teased him about being assigned to protect "that old crab"—but he was won over by Eleanor's warmth. She was attracted to his youth and his rough good nature. In a home movie Eleanor played an innocent maiden and he a pirate-kidnapper. Both were clearly delighted with their roles.

Eleanor and Earl remained close friends throughout her life, and they were sometimes rumored to be lovers. Her son James was certain that they were "more than friends" and conjectured that Eleanor may have become "a complete woman" with Earl. But in view of Franklin's approval of their relationship and Eleanor's statements to Anna about her distaste for sex, it is more likely that they were intimates of another sort, drawing strength from the interplay of their personalities—he fascinated by her mature grace, she by his youthful vigor.

In other respects Franklin remained the chief figure in Eleanor's life. If they could not be romantic intimates, at least they could be friends. If they were not sexual companions, at least they shared many political goals. When Eleanor said that "The light of a true marriage shines" through a couple's common interests, she could easily have been describing her own marriage.

But it was not quite that simple. The balance between Franklin and Eleanor was a delicate one. They retained a capacity to hope for more in their marriage than either was able to give; they could still injure each other. The dark side of their relationship was usually hidden, but it was apparent one afternoon to Nan and Marion at Val-Kill. Franklin was at the big house, but Eleanor had not seen him for two days. They were angry with each other, but only they knew why. Eventually Franklin drove up to the cottage in a Ford he had equipped with hand controls. Eleanor went out and sat in the car and talked with him for two hours. Then they drove off together.

Such moments suggested an antipathy they tried to overcome, or at least to hide. Other moments reveal a persistent yearning each felt to be closer to the other. In 1931 Franklin tried to persuade Eleanor to join him at Warm Springs. Fearing perhaps that she would not come at his request, he wrote Anna telling her how much he wanted to see her. Anna in turn wrote Eleanor, saying that her father was worried about Eleanor's working too hard with speeches, teaching, and meetings and that Franklin hoped she would get a substitute at Todhunter so that she could spend a restful week in Georgia with him. "If you think it would give you any rest at all to go to Warm Springs—do go," wrote Anna. "Pa seems to want you there so badly."

That year Sara was vacationing in Paris and caught pneumonia. Franklin sailed to France to bring her back. When he left, Eleanor looked frazzled. She wrote him, "I think I looked so tired chiefly because I hated to see you go, though I knew it was the best thing for you to do." She told him, "We are really very dependent on each other though we do see so little of each other." This was one of the most revealing sentences Eleanor ever wrote to

Franklin: in spite of flaws in their marriage, they did need each other. "Dear love to you," she concluded. "I miss you and hate to feel you so far away."

It was difficult to be separated, and yet Franklin and Eleanor were most successful as partners when they did keep a distance between themselves, pursuing different interests and developing different friendships. Sometimes these activities enhanced their own relationship—providing material for conversations and acquaintances they could share. But neither was willing to enter fully into the life of the other. Eleanor would not go to Warm Springs whenever Franklin wanted her, and she would not sail to France with him although he urged her to join him. Nor would he consider moving in with her at Val-Kill Cottage. Their implicit distances were as important to their relationship as their periods of communion.

By 1932 Eleanor had gone through several crises in her relationship with Franklin, each of which had threatened her own sense of identity. The Lucy Mercer affair undermined her confidence in herself as a wife; Franklin's election as Governor of New York threatened her ability to take part freely in public affairs. She survived these episodes, becoming a stronger, more self-confident individual after each. But in 1932 she faced an event that seemed at the time the ultimate disaster: her husband was elected President of the United States.

Most American women would have rejoiced at the chance to occupy the White House. Just as schoolboys were taught that no greater distinction could come their way than to be elected President, girls learned that the highest honor available to an American woman was to be First Lady of the land. But to Eleanor the position seemed the ultimate embodiment of the traditional female role she had learned to despise.

It was apparent early in Franklin's term as Governor of New York that he would be a leading candidate for the Presidency in 1932. He was Governor of the nation's largest state and was reelected by a record margin in 1930. In the meantime Herbert Hoover was facing one of the greatest challenges ever presented to an American leader. In October 1929, seven months after he took office as President, the stock market crashed. Soon America was in the midst of the worst depression in its history. The Roosevelts were not gravely affected by the Wall Street crash, but they were surrounded by people who were.

Anna's husband, Curtis Dahl, had taken Anna to live on a thirty-six-acre estate in North Tarrytown, New York. He invested heavily in stocks and was so impoverished after the crash that he and Anna had to move in with Eleanor and Franklin. The streets in New York City were so crowded with men out of work that Eleanor ordered her cook to keep warm coffee and sandwiches ready for the many jobless men whom she met on the street and sent to the house for food. She carried five-dollar bills, earned from her speaking and writing engagements, which she passed out to the needy.

While Eleanor was waging a personal fight against the Depression, Franklin brought the state government into action with a progressive relief program that assisted the needy and added to his national stature. At the Democratic Convention in 1932 he took the nomination in spite of a strong challenge by Al Smith. Eleanor appeared to be fully involved in the presidential campaign. When she flew with Franklin to Chicago, where he accepted the nomination, she impressed a reporter as "one of the calm people of the world." Eleanor organized the Democratic women for the campaign with help from one of her best friends, Molly Dewson. Reporters who came to her for information about her husband went away impressed with Mrs. Roosevelt. "A persistent twinkle in her blue eyes," wrote one, "cannot be transferred into lines of cold type. . . . Though the talk had been entirely about Franklin Roosevelt, our thoughts were increasingly of Mrs. Roosevelt. Gracious, charming, patient, serene, but efficient and plainly the devoted helpmate."

Eleanor was able to create an outward impression of calm devotion, but inwardly she was troubled by the events of 1932. She felt a sense of alienation, detachment, drifting. She attended a World Series game with Franklin in Chicago; it was an exciting game in which Babe Ruth and Lou Gehrig each hit two home runs, but Eleanor slept quietly through the whole show. Her son Elliott commissioned a portrait of his mother in 1932. Eleanor refused to sit for the painter but allowed him to follow her for several weeks gathering his impressions while she conducted meetings, met friends, and attended church. To the casual glance the finished portrait shows a charming woman, her face full of life and compassion. But on closer examination the face is curiously divided: one eye seems to radiate a quiet serenity; the other seems distracted, worried.

When Eleanor saw the completed portrait, she burst into tears. The artist had discovered a sorrow and a confusion that Eleanor wished to hide. During the campaign another person, a journalist named Lorena Hickok, came to know the ambiguity of Eleanor's character. "Hick," as she came to be known, had covered Franklin for the Associated Press since 1928. One of her earliest memories of the Governor's wife was of her unsightliness. Eleanor wore a black skirt that was too long, a knitted green jumper that made her skin look gray, and a hat, "like a black straw pancake," that sat squarely on top of her "tightly netted hair." Eleanor must have been equally startled by her first impression of Hick, who was a short, fat woman with a pugnacious temperament and a face that belonged with a cigar.

On the day that the Democratic Convention voted to nominate Franklin Roosevelt for President, Hick was stationed in the garage of the Executive Mansion in Albany along with an assortment of other reporters and operators and their radios and phones. She and Elton Fay, another Associated Press reporter, left the garage in the morning for a break, and Eleanor spotted them. She was "looking very clean and crisp in a light summer dress" and had just come to the screened side porch for breakfast. She invited the reporters to join her.

Hick was impressed with Eleanor's cordiality but puzzled by her attitude. Eleanor was "rather withdrawn— shut up inside herself." She seemed indifferent to the convention debates and was unwilling to discuss her husband's chances. As they left the house, Hick said to Elton Fay, "That woman was unhappy about something." Later that day Hick attended a press conference. Franklin, fresh and buoyant, laughed and joked with the reporters. Nearby a silent Eleanor sat knitting, "her expression serious—almost unhappy."

In the evening Franklin received a call at the Governor's Mansion telling him that William McAdoo had switched his California delegation to Roosevelt. The nomination was now ensured. Missy Le Hand said, "F.D., you look like that cat that swallowed the canary!" John and Elliott shook hands and tossed paper in the air. Neighbors gathered on the lawn to cheer Franklin, and reporters surged in from the garage. Eleanor and Missy embraced. But at midnight while everyone gathered around her triumphant husband, Eleanor, detached again, went into the kitchen to make bacon and eggs for Franklin.

With that simple gesture—cooking the one meal she had known how to prepare since her early married years—she tried to compose herself. Standing in front of the stove in a pale green chiffon gown, she may have felt unconsciously submissive: Franklin had triumphed, and so with spatula in hand she would revert to a time-honored wifely role. But even in the kitchen she could not escape the events encircling her. A gushing reporter followed her in.

"Mrs. Roosevelt," she exclaimed, "aren't you *thrilled* at the idea of living in the White House?"

Eleanor made no reply but looked at the reporter with an expression, almost angry, that stopped further questions. By chance, Hick saw that expression. Who *is* Eleanor Roosevelt? she wondered.

The Associated Press appointed Hick to cover Eleanor on the campaign. They ate barbecued beef together at a ranch in Prescott, Arizona, and hiked through a cornfield "somewhere in Nebraska or Iowa." Hick was impressed with Eleanor's kindness to her and other reporters. One morning Eleanor arose early to buy Hick coffee, orange juice, and rolls at a station because the train had no diner. In a Pullman compartment she gave the lower berth to Hick, leaving herself a long narrow couch. When Hick protested, Eleanor, who was learning how to handle her corpulent friend, told her, "I'm longer than you are—and not quite so broad!"

As their friendship grew, their conversations became more spontaneous. No longer just reporter and subject, they told each other about their early lives. Both had lived through unhappy childhoods. Eleanor, the orphan, learned about Hick's loss of her mother at age thirteen and Hick's struggle to make her way in journalism. On her forty-fourth birthday Eleanor, who was slowly adjusting to the idea of becoming First Lady, revealed a stoic side of her nature to Hick. "I'm a middle-aged woman," she said. "It's good to be middle-aged. Things don't matter so much. You don't take it so hard when things happen to you that you don't like."

A few weeks later one of those things did happen; Franklin overwhelmingly defeated Herbert Hoover for the Presidency. On the night of the election Eleanor was as calm and detached as she had been when Franklin received the nomination. She sat in front of a mob of reporters; hot newsreel lights glared in her face. Eleanor did her best to smile, but she looked directly at Hick and shook her head "ever so slightly." The expression in her eyes was "miserable." Eleanor reminded her friend of "a fox, surrounded by a pack of baying hounds."

The next morning a police guard and Secret Service men surrounded the Sixty-Fifth Street house. Eleanor arose early to eat breakfast with Louis Howe and her granddaughter, Sisty, who was now a pupil at Todhunter School. After a brief meeting with some reporters, Eleanor went to teach. Her students at Todhunter stood up when she entered the room. One of the girls presented to Eleanor an Egyptian scarab for good luck and said to her, "We think it's grand to have the wife of the President for our teacher." Eleanor thanked the girls but told them not to think of her as changed. "I'm just the same as I was yesterday," she said.

A few days later Eleanor was on a train to Albany with Hick. Eleanor's expression was "wistful" as she looked out the window. A gray rain was falling on the Hudson River and the Catskills. She told Hick what she had told the Todhunter girls and anyone else who would listen: "There isn't going to be any First Lady. There is just going to be plain, ordinary Mrs. Roosevelt. And that's all." They were riding in a coach, instead of a private room in the parlor car, just as Eleanor had always done. She told

Hick, in effect, that she was "serving notice on the American public not to expect her to be the sheltered, conventional White House mistress to which it was accustomed and of which it approved."

During the fall of 1932 Eleanor was more aware of what she was losing than what she would gain. Public service had been the great bulwark of her life. Above all she had loved teaching at Todhunter. She had given inspiring lectures in history and English, and she had given the girls practical lessons in life, taking her wealthy students on field trips to the Lower East Side. "I've liked teaching more than anything else I've ever done," she said, "but it's got to go." They talked for a while, and then Eleanor reached into a bulging briefcase and took out a folder full of student papers and began grading. "A teacher also has homework to do," she said.

They reached Albany at twilight. Standing in the broad station plaza they looked up a steep hill toward the capitol. Eleanor waved away a cabdriver and began walking the two miles to the Executive Mansion. Hick watched her friend set out "with her long, swinging stride." She then went into a cafe and waited for the train back to New York, where she would file her story with the Associated Press. Hick was worried for her friend. "I never wanted to be a President's wife," Eleanor had told her. "Now I shall have to work out my own salvation. I'm afraid it may be a little difficult."

# First Lady

*We are in a tremendous stream, and none of us knows where we are going to land. The important thing, it seems to me, is our attitude toward whatever may happen. It must be willingness to accept and share with others whatever may come and to meet the future courageously, with a cheerful spirit.*

Eleanor Roosevelt, to Lorena Hickok, *1933*

"I, Franklin Delano Roosevelt, do solemnly swear that I will faithfully execute the office of President of the United States. . . ." On the cloudy morning of March 4, 1933, these words boomed over loudspeakers to a vast audience standing on the grass, clinging to trees, and sitting on bleachers high on the roof of the Capitol building. Millions more listened to radios across the country. In a moment Franklin Roosevelt would be President of the United States and deliver a speech designed to bring hope to a troubled nation. In that same moment, by a curious alchemy, Eleanor Roosevelt, who neither pronounced an oath nor delivered an address of her own, would become First Lady of the land. She wore an "Eleanor blue" silk dress, dark blue coat, and orchid corsage—one woman among eighty dark-suited men on the inaugural platform. On her finger was a sapphire ring Hick had given her. During most of the ceremony she stared into her lap, as if trying not to call attention to herself. Reporters remarked that she was curiously passive.

Franklin completed the oath of office and removed his hand from the family Bible, which had been opened to Paul's words, "Though I speak with the tongues of men and of angels, and have not charity, I am become as sounding brass, or a tinkling cymbal." Then he began to speak, his voice firm and reassuring. Eleanor already knew what Franklin would say. He and his advisers had worked on the speech until late the night before in the Mayflower Hotel and had sent Eleanor a copy in the adjoining room, where she was staying with Hick. "It's a good speech," Eleanor told her friend, "a courageous speech. It has hope in it. But will people accept it? Will they believe in him?"

The problems facing the new President were stupendous. During the past four years American industrial production had declined by fifty percent; national income fell from $81 billion to $41 billion per year. The number of unemployed rose from four million in 1930 to almost fifteen million in 1933. Men who had been wealthy now sold apples on streetcorners. Makeshift villages of wood and cardboard sprang up in parks and vacant lots around the country. People foraged for food in garbage cans; some actually starved to death. Confidence in the nation's institutions was so low that thousands of depositors took their money from banks, assuming it would be safer under floorboards or in mattresses. Unable to keep pace with withdrawals, many banks closed their doors. In the crowd that assembled for the inauguration under a cold gray sky were men and women who had lost their savings or were unemployed; almost all had relatives and friends who were out of work. Looking at the faces before her, Eleanor wondered, "How much can people take without blowing up?"

Franklin sought to reassure his listeners. We need not "shrink from honestly facing conditions in our country today," he said. "This great nation will endure as it has endured, will revive and will prosper." America's problem was mainly spiritual: "The only thing we have to fear," he said, "is fear itself—nameless, unreasoning, unjustified terror which paralyzes needed efforts to convert retreat into advance." Confidence had languished because men had given themselves over to "the mad chase of evanescent profits" and forgotten "that our true destiny is not to be ministered unto but to minister to ourselves and to our fellow men."

Eleanor must have liked these phrases. Her personal triumph of the past fifteen years had come from service to family, friends, and community. As First Lady she would have new opportunities for service. But doubts about her own role in the new administration still assailed her. Even as she listened to Franklin speak, Eleanor was worried that she might lose both her privacy and her vocation in Washington. First Ladies were usually esteemed but ineffectual; they sat with their hands in their laps and looked ornamental while their husbands delivered inaugural addresses.

Eleanor's anxiety had been apparent on the morning before when she had taken Hick—who knew better than anyone else her private fears—on an outing to escape the crush of reporters and Secret Service agents surrounding Franklin. Hick arrived by taxi at the side entrance to the Mayflower Hotel, where Eleanor joined her and told the cabbie to drive along R Street. She intended to show Hick the house where she had lived during the 1910s, but as it came into view, Eleanor saw a large sign on the lawn: "Former Residence of Franklin D. Roosevelt." She ordered the cabbie to move on to a more private place, Rock Creek Cemetery.

Eleanor guided the driver unerringly through a maze of driveways to the Adams Memorial and led Hick to the statue of Grief. For a long time the two women sat in silence on a curved stone bench before the figure. Hick saw in Grief "a woman who had experienced every kind of pain, every kind of suffering known to mankind and had come out of it serene—and compassionate." Eleanor spoke in a hushed tone, as if she were in a church. "In the old days," she said, "when we lived here, I was much younger and not so very wise. Sometimes I'd be very unhappy and sorry for myself. When I was feeling that way, if I could manage it, I'd come out here, alone, and sit and look at that woman. And I'd always come away somehow feeling better. And stronger." A decade and a half had passed since those troubled days, and during that time Eleanor had become, in the public eye, an embodiment of serenity and compassion. But now, as she faced the greatest challenge in her personal and public life, she needed once more to draw strength from a statue.

Franklin spoke on. "This nation," he said, "asks for action and action now." Step by step he outlined a program for recovery: people must be put to work, farmers must receive better prices, debtors must find relief, welfare agencies must be strengthened, banks and investment houses must be regulated. Franklin anticipated that these and other reforms could be achieved within "the normal balance of executive and legislative authority." But he warned the people that the nation's problems might require him to seek "broad executive power to wage a war against the emergency as great as the power that would be given me if we were in fact invaded by a foreign foe." Upon hearing these words the audience, which had been restrained until now, burst into loud applause. Eleanor was disturbed by their reaction. Apparently many people would "do *anything*—if only someone would tell them *what* to do." They expected Franklin to be their deliverer. "It was very, very solemn," Eleanor told Hick, "and a little terrifying."

Hick had not gone to the inauguration. She was waiting for Eleanor at the White House in the room that had been Lincoln's bedroom during the Civil War. It would soon be Eleanor's study; now it was filled with ugly mahogany wardrobes and a clutter of old White House furniture. While the inauguration ceremony was drawing to a close a mile away, Hick looked out the tall windows at the Washington Monument and listened to the thumping and hissing of a faulty radiator. Then she heard motorcycles and cheers; a few minutes later the new First Lady strode into the room.

Eleanor had promised Hick an exclusive interview after the inauguration—the first she would give in the White House. They tried to talk in the Lincoln bedroom but were interrupted so often that they retreated to a bathroom. In this unlikely setting Eleanor presented to Hick in a few brief sentences a kind of inaugural address of her own. "One has a feeling of going it blindly," she said. "We are in a tremendous stream, and none of us knows where we are going to land. The important thing, it seems to me, is our attitude toward whatever may happen. It must be willingness to accept and share with others whatever may come and to meet the future courageously, with a cheerful spirit."

Eleanor was quickly involved in her new responsibilities: she attended the inaugural parade and greeted some of the three thousand guests who had come to the White House for an inaugural tea. Next there was a family dinner—with seventy-five in attendance. Then she went to the inaugural ball. In such ways Eleanor was immediately drawn into the traditional role of the First Lady: playing hostess.

The next day the guests departed. Hick had gone back to New York, and that night Eleanor wrote her from her new office. "These are strange days and very odd to me," she said. She apologized for having had so little time for Hick because of her official duties and her family activities. "I hope on the whole," she wrote, "you will be happier for my

friendship." Certainly Eleanor needed Hick's companionship. Surrounded as she was by family, friends, and admirers—and possessed of the highest title held by an
American woman—she still needed the tenderness, the
intimacy, the affinity that had grown up over the past few
months between herself and Hick. She told her friend, "I
felt a little as though a part of me was leaving tonight." In
closing she wrote, "I shall be saying to you over thought
waves in a few minutes:

> Goodnight my dear one
> Angels guard thee
> God protect thee
> My love enfold thee
> All the night through."

Eleanor and Hick had composed this saying as a kind of
nighttime benediction to one another. On this night
Eleanor sealed her letter and climbed into bed. From her
window she could see the great, silent form of the
Washington Monument, illuminated by floodlights
against the black sky. "A great comfort the monument has
always been to me," she wrote Hick the next evening.
"Why, I wonder?"

As she assumed the position of First Lady, Eleanor's
personal world was in chaos. The pleasure of teaching at
Todhunter School was denied her. The husband who had
been her friend, if not her soulmate, would now be more
remote, his attention directed toward the nation's problems. Her children were absorbed in their own interests.
She felt her own individuality threatened by the magni-
tude of her public role. In 1933 her relationship with Hick
was the greatest boon to her private life. Eleanor was,
much to her surprise, deeply in love with her journalist-
friend. During their separations in the ensuing months
Eleanor and Hick showered one another with letters and

phone calls. Three days after the inauguration, on Hick's fortieth birthday, Eleanor wrote saying, "All day I've thought of you. . . . Oh! I want to put my arms around you; I ache to hold you close. Your ring is a great comfort. I look at it and think she does love me or I wouldn't be wearing it." Hick was equally drawn to Eleanor. "There have been times," she told her, "when I've missed you so that it has been like a physical pain."

For several years Eleanor's relationship to Hick was the most compelling of her friendships. When the long Hickok-Roosevelt correspondence, consisting of several thousand letters, was released to the public in 1978, some readers concluded that the two women were more than close friends. Certainly they declared their love for one another. Such declarations were common, however, among women in those days. After all, Eleanor had written her mother-in-law that she wanted to be "kissed all the time" by her. And yet there is a different tone in her letters to Lorena Hickok: "Jimmy [her son] was near," she wrote soon after the inauguration, "and I couldn't say *je t'aime* and *je t'adore* as I longed to do but always remember that I am saying it." Eleanor's reticence about sex and her fundamental loyalty to Franklin probably kept her relationship to Hick within the bounds of convention. But clearly their friendship was a central element in their lives. And what did they mean to each other as friends? Eleanor's attraction to Hick derived from both her generosity and her needs—her ability to venture out and care for someone else and her desire to find in another person some refuge, some escape from life's trials and ambiguities. In Eleanor's love for Hick, her ability to care deeply for another person found one of its purest expressions. At the same time Eleanor sought in Hick, and to a degree found, a kind of shelter. Franklin did not love her sufficiently; her children were growing up and leaving home.

So be it. At least she had Hick, whom she loved and who loved her unreservedly. The assurance of Hick's love helped Eleanor begin life again and find a place in the "very odd" role of First Lady.

Franklin was not burdened with the self-doubt that troubled Eleanor. As President his challenge was formidable, but at least it was concrete: he must develop an economic program that would bring the United States out of the Depression. During his first three months in office—the Hundred Days—he took before Congress a remarkable legislative program including the National Industrial Recovery Act, the Agricultural Adjustment Act, the Farm Credit Act, and the Emergency Banking Act. These bills were passed by Congress along with legislation creating the Civilian Conservation Corps, the Public Works Administration, and the Civil Works Administration. At no previous time in American history had so many significant acts been passed in so little time.

During the Hundred Days Eleanor's achievements could hardly match her husband's, but in many ways she made good her claim that she would not slip into the mold of conventional First Lady. Her servants, many of whom had overseen White House protocol for three decades, soon found Eleanor overturning traditions she considered too formal. When her furniture arrived, she startled moving men by shoving desks and beds across the room in her eagerness to get settled. Laborers were told to work around her rather than wait for her to leave her study. She wanted a phone in her office and wondered why it had not arrived. The phone man was in the hall, she was told. "Oh, spinach!" said Eleanor—for her a salty expression. "Tell him to come in and get started!"

Many of Eleanor's innovations were designed to make the White House and its occupants accessible to the people. By tradition servants greeted guests to the presidential mansion and announced the First Lady to them. Eleanor tried to answer the door herself, just as she would in any other house. A porter would normally run the White House elevator and ring a bell to warn servants of the First Lady's approach. Eleanor learned to run the elevator herself and ignored the formality of announcing her arrival.

The most remarkable of Eleanor's innovations during her months as First Lady was in her handling of the press. Other presidential wives had stayed aloof, refusing even to grant interviews. Eleanor not only allowed herself to be interviewed by Lorena Hickok during her first hours in the White House, but she also instituted press conferences open only to women reporters. A few days after the inauguration she held one of these meetings—before Franklin's first conference. She greeted the newswomen by sharing a box of candies with them.

In such ways Eleanor made herself more accessible to the public than any previous First Lady. But at the same time she fought to preserve a private realm, where she could simply be herself. She refused to be accompanied on her travels by Secret Service agents and insisted on driving her own car without a police escort. The heads of the Secret Service fretted—kidnappers had recently killed Charles Lindbergh's child, and that winter an assassin in Miami had fatally wounded Chicago's Mayor Cermak as he stood beside Franklin. Nonetheless, Eleanor continued to value privacy above safety and refused protection. Finally, a frustrated Secret Service agent placed a gun on Louis Howe's desk and told him to make the First Lady carry it. Eleanor took the gun, and with Earl Miller's help she learned to shoot it, but there her compliance ended: she carried it unloaded in her glove compartment.

During the summer of 1933 Eleanor tested the bounds of her liberty, as if to determine just how much of her private life she could preserve in her new position. First she purchased a car: not a staid black Lincoln or Cadillac as might befit the First Lady of the land, but a light blue Buick roadster, a sporty convertible with a rumble seat. The car was a whim, another sign of Eleanor's refusal to lose herself in the formal persona of President's wife. As if to proclaim her freedom from convention, Eleanor indulged in other whims. She had always wanted to watch the sunrise from Vermont's Mount Mansfield and drive around the Gaspé Peninsula and spend a night in a tourist home. Why not do these things and more? The children had their own summer plans, the White House social season was over, Eleanor was only forty-nine, and life was still an adventure. In this frame of mind she invited Hick to join her in the roadster for three weeks traveling as "ordinary tourists" through New York, New England, and eastern Canada. The Secret Service was aghast, fearing that the First Lady would be abducted.

That idea amused Eleanor as she and Hick sped north in the convertible with the wind whistling in their ears. Eleanor was nearly six feet tall and Hick weighed nearly two hundred pounds. "Where would they hide us?" Eleanor demanded. "They certainly couldn't cram us into the trunk of a car!" As the sun dipped toward the Adirondacks and dusk fell over the forested countryside, they passed a little house with a sign welcoming tourists. "Let's go back and try it," Eleanor said. "I've always wanted to stay in one of those places." The owners—a young couple with a small baby—were startled to see Mrs. Roosevelt walk through their door. But Eleanor behaved like an ordinary tourist, and the hostess, regaining her composure, showed the guests to an ordinary room, small but spotless. The hot-water system was not fully installed, she explained, and so there was water for only one bath.

Alone, Eleanor and Hick argued over who would use the tub. "You're the First Lady, so you get the first bath," said Hick. Eleanor playfully thrust out her long fingers at her friend as if to tickle her into submission. Hick, ticklish but persistent, finally won, and Eleanor bathed. But with her spartan upbringing, she managed to take her bath cold, and Hick found to her surprise that the tap water was still warm. That night before they went to sleep Eleanor read to Hick from one of her favorite books, Stephen Vincent Benét's *John Brown's Body.*

The next morning they visited John Brown's farm and his grave near Lake Placid. With three weeks to themselves they traveled slowly toward Canada, crisscrossing the Green Mountains of Vermont and the White Mountains of New Hampshire. One evening they found themselves in a small town at the foot of Mount Mansfield. It was pitch black, and the village policeman advised them not to attempt the treacherous mountain road in the dark. But Eleanor was determined to see the sunrise from the top. The roadster whined up the trail in low gear, its headlights falling on trees and then into open space as the car rounded hairpin turns on the way to the Green Mountain Inn and a short night's rest.

A few hours later Eleanor and Hick watched the early morning sunlight that broke over the Atlantic and struck the mountains of northern New England. Atop Mount Mansfield they saw the light catch the mountain peaks and drop slowly into the valleys of the silent wilderness; far to the north they could see Mount Royal in Canada, and to the west Lake Champlain caught the pure light of dawn. To the south, out of sight beyond the horizon, the sun brightened the White House and the Washington Monument, five hundred miles away in space, farther still in thought.

The women drove on into Canada, staying at the majestic Château Frontenac in the old stone city of Quebec. For the next few days they drove along the south bank of the St. Lawrence on one of the loveliest roads in all of North America. She and Hick ate meals cooked over woodburning stoves, lay under the sun on a warm beach, and swam in the St. Lawrence. America seemed far away, and their anonymity complete. They stopped at a little church by the water, and the village priest invited them to lunch in his rectory. Hearing Eleanor's name, he asked her, "Are you any relation to Theodore Roosevelt? I was a great admirer of his."

"Yes," said Eleanor, smiling. "I am his niece."

Eleanor and Hick spent their last night in Canada at a tourist camp in a trim log cabin with a huge stone fireplace. The next day they crossed the border into Maine. For the past few days Eleanor had delighted in her freedom. She had not been the First Lady of America; she had been an ordinary person—herself. But that must soon end. With the convertible top still down, looking disheveled with white sunburn cream smeared over their faces, they drove into the town of Presque Isle, where to their "horror" a parade awaited them. They were "wind-blown, dusty, and dirty," and Eleanor felt anything but gracious. But she was trapped and fell dutifully into line with the procession that moved slowly down the main street between rows of flag-waving children. A portable traffic standard loomed ahead, and a flustered Eleanor clipped it. "Damn," she said.

This was the only time Hick ever heard her friend swear. Eleanor may have been surprised at her own profanity, but she managed to drive on through the town. When she realized that a dozen or so cars were still following them, she told Hick, "We've got to get out of this some way." The First Lady then sped around several corners and lost her escort on a country road in the potato fields of Aroostook County. Here they saw a farmhouse with a sign welcoming tourists.

After registering, they settled their nerves with a walk and then sat on a porch swing. Soon the farmer appeared and sat on the steps. Eleanor began talking knowledgeably about potato prices and local agricultural conditions. The farmer's wife came out and sat in a rocking chair; as darkness settled over the farmland, the four of them went on talking. Hick sensed the farmer's growing admiration for Eleanor. At about eleven o'clock they went into the kitchen for a snack of doughnuts and milk. In their room Hick asked Eleanor how she had managed to know so much about farming in Maine. Eleanor explained that she had read a local newspaper; she also gained information from the farmer as she went along—"something I learned to do when I was very young," she said, "to cover my ignorance." She might also have mentioned Franklin's coaching. He had taught her to be a good observer while he was Governor of New York, and he would need her reports even more now that he was President.

After a short visit to Campobello, Eleanor and Hick drove back to Washington. On the night of their return Franklin began a tradition he would observe throughout his Presidency: he dined informally with Eleanor so that she could tell him what she had learned. Hick told him about Eleanor's altercation with the traffic standard, and Franklin's "great, booming laugh" filled the room. Franklin asked about the country they had seen. What was the hunting and fishing like in Quebec, he wondered. How did the people live: what were their houses like, what did they eat, did the Catholic Church control education? And what about Maine: how were the farmers getting along, what had she learned about the Indians? Eleanor answered these questions and others. It was soon apparent to Hick that although Eleanor had relaxed on their vacation, she was constantly registering information for herself and for Franklin, even making mental notes about the state of laundry hanging on clotheslines—any detail that would help them both understand more fully the condition of the nation they served.

In such ways Eleanor brought together her private and her public life, even while touring in a Buick convertible. The vacation had been an escape from Washington, a part of Eleanor's personal life; at the same time it served her public role and her relationship with Franklin. The personal distance between Eleanor and Franklin remained great. He could relax more easily with Missy and Anna than with his wife. In the White House there were rooms enough for the President and First Lady each to have their own suites. When guests came for dinner, they often had cocktails with Franklin *or* with Eleanor in their separate White House apartments before coming together for dinner.

But even while their personal ties remained tenuous, their political partnership grew. Denied the physical and emotional intimacy of lovers, they continued to find another sort of intimacy in their shared goals and in the mingling of their careers. During the presidential years many of Eleanor's best times with Franklin came during their discussions of common political matters—their observations on national conditions, their exchanges on legislative and administrative questions, their conversations about political and moral values. Because Eleanor could travel more freely than Franklin—she covered forty thousand miles in 1933 alone— she became his eyes and ears, bringing him personal reports from around the world. Franklin developed the habit of throwing arguments at Eleanor to test her reactions, sometimes adopting her point of view. As she left the room after one conversation he told an adviser, "There goes the opinion of the average man in the streets."

Although Eleanor and Franklin developed independent circles of friends, these circles often overlapped. Henry Morgenthau was Franklin's crony and his Secretary of the

Treasury; his wife, Elinor, was one of the First Lady's best friends. Louis Howe continued to be the companion and political adviser of both Roosevelts. And Franklin established a lighthearted rapport with Hick. One afternoon Eleanor suggested that Franklin join her and Hick for tea at Normandy Farms, a country restaurant fifteen miles outside of Washington. Franklin agreed but insisted that the outing must be completely informal. "Either I go with my Missis alone, in her car," he said, "or I don't go." He refused to allow a Secret Service agent to sit in the rumble seat and insisted that the agents stay at least a half block behind Eleanor's car and not ride on the running board. Hick traveled in a third car, the presidential limousine, with Missy Le Hand. At the restaurant Missy and Hick stationed themselves on either side of the door and whistled "Hail to the Chief" as two Secret Service agents carried the President inside.

Hick was somewhat self-conscious in Franklin's presence—partly because of his eminence and partly because of her intimacy with his wife. But Franklin seemed completely at ease with Eleanor's friend. Hick spent a few days in the White House when the Roosevelts were away and made the mistake of opening her bedroom windows while a dehumidifier was running in her room. She awoke to find the room several inches deep in water. A rug was soaked, and the water had seeped under her door into the presidential bedroom. The Chief Usher of the White House, Ike Hoover, told Hick she had "been trying to dehumidify the whole city of Washington." When Franklin learned about the incident, he used it as an occasion to tease Hick. At lunch or dinner he would raise his head, sniff the air, and remark: "It seems to me that Washington is a little less humid than it was."

Then with a knowing glance at Eleanor's friend, he would add, "What do you think, Hick?"

In the summer of 1933 Hick went to work for the Federal Emergency Relief Administration, the agency created during the Hundred Days to provide a half billion dollars in assistance to the nation's poor. She was to travel across the country investigating the success of the relief program and writing reports to her boss, Harry Hopkins, who would pass them on to the President. Hopkins told Hick to be honest and compassionate. "I just want your own reaction," he told her, "and don't pull any punches." When she interviewed relief clients, she should tell herself, "But for the grace of God, I'd be sitting on the other side of this table."

Hick's reports to Hopkins were vivid accounts of the war waged by the New Deal against the Depression, and Hopkins often passed them on to Congressmen and the President. Hick also wrote daily letters to Eleanor, some extending to ten and twelve pages, giving her a personal glimpse of places like Dickinson, North Dakota; Hibbing, Minnesota; and El Centro, California. Just as Eleanor's travels made her the eyes and ears of the President, Hick's letters to Eleanor widened the First Lady's view of the Depression. One of Hick's letters early in her travels introduced Eleanor to Scott's Run, West Virginia, the place that became for her the essential example of what poverty and relief were all about.

After World War I the coal-mining districts of West Virginia had prospered with the industrial progress of the 1920s. Men sold out their small homesteads and came to work in the mines for ten to twenty-five dollars a day— enormous wages for that time. But with the Depression the demand for coal fell, and many of the mines shut down. Thousands of workers were stranded in dreary mining camps throughout the state. Hick toured West Virginia in August 1933. She saw miners living in tents because they had been driven from company housing after a strike, babies with distended bellies and eyes vacant from hunger, and children who took turns wearing the only pair of shoes in the family. She heard about a mother of eight who was dying of appendicitis and was denied admission to a hospital because she was too poor.

Hick came to Scott's Run, a scattering of mining camps along a tributary of the Monongahela River. A primitive dirt road followed a dirty little stream; steep hills rose on either side. Clusters of shacks, black with coal dust, stood beside slag heaps from the mines. Outhouses hung over a filthy stream that flowed down the mountain, and yet the people washed in the creek and used its water for cooking. The houses were small, ramshackle, leaky, hardly fit for pigs. "And in those houses," Hick wrote, "every night children went to sleep hungry, on piles of bug-infested rags, spread out on the floor."

When Eleanor heard about conditions in West Virginia, she arranged to visit Scott's Run. She found the houses "scarcely fit for human habitation." In some the parents and younger children slept together on the only bed—often bare springs covered with a blanket—and the older children slept on rags on the floor. In the town of Jere everyone drew water from a single spigot. "You felt as though the coal dust had seeped into every crack in the houses," Eleanor later wrote, "and it would be impossible to get them or the people clean." The families were large, but most had no more than two or three chipped cups and plates on the shelves. Children missed school because there was only one dress or pair of pants between them, and so they had to take turns dressing and going to class.

When Eleanor visited Scott's Run, the place became for her the embodiment of economic injustice in America. She went to the coalfields often, as if to immerse herself in their dirt, their poverty, their despair. A Quaker worker remembered her sitting in a dirty hovel, talking to a bedraggled mother, listening intently to her story. The woman's baby sat on Eleanor's lap. Eleanor saw a little boy holding a pet rabbit fondly in his arms. His sister remarked mischievously, "He thinks we are not going to eat it, but we are." The boy fled down the road clutching the doomed bunny closer than ever. When Eleanor returned to Washington, she told the story of the pet rabbit at dinner. One of the guests sent her a check the next day for one hundred dollars, hoping she would use it to keep the animal alive. Through his generosity the rabbit may have grown to a ripe old age, but Eleanor realized that the hardships of Scott's Run could not be cured one by one.

In his inaugural address Franklin had said, "Our true destiny is not to be ministered unto but to minister to ourselves and to our fellow men." On Inauguration Day Eleanor told Hick that Americans must be "willing to accept and share with others whatever may come." These ideals lay at the heart of Franklin's administration. The New Deal was more than the Agricultural Adjustment Act or the National Industrial Recovery Act or the other measures passed by Congress. It involved a commitment to use the machinery of government to provide for the well-being of all Americans. Clarence Pickett of the American Friends Service Committee saw the change in Washington as a "growing sense that the chief function of the state should be the welfare of its whole citizenry."

During his first two terms as President of the United States Franklin Roosevelt presided over the shift in national policy that put the government to work to alleviate economic suffering. Franklin was the principal statesman and administrative leader of the new movement. Eleanor too contributed to the revolution of the 1930s; if Franklin was its head, she was its heart. Naturally their roles overlapped: Eleanor brought brains as well as sympathy to her work, and Franklin's personal warmth was as important as his administrative policies. But Eleanor immersed herself more deeply in the particulars of some of the nation's problems than he was able to. He heard about places like Scott's Run; she came home with coal dust in her pores.

Eleanor was determined to do something for the people of Scott's Run. She helped by making contributions to the American Friends Service Committee for its relief work, just as she had fought hunger in New York City by supplying beggars with sandwiches and coffee. Eleanor had been raised believing that people were responsible for one another. Her grandfather Theodore had founded the Newsboys' Lodging House out of a sense of obligation to the needy. "Greatheart" taught Elliott a sense of charitable duty, and Elliott in turn taught Eleanor. She would continue to visit poor people and make personal contributions to charity. But she realized that individual acts of generosity could not begin to solve problems like the Depression in West Virginia. The government itself must care for the needy, and even more important, the people as a whole must acquire a higher sense of responsibility for human welfare.

Fortunately, Congress had already passed a bill that would provide assistance to people in places like Scott's Run. One section of the massive National Industrial Recovery Act set aside $25 million in loans for "subsistence homesteads," for people who could not afford to buy their own houses. The homestead program would demonstrate the value of government planning and provide a way for "stranded populations"—people thrown out of work by industrial decline—to make their own living on the land. The program's backers anticipated that families settled by the government on small plots of land could combine subsistence farming with work in small manufacturing plants.

More than fifty subsistence homestead communities would be established throughout the United States during the New Deal. The most famous, Arthurdale, became Eleanor Roosevelt's pet project. She realized that a resettlement community would be ideally suited to help the people of Scott's Run and met with Louis Howe and Secretary of the Interior Harold Ickes to discuss the matter. She had an advantage over both men in knowing the conditions in West Virginia at first hand and easily persuaded them that a community should be established near Scott's Run. "I'll buy the houses," said Howe. "Ickes, you buy the land. And Eleanor, you'll put the families in the houses."

The government bought the houses and the land. Louis Howe negotiated with Richard M. Arthur to buy his twelve-hundred-acre farm outside of Reedsville, West Virginia, as the site for a planned community. During the fall of 1933 some fifty families were chosen from Scott's Creek to be pioneers in Arthurdale. Louis ordered fifty prefabricated houses from Cape Cod, road crews went to work, and the new community was on its way. Eleanor visited the homesteaders often and came to know many by name. In June 1934 the homes were ready to occupy. At a ceremony marking the event the leader of the new community introduced Eleanor as a person "whom we all love and, with her husband, deeply respect." Eleanor told the "pioneers" their hard work would inspire other Americans. They presented her with onions and radishes grown in their gardens.

Arthurdale was an attractive community. Neat white houses, each with its own barn, stood side by side on five-acre plots. A community center housed a school, auditorium, post office, and shops for local crafts. Esther Clapp, a distinguished educator, established a progressive school for the village. Near the school was an old log cabin where the children learned crafts and built a loom, a spinning wheel, and wooden dishes. Eleanor gave money to the school and persuaded her friend, Bernard Baruch, a wealthy financier, to make substantial contributions. The First Lady often visited Arthurdale during the 1930s, taking part in village square dances and attending high school commencements.

Because of Eleanor's interest, Arthurdale attracted the attention not only of the government but also of the press. Soon stories began to circulate about the flaws in this planned community: Howe's Cape Cod houses had cost twice what they should because they had to be rebuilt for local conditions; the homesteads had one well apiece instead of sharing a community water supply; the pipes and gutters were of copper instead of less costly materials. No major business had located factories in the town, and so the idea of overcoming the split between rural and urban America with factories in the farmlands could not be tested.

Because no businesses were there to employ the pioneers, they could not make the payments on their houses, and their obligations had to be continually rescheduled. Consequently the homesteaders tended to become overly dependent on the government. One complained that he could not sit down to dinner without someone wanting to interview him. Another indicated his addiction to government assistance by driving the school bus to the White House garage when it needed repairs. A journalist concluded in 1940 that "Arthurdale seems to reaffirm a belief still strong that men must find their own places in life, must work out the solution of their own problems."

Eleanor eventually admitted that Arthurdale was not the economic and social panacea she had hoped for. But she knew another side to the experiment at Arthurdale. Some reporters saw only a picturesque village that was costing the government a lot of money. Eleanor had seen what came before. One woman's experience told the whole story: she was a homesteader whom Eleanor visited shortly before Christmas 1934. The woman had three small girls and carried a baby in her arms. She was living in an attractive house with a cellar full of canned goods. Last Christmas, she told Eleanor, she had been in a hovel with two rooms and no windows. Christmas dinner had consisted of carrots. Because she and her husband had no money for presents, she had not even told the children it was Christmas. "This year," she said, the children "will each have a toy and we have a chicken, one of our own, that we are going to eat. It will be wonderful." "Oh, yes," Eleanor wrote, summarizing her defense of Arthurdale, "the human values were most rewarding, even if the financial returns to the government were not satisfactory."

Arthurdale owed much to Eleanor's initiative. She helped develop the idea of the settlement, she discussed its progress with politicians and with the homesteaders, and she raised money to supplement government spending. In all these things she exercised the moral and administrative leadership of the President himself. Had she done nothing in public affairs but sponsor Arthurdale, she would have achieved more than most First Ladies. But Arthurdale was only one of many projects that Eleanor supported.

With her friend Molly Dewson, head of the Women's Division of the Democratic Party, Eleanor helped many women find government posts in Washington. A woman who had spent many years in the capital remarked that when women administrators had wanted to dine together in the past, a small club could seat them all. "Now there are so many of them," she remarked, "that we need a hall." Eleanor also encouraged women journalists in Washington by holding press conferences for them and by hosting a "Gridiron Widows" buffet supper on the night when the Gridiron Club held its annual banquet. The

Gridiron Club consisted of male journalists; Eleanor's "widows" included newswomen, Cabinet wives, and women in the government. Eleanor was sometimes criticized for not embracing complete equality for women. More militant women, such as Alice Paul, favored picketing and other confrontational tactics and considered social reformers such as Eleanor Roosevelt and Labor Secretary Frances Perkins too "ladylike" in their approach to women's issues. Eleanor was not a vigorous supporter of the women's equality movement, yet in practice, by her own example and by providing opportunities for women, she was instrumental in encouraging women to expand their horizons.

Eleanor's care for human values brought her inevitably into contact with the area of greatest injustice in America, the treatment of African Americans. As a young woman Eleanor had, like most white Americans, overlooked the indignities suffered by blacks. When Franklin was in Washington during the race riots of 1920, Eleanor had worried about his safety but did not appear to give a thought to the reasons for the riots. Her main contact with blacks at that time was through servants; she had built up a staff of tractable "darkies" who cared for the house and the children.

During the 1930s prejudice against blacks was so pervasive that the Roosevelts themselves were unable to avoid practicing discrimination. Franklin's Warm Springs was closed to blacks, and the homesteaders at Arthurdale voted to admit only whites. Blacks were not even invited to Eleanor's or Franklin's press conferences. Despite her acquiescence in such discriminatory measures, however, Eleanor grew increasingly upset about the treatment of black Americans. For the first time in her life she was in constant contact with black leaders, befriending them and learning firsthand about racial injustice in America.

Discrimination barred blacks from schools, restaurants, and hotels. Movie theaters in downtown Washington were segregated, and throughout the South most non-whites could not vote. Blacks were kept "in their place" by laws, social pressure, and the brutal sanction of lynching—in the year of Franklin Roosevelt's inauguration, blacks were killed by vigilante mobs at the rate of one every two weeks.

Despite these facts New Deal reformers refused to think of blacks as a group deserving special attention. They claimed to be color-blind, assuming that blacks would prosper with other Americans if the Depression could be ended. But often their "impartiality" led to another kind of blindness—allowing racial injustice to continue unabated. Agencies such as the Civilian Conservation Corps failed to hire blacks in proportion to their numbers in the population, and the Agricultural Adjustment Administration adopted policies that resulted in loss of work for black sharecroppers in the south. A White House receptionist greeted a group of black leaders with the cold remark, "What do you boys want?"

Eleanor learned how deeply race prejudice was embedded in the American political system when she tried to persuade Franklin to support an antilynching bill. In many cases whole towns witnessed vigilante murders, but the killers were almost never brought to trial. A federal law against lynching would allow the government to intervene when local officials would not. Eleanor strongly favored such a bill, but popular as it was, Franklin believed it would be political suicide to support it. Most of the southern Democrats would regard such an act as undue federal interference in their affairs, and Franklin could not afford to alienate the southern wing of the party.

Despite the administration's failure to support civil rights legislation, when blacks voted in 1936, they swung overwhelmingly to the Democratic fold, ending their traditional alliance with the Republican Party. This change came about for several reasons. Although blacks did not benefit as much as whites from New Deal legislation, many did find work in relief programs. The administration included a few men like Interior Secretary Harold Ickes who cared about the blacks and established rigorous quotas for black employees in the Public Works Administration. Although Franklin Roosevelt failed to adopt a civil rights program, he made a few symbolic gestures—such as visiting black college campuses—that pleased black leaders.

The administration's greatest asset in attracting black voters, however, was Eleanor Roosevelt. She had grown up thinking of blacks affectionately as "darkies"—a charming but somewhat shiftless people who were the equal of whites in emotional integrity but not in brains or industry. Her liberation from these stereotypes came slowly, and mostly through her acquaintance with black leaders who became her friends.

Walter White, the intense leader of the National Association for the Advancement of Colored People, found in Eleanor a person who would listen to his pleas for better treatment of blacks. Eleanor befriended him and served as his advocate. When he came to discuss antilynching legislation with the President, Eleanor and Sara sat with him on the White House veranda until the President arrived. He found the three of them—even his conservative mother—a solid phalanx for stiff antivigilante laws.

Eleanor formed a close friendship with Mary McLeod Bethune, the most influential black woman of her time. Initially Eleanor was somewhat awkward with this, her first close personal friend of another race. But in time she came to greet Mary as warmly as any other friend, rushing down the White House drive to greet her and walking arm in arm to the main door. Eleanor was primarily responsible for Mary Bethune's appointment to the advisory board of the National Youth Administration, a position Bethune used to ensure black representation in NYA programs.

In her personal conduct Eleanor left no doubt that blacks were her friends, her kin in the human family. During the years of the Hoover Presidency black servants in the White House had been trained to scurry out of the way when the First Lady walked down the hall. In contrast, Eleanor greeted the servants cheerily, and if one were near the elevator when she was entering, she often said, "Come in and ride along." Eleanor entertained blacks at the White House and visited black schools and communities. Newspaper photos showed the First Lady beaming down at a black child who was handing her a flower or mingling in a playground with black nursery school children.

Southern racists complained that "Eleanor Clubs" were being established to persuade black domestic servants to refuse to work, and they predicted a race war. Within the administration bigoted New Dealers, who regarded blacks as inferior, and practical New Dealers, who worried about political support, criticized Eleanor for her liberalism. But Franklin was unwilling to curtail his wife's gestures of friendship toward black Americans. In part he went along because he realized she was building political allies, while he kept his southern supporters faithful by being less progressive. In part he accepted her liberalism because he too sympathized with the blacks, and in part he supported her because he was too wise to try to dissuade his wife from taking part in any cause she genuinely embraced.

Eleanor could not give disenfranchised blacks the right to vote or to attend unsegregated schools, but more than any other public figure in the 1930s she communicated to blacks and to the nation as a whole a sense that they were all human beings and Americans. In 1938 she attended a meeting of the Southern Conference for Human Welfare in Birmingham, Alabama. Municipal law decreed that blacks and whites must not sit together in public gatherings, and so as the meeting began, Eleanor was seated on the white side of the hall, separated by an aisle from the blacks. She abhorred this separation of peoples, but Franklin had taught her to be discreet. She could not attend an antilynching rally; she should not place her chair squarely among the blacks. So in a gesture both subtle and brilliant, she edged her chair over to the middle of the aisle.

In 1939 she was called on again to accept an act of racial discrimination and refused. The Daughters of the American Revolution barred the great singer Marian Anderson from their auditorium because she was black. Eleanor had once been proud of her association with the DAR, as she was proud of her ancestors who had taken part in the Revolutionary War. But she decided that remaining in the organization after this outrageous display of racial discrimination would condone that bigotry. She resigned from the DAR and helped Harold Ickes arrange an outdoor concert for Anderson on the steps of the Lincoln Memorial.

On the cold afternoon of April 9, 1939—Easter Sunday—Marian Anderson stood before a crowd of seventy-five thousand men and women. Wearing a dark dress and a fur coat, she seemed the embodiment of stately self-control. But inwardly she quaked: "There seemed to be people as far as the eye could see," she later wrote. When the crowd grew still and she prepared to sing, she felt for a moment as though she was choking and feared that the words would not come. She may have thought of the years of hardship she had experienced and the centuries of injustice her people had known. But, she wrote, "a great wave of good will poured out from these people, almost engulfing me." And the words did come: "My country 'tis of thee, sweet land of liberty, of thee I sing. . . ."

Harold Ickes was there; he called it "the most moving occasion" of his life. Mary Bethune said she "came away almost walking in the air." Years later Marian Anderson wrote, "It seemed that everyone present was a living witness to the ideals of freedom for which President Lincoln died. When I sang that day, I was singing to the entire Nation." Eleanor Roosevelt did not go to the concert. A prisoner of her time and her position, she could not go any further than she already had to express her hostility toward racial prejudice. But Eleanor's action in resigning from the DAR carried many people with her; two-thirds of the people interviewed for a Gallup poll approved of her action. Behind Marian Anderson that Easter Sunday had been not only the bronze form of Abraham Lincoln but also the infectious goodwill of Eleanor Roosevelt.

Eleanor's Uncle Ted had called the Presidency a "bully pulpit." Eleanor discovered—while visiting Arthurdale, holding press conferences, and helping blacks—that the same could be said of the "office" of First Lady. Eleanor's work for coal miners, women, and blacks was only part of a White House career that ranged across the whole spectrum of American society and included many other activities. She continued to tour the country for herself and for Franklin, visiting farms, slums, and relief projects. She used her press conferences to air her views on important issues and to introduce people she admired.

Eleanor always claimed that she did not like to give speeches, but as First Lady she became one of the most admired lecturers in America. She enlisted a voice coach to help her overcome the high-pitched, girlish tones that sometimes spoiled her talks, and she hired an agent to arrange her lecture trips. She also developed as a journalist. She had contributed many articles to magazines since 1920; in 1936 she began to write a daily syndicated column called "My Day" that contained observations on her own life in the White House and on her trips. And she undertook several series of radio broadcasts. She used the media to publicize her views on human rights and to cultivate a closer relationship between the people and the White House: her topics ranged from discussions of policy issues to descriptions of the square dancing at the Executive Mansion. She even broadcast advertisements for coffee, mattresses, and other products, using her considerable earnings to support the American Friends Service Committee and other charities.

Eleanor traveled so widely, used the media so thoroughly, and supported so many issues that she acquired the nickname "Eleanor Everywhere." People came to think of her as a person who could solve their personal problems. Among the hundreds of letters she received every day were many asking Eleanor to help them financially. I am a "worthy, honest blind man," wrote one correspondent, "asking you to assist me by sending me your subscriptions for all magazines." A woman in Kentucky wrote Eleanor asking her to help the woman's son, Woodrow, buy a "9 or 10 tube" radio by purchasing a wool quilt belonging to the boy. An Indiana farm woman wanted Eleanor to buy a handmade comforter to help her pay off her mortgage: "I have noticed the poor and the once rich are becoming more like one big family," she wrote, "and that includes most of our population of our dear United States."

Many of the letters to Eleanor indicated how much people whom she had never met had come to think of her

as a close friend—or a generous aunt. One woman wanted the First Lady to buy a crocheted bedspread and told
about her ailments: fallen arches, hemorrhoids, "female
troubles," a hernia, a poor liver, and other weaknesses.
"Thank goodness," she wrote Eleanor, "it doesn't all hurt
at once." Most of the people who wrote the First Lady
asking for assistance indicated that they had heard of her
generosity.

"I have heard, or read, of so many fine things you have
done for those in need . . . and you always seem able to find,
or make a way, to solve every problem presented to you."

"I am an entire stranger to you, but I often see in the
papers where you have done so many good deeds for so
many poor folks."

"I have read and heard so many nice things about you,
it's almost like writing to a friend."

"No one seems to care so much or realize how to help
folks in the way they need help," wrote a woman who
wanted Eleanor to buy an "embroidered panel" from her.
I "hope you won't object to my sending this on for your
consideration, as it will really and truly mean a New Deal
to me. . . ."

Eleanor's standard reply to such requests for personal
help was a letter indicating that she could not make pur-
chases from individuals. Her "New Deal" did not extend
that far. But simply by taking the side of the underdog—
whether in sponsoring Arthurdale or identifying herself
with oppressed blacks—she created a feeling among millions of Americans that someone in high office *cared*
about their condition. For a girl considering a career in
journalism or a black leader wanting to be heard,
Eleanor's support was enormously valuable.

In various ways she interested Franklin in her issues. She
brought southern sharecroppers and northern garment

factory workers to the White House. She arranged his social schedule so that at dinner he would sit next to representatives of minorities and laborers. As President and First Lady they worked together more effectively in public affairs than any previous White House couple. Franklin would send Eleanor to a forgotten place like Puerto Rico to indicate his interest in the people there; she surveyed conditions on the island and urged Franklin to "send down some labor people and industrialists to look over the situation."

Franklin sometimes used Eleanor's care for the needy to his own advantage. Through her influence he won votes with disadvantaged groups while keeping conservative Democrats happy by remaining more neutral himself. But often he bent to her will, showing an interest in measures she brought to his attention. "Never get into an argument with the Missis," he told Lorena Hickok. "You can't win. You think you have her pinned down here . . . but she bobs up right away over there somewhere! No use—you can't win." Economist Rexford Tugwell witnessed many discussions between Eleanor and Franklin and was impressed. "No one," he wrote, "who ever saw Eleanor Roosevelt sit down facing her husband, and holding his eyes firmly, say to him, 'Franklin I think you should . . .' or, 'Franklin, surely you will not . . .' will ever forget the experience."

As Eleanor became better known, she found it increasingly difficult to travel as an ordinary tourist. She and Hick took a West Coast trip in 1934 that ended any further efforts to go incognito. Their only real privacy came during an idyllic sojourn in the backcountry of Yosemite National Park. They were met by rangers who escorted them high into the mountains, where they set up camp at ten thousand feet. For Eleanor these were "days of enchantment." She climbed peaks surrounding the camp and looked down over a vast wilderness of lakes and mountains. At night she sat by a campfire and listened to the rangers telling stories; she slept outside her tent under the stars and rose early in the morning to watch the head ranger fishing. Hick, a heavy smoker with a weak heart, was less comfortable, but even for her the privacy of the wilderness was preferable to traveling in settled areas.

Everywhere else they went they were pursued. On a highway outside Sacramento a group of reporters forced them to pull over and talk. The journalists insisted on knowing Eleanor's travel plans. She pulled her knitting out of the car and sat under some trees. "It's nice here in the shade," she said amiably, "and I like to knit. I'm willing to sit here all day if I have to, but I am not going to tell you where we're going."

These reporters finally left, but others were more persistent. Photographers pursued them in San Francisco, snapping pictures while the two women ate, and souvenir hunters pilfered odds and ends from their car. As Eleanor and Hick toured the city, they were followed by so many people that they were "hardly able to exchange a dozen words in private." They traveled on to Bend, Oregon, where they ate a quiet meal in a restaurant only to come out and find the town's leading citizens formed up in a reception line. In Portland they entered their hotel room to find it "literally filled" with roses. "All you need," said Hick, "is a corpse."

The West Coast trip made Eleanor aware that she could no longer lead the life of an ordinary citizen. When Eleanor became First Lady she had worried that her position would deprive her of both autonomy and privacy. By taking part in many projects of her own, she stepped out of her husband's shadow and created a unique role for herself.

Having "liberated" herself in the 1920s and 1930s from the limited role usually assigned to women, she became both the supporter and embodiment of the aspirations of laborers, women, and blacks seeking their own liberation.

But in the very act of embracing new opportunities for public service—and thus achieving remarkable autonomy—she limited her own opportunities for a rich private life. With each public act she identified herself more with the persona of the First Lady. Even her relationship with Hick suffered. As the first intensity of their attraction waned and Eleanor became more preoccupied with her official role, they saw each other less often and their letters became more perfunctory. Years later Eleanor wrote: "It was almost as though I had erected someone a little outside myself who was the President's wife. I was lost somewhere deep down inside myself. That is the way I lived and worked until I left the White House."

This detachment may have been in part produced by Eleanor's new role, but it was also a feeling she had experienced throughout life. Her personal life was never as full as she could wish; the things she loved always brought sorrow as well as joy: a father who drank himself to death, a husband who failed to supply her needs for companionship, an intimate friend with whom she could not live happily ever after.

But Eleanor's detachment was only a mood, only a part of her temperament. She found satisfaction in her many acts of public service, and if she was the prisoner of her "office," it was above all because she gave so much of herself to it, her great heart finding satisfaction in work as well as in friends. Across the United States were individuals and groups who needed her help, and she was willing to serve, serve, serve. In this enterprise of public service she and Franklin, who were so distant in many ways, formed a remarkable partnership.

Devoted as Eleanor was to public life, she found time for many individual gestures of goodwill. Her attachment to scores of people was apparent in a White House room she set aside as the "Christmas closet." Here she began storing Christmas presents early in the year—for people at Arthurdale, for White House servants, for friends and relatives. She bought so many that during the fall she enlisted guests to help her wrap them. Then came Christmas: parties for the White House staff, a visit to the poorer neighborhoods in Washington and New York, and finally a holiday at Hyde Park, where Franklin in his wheelchair directed the placement of every ornament on the Christmas tree.

New Year's Eve usually found them back at the White House. With a few friends they gathered in the Oval Office to sip eggnog and listen to the radio. Midnight arrived. Franklin, sitting in a big presidential chair, raised his cup and said, "To the United States." The guests standing nearby raised their glasses and repeated the toast. Eleanor joined in the benediction.

Yes, Franklin . . . yes, my darling. "To the United States."

# 9

# The Democratic Crusade

*Somehow or other, human beings must get a feeling that there is
in life a spring, a spring which flows for all humanity, perhaps like
the old legendary spring from which men drew eternal youth. This
spring must fortify the soul and give people a vital reason for wanting to meet the problems of the world today, and to meet them in a
way which will make life more worth living for everyone. It must be
a source of social inspiration and faith.*

Eleanor Roosevelt, *The Moral Basis of Democracy*

In June 1939 Britain's King George VI and Queen
Elizabeth came to the White House. Eleanor, an aristocrat
herself, was eager that the royal couple be treated like royalty. "Even in this country," Eleanor remarked, "where
people had shed their blood to be independent of a king,
there is still an awe of and an interest in royalty and in the
panoply which surrounds it." But the democrat in Eleanor
demanded that George and Elizabeth also be exposed to
things American. She drew up a menu featuring American
food and planned "a sort of folk festival" with Kate Smith
singing "When the Moon Comes Over the Mountain"
and Marian Anderson performing Negro spirituals. The
visit would not only expose the royal couple to the products of democratic culture but would also sharpen
Eleanor's thinking about the nature of political leadership
and the character of democracy.

On the morning of June 7 a train bearing the King and Queen arrived at Union Station, where Eleanor and Franklin met them. As they rode through Washington in two limousines, Eleanor was impressed with the Queen's energy as she continually rose from her seat and bowed to the people who lined the way. She later discovered that Her Majesty had been sitting on a spring cushion: clearly the First Lady, seasoned politician though she was, had something to learn from the Queen about meeting the public.

In some respects Their Royal Majesties were unlike anyone Eleanor had met before. The Queen continually amazed Eleanor by appearing without a hair out of place. She was so lovely one evening in a white spangled dress and a jeweled crown that Harry Hopkins's eight-year-old daughter, Diana, who was allowed to meet her for a moment, told her father, "Oh, Daddy I have seen the Fairy Queen." Despite their royal bearing, however, the King and Queen showed a solicitude for the well-being of others that exceeded, in Eleanor's view, that of many a self-styled democrat. At a Civilian Conservation Camp under a "broiling sun" they walked down a long reception line; the King stopped and spoke to every other man in the line, and the Queen spoke to the intervening men. How was the food, they asked, what were they learning, would they be able to find work after leaving the camp? Coming to the end of the first line, the pair turned and spoke to every man in the second row as well. Then they inspected the mess hall and barracks: looking into pots and pans on the stove, feeling for lumps in the mattresses, and overturning a table to see how it was made. The King was determined to learn everything he could on the chance that similar camps might be established in Britain. Eleanor was impressed by his desire to improve life for others—here was the essence of wise leadership. That day the King had gone to Mount Vernon and laid a wreath on George

Washington's tomb; it was a fitting gesture, the descendant of George III paying homage to the revolutionary leader.

After several days in Washington George and Elizabeth joined the Roosevelts at Hyde Park. Eleanor and Franklin had gone ahead, taking with them the White House butlers to serve Their Majesties. Sara was upset, believing that her servants were better than those from the Executive Mansion. As they waited on the evening of June 10 for Their Majesties to arrive, Franklin sat on one side of the fireplace in the living room with a tray of cocktails. On the other side sat his mother, looking disapprovingly at him. Surely, she said, the King would prefer a nice cup of tea to a cocktail.

The King and Queen arrived. "My mother does not approve of cocktails," Franklin said, "and thinks you should have a cup of tea."

"My mother would have said the same thing," the King replied, "but I would prefer a cocktail." Franklin must have grinned mischievously at Sara.

The next day the two couples went to church and then to a picnic at Val-Kill, where dozens of friends and neighbors joined them. Dispensing with formalities, Eleanor served up barbecued hot dogs, smoked turkey, cured hams, and baked beans, followed by Dutchess County strawberries. For entertainment an Indian princess from Oklahoma sang songs and told stories. After the meal Franklin and the King went swimming. He invited the Queen to join them, but as Eleanor discovered, "if you are a queen, you cannot run the risk of looking disheveled." While the men swam, Elizabeth and her lady-in-waiting sat by the side of the pool with Eleanor.

After an informal dinner the royal couple went to Hyde Park station to take a train to Canada. As she was about to board the train, the Queen suddenly turned back and asked after the man who had been their driver. She wanted to thank him. Eleanor was impressed with this final example of noblesse oblige. "How kind and thoughtful," she reflected, "and what training this must take."

As the train pulled out, George and Elizabeth stood on the rear platform and waved. A crowd had gathered along the banks of the Hudson to watch them leave and began to sing "Auld Lang Syne." For Eleanor there was "something incredibly moving about this scene—the river in the evening light, the voices of many people singing this old song, and the train slowly pulling out with the young couple waving good-bye."

The royal visit was one of the most memorable events of Eleanor Roosevelt's White House years. It had been a meeting with the foremost representatives of royalty, but in many ways the King and Queen displayed the essential traits of democratic leaders. In their consideration to others—whether to CCC workers or to a chauffeur—Their Majesties had been better democrats than many American politicians. Her encounter with the King and Queen encouraged Eleanor to ask herself: Just what is the essence of democracy? How does it draw upon and nourish individual and communal responsibility? How can it create of average American citizens human beings who are as sensitive to the worth of others as the King and Queen?

A year later Eleanor published a book titled *The Moral Basis of Democracy* in which she probed the meaning of American political ideals. The book was both an essay on democracy and a personal testimonial, drawing on Eleanor's political experience, religious beliefs, and sense of life's meaning. During much of her adult life she had struggled to achieve both personal autonomy and a sense of communion with others. She understood democracy better because of this personal struggle: it was a political system that valued both the individual and the community.

Eleanor argued that democracy required, first, a profound

sense of responsibility for the well-being of others. "The motivating force of the theory of a Democratic way of life," she continued, "is still a belief that as individuals we live cooperatively, and, to the best of our ability, to serve the community in which we live, and that our own success, to be real, must contribute to the success of others." Democracy could not be fully realized in America until the great blemishes of poverty and prejudice were eradicated. "No one," she said, "can honestly claim that either the Indians or the Negroes of this country are free. . . . We have poverty which enslaves and racial prejudice which does the same." She insisted that "a minimum standard of security must at least be possible for every child" and there must be "an economic level below which no one is permitted to fall." Our love for our neighbors should extend far beyond our immediate circle of friends: "That means an obligation to the coal miners and sharecroppers, . . . to the tenement-house dwellers and the farmers who cannot make a living. It opens endless vistas of work to acquire knowledge, and when we have acquired it in our own country, there is still the rest of the world to study before we know what our course of action should be."

Some sorrows, Eleanor admitted, were purely individual and could not be eradicated by public action—politics could not bring back her mother and father or her baby. "But hunger and thirst, lack of decent shelter, lack of certain minimum decencies of life"—these things, she said, "can be eliminated if the spirit of good will is awakened in every human being." Because she advocated a reform program that extended far beyond even the legislative reforms of the New Deal, Eleanor was sometimes branded a "Communist." Her program was definitely "left-leaning," and she echoed the words of Karl Marx when she castigated people who used the concept of property rights "to retain in the hands of a limited number the fruits of the labor of many." But Eleanor was critical of the totalitarian regimes of the left and the right. In Communist Russia and Nazi Germany, she believed, human beings were "trained for cruelty and greed." In America, at its best, they were trained "for gentleness and mercy and the power of love."

Totalitarianism was wrong because it emasculated "the fundamental ideal of self-confidence which arises out of individual liberty." Democracy, in contrast, was "a method of government conceived for the development of human beings as a whole." As Eleanor probed deeply into the meaning of democracy, she found in it an ideal that was both political and personal. The democratic ideal offered a solution to the heart-numbing sorrows that men and women feel in their isolation. Democracy taught that people were responsible for one another and that those who assumed that responsibility could overcome their own loneliness. Eleanor had known times when people, meeting to discuss public policy, were so united in their goals that they experienced "a moral feeling of unity brought about by a true sense of brotherhood." One of the finest products of democracy, she argued, was "a sense of brotherhood, a sense that we strive together toward a common objective."

In serving others one led a richer life oneself. Eleanor's experience with sorrow and loneliness had developed in her great compassion for other men and women. That compassion, in turn, enabled her to feel a life-enhancing kinship with humanity. Trying to describe the source of her own strength, she wrote: "Somehow or other, human beings must get a feeling that there is in life a spring, a spring which flows for all humanity, perhaps like the old legendary spring from which men drew eternal youth. This spring must fortify the soul and give people a vital reason for wanting to meet the problems of the world today, and to meet them in a way which will make life more worth living for everyone. It must be a source of social inspiration and faith."

Eleanor Roosevelt believed that people like the King and Queen of England were in touch with that "spring" of human compassion. But when they left Hyde Park, she realized they were returning to Europe, where another principle, fascism, had come to power. As the train left Hyde Park station she "thought of the clouds that hung over them and the worries they were going to face, and turned away and left the scene with a heavy heart." For the first time in twenty years Eleanor and other Americans had to face the possibility of war. Since the end of World War I Eleanor had believed that warfare "is the result of spiritual poverty." She argued, "It is the fact that human beings have not developed the ability to rise above purely selfish interests which brings about war." After the Great War Eleanor had wondered whether any future conflict could be justified. She and Franklin were staunch supporters of the League of Nations, and probably no political act had disturbed either of them more than the Senate's rejection of American entry into the League.

Although the United States turned down the League, the country backed a number of measures during the 1920s and 1930s designed to prevent war. In 1921 and 1922 the Washington Arms Conference resulted in a five-power pact to limit naval development. Between 1935 and 1937 Congress passed several "neutrality acts" to prevent the country from being dragged unwittingly into another global conflict by trade with the belligerents. During the 1930s the United States debated the possibility of joining the World Court; Eleanor was a strong supporter of the court. "We cannot escape being a part of the world," she argued. "Therefore, let us make this gesture for peace, and remember there was no world court in 1914 when the

Great War began." On the same basis—that we cannot escape being a part of the world—she defended her husband's recognition of the Soviet Union in 1933. Isolation and ignorance only increased the chance of war.

Eleanor tried to impress upon her children the horror of battle. In 1929 she toured Europe with Franklin Jr. and James and pointed out to them all the signs of war: monuments in English villages listing war dead, whitened stumps on French hillsides where whole forests had been mowed down by shells, cemeteries with "rows and rows of crosses," and in the fields "curious holes made by bursting shells, now covered with grass." One afternoon in France young Franklin said to his mother, "This is a funny country. There are only boys our age and old men coming out of the fields. We've seen young men in uniform doing maneuvers, but there don't seem to be any men of father's age." Strange indeed.

Like many other Americans who leaned toward pacifism during the two decades following World War I, Eleanor came reluctantly to regard the rise of aggressive, totalitarian regimes in Germany, Italy, and Japan as a greater threat to human values than war itself. During the early years of the Roosevelt Presidency news of foreign affairs had been driven into the background by the domestic crisis of the Depression. The condition of the miners in West Virginia seemed more important than the fact that Japan had invaded China or Italy attacked Ethiopia. But in the late 1930s the economy was slowly recovering, and the news of aggression in Asia and Europe was so persistent that it became the preeminent problem in American policy.

One morning in the fall of 1939 Eleanor was awakened at five in the morning by a call from Franklin, who gave her the news that the Germans had just invaded Poland. She was so upset by a "sense of impending doom" that she stayed up, despite the early hour. A few thousand miles away the world had slipped into chaos, and America herself might soon be "dragged into the vortex."

Eleanor recalled uneasily her feelings twenty-five years before on the eve of another war. She had worried that Franklin might quit his position in the Navy Department to enlist, and she feared for his life when he visited the front in 1918. At the same time she had felt an obligation to be "doing something in the actual danger zone." The old conflicts and anxieties passed through her mind "like the fragments in a kaleidoscope." The sense of danger was familiar, but the personal risk was even greater now than in 1917. Then the four boys had been too young to fight, but in 1939 the youngest was twenty-three and the oldest thirty-two.

The war came slowly to America. France fell, England was bombed daily, and Hitler invaded Russia. In the United States isolationists argued that America should stay out of the "European conflict." But the government slowly prepared for war, increasing military spending and sending assistance to the Allies. Had there been no war Franklin probably would have retired from the Presidency in 1941. Eleanor believed that in retirement he "would have lived his life very happily." But with the outbreak of the war in Europe his advisers urged him to run for an unprecedented third term.

During the 1940 Democratic Convention Eleanor was drawn into politics as never before. Franklin's nomination was ensured, but many delegates opposed his chosen running mate, Henry Wallace. Franklin would not go to the convention himself to address the delegates, and so Eleanor was invited to speak for him. When Eleanor arrived, she found the convention in disarray. Franklin had not even made his choice of Wallace clear to Jim Farley, his campaign manager. Her own son, Elliott

Roosevelt, at the convention as a delegate from Texas, was planning to second the nomination of another candidate. The crowded hall was full of noisy partisans, shouting their support for various nominees.

Eleanor came to the podium, and the crowd grew still. Accustomed now to public speaking and still remembering Louis Howe's good advice—"Say what you have to say, and sit down"—she declared that the next four years would be difficult for the President and that he would need a man he could depend on to help him. The man he wanted was Henry Wallace. She urged the delegates to "sink all personal interests in the interests of the country"—and sat down. Wallace won the nomination.

As her plane began to taxi down the runway someone waved frantically to the pilot, and he turned back to the terminal. Franklin was on the phone; he had heard Eleanor speak, and he wanted her to know that she had done "a very good job." Supporters of the Republican candidate, Wendell Willkie, tried to make the First Lady one of their campaign issues and wore big "We Don't Want Eleanor Either" buttons. But the tactic backfired, for Eleanor was just as popular as Franklin, and together they won a third term.

When the news of victory reached Hyde Park, Eleanor was, as usual, both supportive and detached. She "wanted him to win, since that was what he wanted." But she was still ambivalent about being a President's wife. Too often her triumphs as First Lady had been at the expense of her private life. She wrote Lorena Hickok, "I only like that part of my life in which I am a person." She worried, too, about Franklin. He seemed to Eleanor—who had lived with him now for thirty-five years—to be "weary." Franklin still enjoyed being President, and the nation, on the brink of war, needed his leadership. But Eleanor could imagine him being happy in retirement with time to read and write and think.

The year following the 1940 election was one of the most difficult Eleanor ever faced. She hated war, but she believed that Japan and Germany must be defeated for the sake of humanity. Slowly the face of the country was changing in preparation for battle. In September 1940 Franklin had signed the Selective Service Act, authorizing the draft. In March 1941 she met Franklin at Fort Bragg, North Carolina; the enormous size of the camp, she said, "took my breath away; it brought home to me the fact that war was drawing near." Franklin spent more and more time in his study alone or with advisers. Often he sent word at the last moment that he could not come down for dinner, and Eleanor would entertain guests by herself.

In August 1941 Franklin told Eleanor he was going to take a trip through the Cape Cod Canal to do some fishing. Then he smiled as if to signal her that something else was happening that he could not tell her about. Franklin went through the canal in the presidential yacht, and for several days the crowds along the shore thought they saw the President with a cap pulled down over his eyes sitting on deck and waving amiably. In the meantime, however, Franklin had transferred to a ship, and a man who looked like him had boarded the yacht to go fishing. Franklin steamed north to the coast of Newfoundland, where Winston Churchill joined him, and together they drafted the Atlantic Charter, a plan for a postwar world characterized by self-determination of nations, freer international trade, and disarmament of aggressor nations.

If Eleanor could see any purpose in the war to come, it was in goals such as these. War could be justified only if it contributed ultimately to the "moral sense of unity" that the nation and the world so needed. But Eleanor's mood in 1941 was far from triumphant. Already two of her sons, Franklin and Elliott, were in the armed services. Elliott was in the Air Force in Newfoundland flying reconnaissance missions to locate emergency landing fields. Franklin Jr. was convoying merchant ships to England through the submarine-infested North Atlantic. She could find rational reasons for their involvement, but inside she said, "You feel a kind of rebellion when those you love are in danger, or may be in danger, and you must sit safely and idly by."

During these strange months when America was preparing for battle but not yet at war, Eleanor's personal world was further shaken by death. Sara had been weak for some time. In September, shortly after Franklin visited her, she fell into a coma. She died, as she had wished, in her own room at Hyde Park. Eleanor had known Sara for almost four decades, but as she admitted to a friend, she "felt no deep affection or sense of loss." They had been, perhaps, too close and then too distant. Sara had been the mainstay of Eleanor's life when the young bride thought that to be a good wife and mother was her whole purpose in life; when Eleanor grew beyond that role, she resented her own earlier dependence on her mother-in-law. It was perhaps not fair to blame Sara, for the orphaned Eleanor had invited and even yearned for Sara to take the role of mother. Eleanor's later hostility was in part hostility toward the person she herself had once been.

For years Sara had resisted the idea that Hyde Park should become a museum after her death, but she left a memorandum requesting that the room in which Franklin was born be returned to its original condition. That request suggested that she had come to approve transformation of Hyde Park into a national shrine. It may also have shown her own yearning for an earlier, simpler time when women stayed at home and Franklin was her own baby son.

Sara died after a full life, greatly admired as the grande dame of the presidential family. A few weeks later Eleanor faced another, more disturbing death. Her brother, Hall, had led a desperate life, failing in marriage and business and giving himself to drink. Eleanor still thought of Hall as her child and tried to help, although his drinking caused "many heartaches and many moments of great embarrassment and anxiety." He died in Walter Reed Hospital, where Eleanor had watched over him during the final weeks of his life. Funeral services were held in the White House; then Hall's body was taken to Tivoli and laid in the family vault.

Hall was now buried near his father, Elliott; his mother, Anna; and his brother, Ellie. Of that star-crossed family only Eleanor was left alive to ponder the meaning of their existence. Hall was "one of the most generous people in the world," she wrote. He was a "warm friend," and he "loved children." While working as a relief administrator in Detroit, he had lived voluntarily on the same allowance as his clients so that he could experience their poverty. But he was unable to apply himself for long to any job, and as he aged, Eleanor had to watch his "fine mind gradually deteriorate" with drinking. He never learned "complete self-discipline," Eleanor later wrote. Hall's personality was so like their father's that Eleanor must have felt at times that she was reliving the great tragedy of her childhood. Both men had great hearts but were unable to lead full, constructive lives.

The world was flawed by social injustice and by international hostility; it was flawed too by man's failure to fulfill his own potential. Where was life's "spring" when Elliott and Hall died in drunkenness? Looking back on Hall's death Eleanor later wrote, "Sorrow in itself and the loss of someone whom you love is hard to bear, but when sorrow is mixed with regret and a consciousness of waste, there is added a touch of bitterness which is even more difficult to carry day in and day out."

In the past during times of personal crisis Eleanor had given herself to work. Now she added to her White House chores an official position as codirector of the Office of Civil Defense, an agency devoted to preparing the American people for war. It was in part to numb the pain of Hall's death that she "went to work in earnest" at the OCD after returning from his funeral. One morning Franklin said to her, "What's this I hear? You didn't go to bed at all last night?" Eleanor had been working on her mail without watching the time; suddenly it began to get light outside and she saw no point in going to bed. A watchman on hourly rounds had noticed that her light never went out and told Franklin. In such ways husband and wife buried themselves in work, preparing for a war that must soon come.

Eleanor learned about Pearl Harbor from a White House usher. She went to Franklin's study but found him so busy that she went on with her work. That evening she made one of her weekly radio broadcasts on current affairs. The show featured Eleanor interviewing a soldier about army morale. As if the meaning of Pearl Harbor had not yet sunk in, they went on with prearranged questions about camp life. But Eleanor did begin her remarks by saying, "I have a rock, and that rock is my faith in the American people."

Cabinet members and generals gathered around Franklin in the Oval Office late into the night. Reports were still coming in of damage to the Pacific fleet: two battleships destroyed, six others and a dozen smaller ships put out of action, one hundred fifty planes destroyed, and thirty-four hundred American servicemen killed or wounded. The losses were staggering; with this disaster the nation had moved from the shadow world of isolationism into the brutal reality of twentieth-century war. Finally Eleanor and Franklin had a chance to talk. He seemed to her "more serene than he had appeared in a long time."

Franklin's address to Congress the next day embodied a sense of remorseless fact: "Yesterday, December 7, 1941—a date which will live in infamy—the United States of America was suddenly and deliberately attacked by naval and air forces of the Empire of Japan. . . ." Eleanor sat listening, and for the second time in twenty-five years she heard a President call for a declaration of war. The cause was just, but the danger to her own children was tremendous, and she was "deeply unhappy."

That night she boarded an airplane with Fiorello La Guardia, Mayor of New York and codirector with Eleanor of the Office of Civil Defense. They were bound for Los Angeles, where they would help local officials plan the defense of the West Coast, which might at any moment be attacked by the Japanese. As the plane droned on through the night, the pilot received a disturbing report by radio from San Francisco. A messenger took the word to Eleanor in a small forward compartment: the Japanese had bombed San Francisco. Stunned, Eleanor walked back to where La Guardia slept in a curtained berth and told him the news.

At the next stop Eleanor went to a phone and found that San Francisco had not been bombed. The rumor, however, indicated the panic felt along the West Coast. She and La Guardia toured the region, helping fire departments and hospitals prepare for war. Eleanor traveled from city to city by night. The trains' headlights were dimmed. The frightened people of California, Oregon, and Washington had darkened their houses so effectively that all was blackness outside the train.

Back at the White House she encountered other signs of war. Blackout curtains were placed on all the windows. A steam shovel worked day and night on the front lawn, digging a trench for a bomb shelter. Everyone was given gas masks and run through air-raid drills. Gun crews were placed on the roof and wings of the White House, and an order was issued against flying over the presidential grounds. Franklin complained good-naturedly about all the fuss. After learning that he might have to go to a shelter under the Treasury Building, he told his Treasury Secretary, Henry Morgenthau, he would not go unless he could "play poker with all the gold in your vaults."

Eleanor continued to work in the Office of Civilian Defense. Remembering the role of volunteers in World War I, she hoped that the OCD would organize millions of volunteers nationwide to help the war effort. But she came under attack for some of her ideas, including civil defense–related programs in drama and dance. As one of the most outspoken liberals of the time, she inevitably aroused hostility among those who opposed the social changes of the Roosevelt years.

Eleanor came reluctantly to the conclusion that her status as wife of the President hindered rather than helped the programs she favored in the OCD, and so she resigned in February 1942. She was pleased "when the weight of that office" was removed from her shoulders, but she immediately found new responsibilities. One of her major activities was visiting American troops on bases and in hospitals at home and abroad. She said of Franklin that his insistence on taking trips during the war was motivated in part by "a strong subconscious desire" to share the dangers his four sons faced. She may have felt the same desire, for her wartime travels were almost as extensive as the President's.

On October 21, 1942, Eleanor boarded a plane for Great Britain. A few hours later she looked down at the ocean and saw a convoy of merchant ships steaming along with a protective shield of destroyers zigzagging around them. Her craft, a seaplane, landed in a rainstorm at Foynes, Ireland, and a small boat came out to take the passengers off. Eleanor's raincoat and umbrella were stowed with her bags in the wings of the plane; she arrived on shore with hair disheveled and clothing soaked with rain— a fitting welcome to the austerities of a continent at war.

In London she was given a more comfortable greeting: a red carpet in the train station and a royal reception from the King and Queen. Eleanor spent three weeks touring England. Someone "with a sense of humor"—she suspected Franklin—had assigned her the code name "Rover" for the journey. She met with the King and Queen and with Prime Minister Winston Churchill; she visited paratroopers who were about to be flown to the front in North Africa, and she delivered a radio address to the British people. Eleanor was particularly interested in learning how women were involved in the war and was pleased to see the variety and complexity of their tasks. She visited war plants, where she met women working on "every kind of truck and motor car." She also encountered women who served on gun crews or flew warplanes from place to place within the country.

Everywhere Eleanor went she was reminded that England was at war. In the royal palaces the rooms were cold because of fuel rationing, and on the tub in Buckingham Palace a black line indicated the maximum depth for a patriotic bath. With the King and Queen she toured the poor sections of London that had taken the worst pounding from the Nazis during the Battle of Britain. Streets were lined with shell holes, and whole blocks had been erased from the earth. She met workers along the Clyde River, whose nearby towns had been bombed. The worst thing, they told her, was to go on working when the bombs were falling a few miles away in your own neighborhood—to go on building ships when at that very moment your home and your family was perhaps being obliterated.

Eleanor went home to the United States with a stronger conviction that a better world must rise out of the ashes of the world war—a conviction she reaffirmed during her journey to the South Pacific the following year. She associated this better world with the humanitarian programs begun in the United States during the New Deal, and she declared that the reform movement of the 1930s must not be allowed to die during the war. Many Americans still lacked good medical care and suffered from discrimination. She tried unsuccessfully to interest Franklin and others in further reforms: they were too occupied with the war, and the cost of further reforms seemed too great.

Eleanor could do nothing on her own for improved medical care for the poor, but she continued to help women and blacks. Whenever women assumed new responsibilities in commerce and industry, Eleanor publicized their activities in her radio broadcasts and newspaper articles. She made a point of seeking out and encouraging black servicemen and argued for fair treatment of blacks in the armed forces. Because of her pressure on War Department officials, directives were issued forbidding the segregation of armed service recreational areas by race. Eleanor also provided access to the White House. One night a visitor was surprised at the number of African Americans he met there. To Eleanor he said, "Looks like we're entertaining most of the blacks in the country tonight." She replied, "You must remember that the President is their President also."

Eleanor also played an active role in White House discussions of such matters as the allocation of defense contracts, arguing that small contractors should receive opportunities along with giant corporations. She took part in discussions of economic policy with labor leader Walter Reuther. During the war women were moving into factories to replace men in the armed forces: Eleanor was instrumental in securing day-care centers to encourage this trend.

The war could be justified only insofar as it was a humanitarian crusade, Eleanor believed, but other Americans, more conservative, criticized her for seeking to change a world in which they were comfortable. After reading an article that described Eleanor's attendance at a party where blacks and whites had mingled, a woman from Tennessee wrote her, "It is heart breaking to know our leaders act in such a manner." A woman in Arkansas claimed that due to Eleanor's support of civil rights, "the negroes are refusing to work on the farms and in the homes." And a twelve-year-old girl from Louisiana, well schooled in bigotry, wrote Eleanor, "I am very much against the white people mixing with the colored." Throughout these criticisms was the notion that America was better before the New Deal, when blacks "knew their place." A woman from Alabama summarized that attitude in these ominous words: "When your sons and my brothers and my husband and all the rest of the boys come home, they want to have peace and the wonderful country they left, not another war."

Eleanor received criticism for particular stands. She also was criticized for what she was: a woman with a sense of mission and the energy to carry out that mission. Her highly publicized travels drew out critics who were disturbed by the spectacle of a woman making a mark in the world. "Why don't you buy yourself some stuff to knit with instead of using the army's gas to go on your pleasure trips," wrote a man from Iowa. "If you would stay home and make a home for your husband, it would be O.K." Other citizens wrote Eleanor telling her to "keep Franklin company (as a real good woman should do)" and "tend to her knitting as an example for other women to follow." She was characterized as a "female-dictator who would advise her husband" and as a "selfish, pleasure-loving woman."

Brutal as these comments were, they show how deeply Eleanor's personality had registered on the American psyche. For every racist who criticized her for supporting civil rights and every conservative who believed women, even First Ladies, should tend to their knitting, many other men and women shared Eleanor's vision of how they might improve their lot or that of others less fortunate. George Gallup had begun his polls by now, and Eleanor usually won a two-thirds approval rating, often running ahead of Franklin. Her vision of a more humane nation, though rankling some, inspired others who hoped with her that the world would become a better place after the defeat of the Axis Powers.

Throughout the war Eleanor continued to be troubled by the conflicting demands of her public and private life. The war drove a further wedge into her relationship with Franklin. He had less time to spend with her now and, beset as he was with military problems, less energy for her reform schemes. As the war went on, the pressures began to wear away at Franklin's health. He had no time for swimming, and even the children had to make appointments to see him. Franklin's advisers worried about his declining health; some felt that Eleanor failed to realize how weary he was and "bugged" him with her unending suggestions and requests.

As in the past Franklin turned to other friends for companionship. Missy had died after a long illness. Her passing left a gap in his life that was filled partly by his friendship with his daughter Anna. She was so sympathetic to his need for companionship that she helped him renew one of the most compelling, if disturbing, relationships in his life. Lucy Mercer was recently widowed. With Anna's connivance and without Eleanor's knowledge, she visited Franklin at the White House and in Warm Springs.

Eleanor might have been devastated had she known that Franklin was seeing Lucy, but as in the past, she had her own circle of personal friends. Her relationship with Lorena Hickok had lost the intensity of the mid-1930s, but their friendship was still warm. Hick was working in Washington and at Eleanor's invitation lived in the White House in the small bedroom once occupied by Louis Howe. She and Eleanor went through days without seeing one another, but they often breakfasted together, and in the evenings Hick sometimes visited with Eleanor in her sitting room while the First Lady worked over her mail, or Eleanor went to Hick's room and sat chatting at the foot of her bed.

The most intense of Eleanor's relationships during the war was with Joseph Lash. They met in 1939, when the American Students Union, of which Lash was executive secretary, was under investigation by a congressional committee for possible subversive activity. Eleanor was one of the chief supporters of the National Youth Administration, a New Deal agency designed to help young people find work and a sense of purpose during the Depression. Liking young people and believing that "it was essential to restore their faith in the power of democracy to meet their needs," Eleanor befriended many of the leaders in the American youth movement.

In 1939 the Dies Committee, which Congress had established to ferret out subversives in the United States, called a number of youth leaders to Washington for questioning.

Eleanor began attending the Dies Committee hearings, sitting conspicuously with the students, like a mother protecting her children. At one time she felt that the "questions were so hostile as to give the impression that the witness had been haled before a court and prejudged a criminal." Eleanor rose from her seat and walked over to the press table. She had, of course, no official standing before the committee, but she carried much moral authority as First Lady. She took up a pencil and pad, as if she were about to write some disapproving comments on the committee, and suddenly the questioning turned less hostile.

Eleanor invited some of the youth leaders back to the White House for meals. One she particularly liked was an earnest young man who had just returned from fighting with the Loyalists in the Spanish Civil War. When his turn for questioning arrived, he brought a guitar to the stand and sang civil war songs for the startled committee. This was Eleanor's first meeting with Joseph Lash, soon to be known simply as "Joe," who became her most trusted confidant within the youth movement and a source of emotional strength and communion.

When Eleanor had to say goodbye to two of her boys who were bound for war, she allowed Joe to see her tears. When he wanted support in his pursuit of Trude Pratt, a woman who was unhappily married to another man and whom Lash wished to marry, he went to Eleanor. During the war the overeager Army Intelligence followed Joe and Eleanor and tried to find evidence of a sexual relationship. Certainly there was an element of passion in the First Lady's attachment to the energetic young veteran of the Spanish Civil War. With him, as with Hick a few years before, she could expose the emotional side of her personality.

Despite the presence in her life of close friends like Joe and Hick, Eleanor continued to live much of her White House life "impersonally." The forces of history—the war, the New Deal, the Presidency—were so towering that there seemed no time for intimacy. Eleanor's loneliness was increased by the events of April 12, 1945. That afternoon when she was at a meeting, Franklin's cousin, Laura Delano, called from Warm Springs to say that the President had passed out while having his portrait painted. Eleanor went on with her afternoon's engagements, but she knew in her heart "that something dreadful had happened." Franklin had been frail for several months. On election night in 1944, when he won his fourth presidential victory, he had gone out to greet his Hyde Park neighbors in a wheelchair, instead of standing with braces. When he returned from a meeting with Churchill and Stalin at Yalta, he addressed Congress while seated—something he had never before done.

Later that afternoon the dreaded news arrived: Franklin had suffered a massive cerebral hemorrhage and was dead. Eleanor felt her insides freeze, but she moved automatically: telegraphing the children, discussing funeral arrangements, planning her trip to Georgia. She sent for Vice President Harry Truman to tell him the news.

"Harry," she said, "the President is dead."

Truman was speechless. He finally said, "Is there anything I can do for you?"

"Is there anything *we* can do for *you?*" Eleanor replied. "For you are the one in trouble now."

Eleanor flew to Georgia, where she first saw her husband's body. Friends there told her about Franklin's last hours. He had been sitting for a portrait artist, Mme. Shoumatoff, when suddenly he collapsed. That part of the story was easy to tell. The rest was more difficult. The portrait had been for Lucy Mercer's daughter, and Lucy was with Franklin when he suffered the attack. Eleanor, who had not even been aware that Franklin and Lucy were seeing one another, was shocked by the news. But this final piece of intelligence only confirmed a lifetime's experience: she knew Franklin, and yet she did not know him.

That night she lay in a berth on a Pullman car bound for Washington, D.C. In the rear of the car a military guard surrounded the coffin. Eleanor was so numb that she had "an almost impersonal feeling about everything that was happening." She later tried to analyze this feeling. She reacted this way in part because during the war she had prepared herself for the possibility that one of her sons would be killed in action or that Franklin would die. Many people were dying horribly every day on the battlefields, and she had seen so many wounded men in hospitals, that whatever might happen to her had merged in her mind "with what was happening to all the suffering people of the world."

Perhaps too she was stunned by the further evidence that Franklin's heart did not belong to her alone. Had she looked into her own heart, she would have discovered that she too had found intimate companionship with people other than her spouse. But a part of her still resented Franklin's affair with her own friend and social secretary, Lucy. She resented Franklin, and yet she accepted him, as he accepted her. "A man must be what he is," she later wrote, "and life must be lived as it is." She realized that she had not been the light-hearted, uncritical wife Franklin might have desired, but she knew that she had "sometimes acted as a spur" and "served his purposes." She had made certain that her young husband paid the bills on time, she had cajoled her middle-aged spouse into exercising his paralyzed limbs when he had wanted to rest, and she continually reminded her aging companion of the poverty and discrimination that they, as President and First Lady, must fight.

With such austere thoughts Eleanor, no longer the First Lady, sought to summarize and comprehend her four decades with Franklin Roosevelt. They had been the closest of colleagues and the most distant of antagonists. To the end each had hoped for a warmer relationship with the other. Shortly before his death Franklin told Elliott he wished he could get to know Eleanor better, but she was so busy it was hard to be with her. Eleanor's enduring affection for Franklin was apparent in her sorrow at learning that he was seeing Lucy again. No one word seems to describe their complex relationship: neither love nor hostility nor admiration nor annoyance was the all-encompassing ingredient of their life together.

As the train carrying Franklin's body moved north, Eleanor stared out the window at the darkened country-side Franklin had loved. She could not fully comprehend on this night her years with Franklin or what the future would hold for her or for the nation. She only knew that "something was coming to an end and something new was beginning." For other Americans, too—for the millions who had been inspired by Eleanor and Franklin's vision of a just society—something had ended.

At every station and crossroad men and women stood silently watching the train roll by with its burden of a dead President and his widow. Unseen, Eleanor looked out her Pullman window at their grief-stricken faces.

# On Her Own

*The thing which counts is the striving of the human soul to achieve spiritually the best that it is capable of and to care unselfishly not only for personal good, but for the good of all those who toil with them upon the earth.*

Eleanor Roosevelt, *The Forum*

During the first two years following Franklin's death, Eleanor wore black. She gave away clothes and suitcases that were too brightly colored for the traditional ceremony of mourning. And she occupied herself with the details of Franklin's estate, spending much of the summer of 1945 going through cupboards and closets in Hyde Park and sorting through boxes and barrels from the White House. The accumulated goods of Franklin's lifetime and of Sara's—jewelry, furs, silver, pictures, furniture, linen, china—she distributed to children and charities and to the Roosevelt museum at Hyde Park. To Eleanor "possessions seemed of little importance," and she kept only a few things for herself. She held on to the Turner watercolors Franklin had given her, and she kept her husband's Ford convertible. The roadster was so cold in the winter that Eleanor and her secretary, Malvina "Tommy" Thompson, wrapped themselves in blankets for their frequent drives between Hyde Park and New York City.

Eleanor was lonely without Franklin. Although the distances between them had been great, his life had been the major force in hers for forty years. Now there was a void where once had been a vital human being. Fala, Franklin's black Scottie, grieved too. One day he heard sirens on the Hyde Park grounds as General Eisenhower, accompanied by a police escort, arrived at the house with a wreath for Franklin's grave. Fala's legs straightened and his ears pricked up at the sounds that had once heralded Franklin's return. It seemed to Eleanor that the disappointed dog "never really forgot" his master. Eleanor fed Fala herself, as Franklin had done, and let him sleep in her room and took him every morning on long walks. When Eleanor returned from a trip Fala would stand "on his hind legs, making a chortling sound in his throat, his lips curled back showing his teeth in a truly entrancing dog smile." Hick, who wrote these words, believed that Fala was "devoted" to Eleanor. But Eleanor, with her usual self-deprecation, believed Fala considered her merely "someone to put up with until the master should return."

During the intensely personal summer of 1945, while Eleanor was sorting through Franklin's things, President Truman called her with the news that Japan had surrendered and the war was over. Eleanor had looked forward to this moment for four years. Now her sons would return home; now the politicians of the world had a chance to build a lasting peace. With Franklin gone, however, she doubted her own importance in shaping the postwar world. Shortly after his death she told a reporter, "The story is over." She attributed most of her own influence to her position rather than to her person, and she was no longer First Lady. Sixty-one years old, she told her friends, half-seriously, that she expected someday soon to settle in front of the fire, an old lady in a shawl. The shawl, she said, was protected with tissue paper and mothballs and stored in a bureau at Hyde Park, ready for use.

Despite her furtive thoughts about retirement, however, and her persistent feelings of insignificance, Eleanor had achieved by 1945 a momentum in public affairs that survived the death of her husband. She had, at first, no definite plans. She knew only that she did not want to "run an elaborate household" or "feel old" and that she wanted to continue being "useful in some way." Eleanor made herself "useful" in many of the same ways as in the past: playing hostess, writing letters, delivering speeches. She entertained so many guests at Val-Kill Cottage that Hick observed, "arms and legs practically stick out the windows." She continued to receive, and with Tommy's help, to answer roughly a thousand letters a week. Three hours a day went to answering letters from people she did not even know.

Eleanor divided her time between her cottage at Val-Kill and a New York apartment on Washington Square. In the city she had two phones to handle all her calls. The apartment was a maelstrom of activity: visitors arrived for appointments; flowers and telegrams were delivered to the door; Eleanor and Tommy discussed lecture invitations. During a normal week Eleanor received a hundred requests for public appearances. She had to decline most, but those she accepted kept her busy with as many as three or four appearances a day. Eleanor began one spring morning with a breakfast conference at Bryn Mawr, took a train from Philadelphia to New York for a fundraising luncheon for a boys' school, drove to Poughkeepsie to deliver a late-afternoon talk at Vassar on the United Nations, went home to Hyde Park for a quick dinner, and returned in the evening to Poughkeepsie to attend a Girl Scout powwow. A good day's work.

On her lecture circuit Eleanor did not use notes, but she was so sure of her thoughts that the most impromptu speech seemed carefully prepared. She had still not completely eliminated the girlish giggle that sometimes appeared in her talks—an unheralded and embarrassing reminder of the shy young woman she had been. But her enunciation was so clear, her manner so sincere, and her ideas so compelling that she was one of the most popular speakers in America. *Variety,* the entertainment newspaper, said her radio talks ranked with the "finest pieces of speaking ever done by a woman on the air." Eleanor also continued to write her daily newspaper column, "My Day," and a monthly magazine column consisting of answers to readers' questions.

Her efficiency, which had won public attention as early as 1917, when her home in Washington was described as a model household, was an enduring trait. She even kept a notebook—two inches thick by 1945—listing the presents she had given each year to some two hundred relatives and friends so that she would not send the same gift twice. In order to find the time for all her engagements Eleanor stayed up late every night and made up for lost sleep with catnaps, taken inconspicuously at public gatherings. In 1946 she accidentally napped at the wheel of her car and ran into two other cars, breaking her two prominent front teeth. They were replaced with less obtrusive porcelain caps—to her great pleasure.

Eleanor was so much of a public phenomenon that a lawyer and longtime friend, Henry Hooker, got together with theatrical producer John Golden to form a committee to organize her schedule. Calling at her Washington Square apartment, Golden announced: "We would like to have you consult us in connection with the various things you have been asked or will be asked to do. Then we could pass on whether such proposals are a good idea." Tommy was standing nearby, her mouth open in astonishment.

"Did I hear you correctly?" she asked. "You want to plan her life?"

"Exactly," Golden replied. "As old friends of the family, we feel that she should be careful to do only things that count. Now our idea is that I will provide whatever showmanship is necessary and Major Hooker will pass legal judgment. . . ."

Eleanor, on the verge of bursting into laughter, answered, "Look, my dears, I love both of you dearly. But you can't run my life. I would probably not like it at all."

Popular as Eleanor was, she often had to handle overzealous admirers, like Hooker and Golden, who wanted to rearrange her schedule. In 1948 she planned to go to England as a guest of the Pilgrims of Great Britain, who wanted her to attend the unveiling of Franklin's statue in London. On learning of her trip, an official of the United States Line called, urging Eleanor to lend her prestige to American shipping by traveling on board the *America*. Eleanor explained that because she was traveling as a private citizen and the Pilgrims had arranged for her passage on the *Queen Elizabeth,* she could hardly change her plans. Desperate for her favor, the man tried one last argument. "But Mrs. Roosevelt," he pleaded, "you *christened* the *America*."

Because of Eleanor's popularity, people often suggested that she run for office, even for the Vice Presidency in 1948 under Harry Truman. She always discouraged such suggestions but continued to exercise considerable influence within the Democratic Party. Truman asked her to evaluate men and women who had served under Franklin Roosevelt. She in turn wrote Truman letters pressing for various liberal measures: more women in government, civil rights legislation, and efforts to improve international understanding. Truman, eager for her approval, listened. Needing her following among liberals and blacks, he told his advisers she was one of the people whose support was essential to his administration.

Eleanor believed that the reform program of the New Deal should be continued and expanded, but she realized that reform would progress slowly. In 1947 she was urged to support the newly formed Progressive Party, which ran Henry Wallace as a presidential candidate the following year. Eleanor admired Wallace's humanitarian views, but she considered him impractical. "Mr. Wallace," she wrote, "is perhaps too idealistic—and that makes him a bad politician." She had long since learned from Franklin and from her own experience that patience and moderation were essential in politics. Her reform interests were best expressed in her helping to found Americans for Democratic Action, which drew together liberals within the Democratic Party.

She also helped shape postwar liberalism with her newspaper columns and through guest editorials in the *New York Times* and other periodicals. During the 1950s anti-Communists such as Joseph McCarthy sought to associate civil rights advocates and other reformers with Communism. Eleanor Roosevelt wrote a blunt assessment of these smear tactics: "I am beginning to think that if you have been a liberal, and if you believe that those who are strong must sometimes consider the weak, and that with strength and power goes responsibility, automatically some people will consider you a Communist."

Eleanor continued to have an important role in Democratic politics, but surely her most significant part in public affairs was in the United Nations, as one of five American delegates. Truman offered her the position in part because he needed Eleanor's political support and in part because he felt that she would lend strength to the American delegation. Eleanor accepted because she "believed the United Nations to be the one hope for a peaceful world," and she knew that Franklin "had placed great importance on the establishment of this world organization."

Approval of Eleanor's selection was widespread but not universal. Several Senators disapproved of Eleanor's appointment because of her attitude toward civil rights, but only one, Theodore G. Bilbo of Mississippi, voted against her confirmation. When asked by a newsman why he disliked her, he answered that he would have to write a book to give all his reasons. Even in the American delegation several of Eleanor's colleagues, including John Foster Dulles and Senator Arthur H. Vandenberg, thought she was too liberal or too naive for the position.

The first meeting of the United Nations General Assembly was to take place in London during the winter of 1946. On the day that American delegates left New York, most arrived at dockside in limousines with retinues of followers and basked in floodlights, reading farewell statements to newsreel cameras. Eleanor arrived by taxi and boarded the ship without fanfare. She set forth her hopes for her UN work in her newspaper column. "Some things I can take to the first meeting," she wrote, are "a sincere desire to understand the problems of the rest of the world and our relationship to them; a real good-will for all the peoples throughout the world; [and] a hope that I shall be able to build a sense of personal trust and friendship with my co-workers, for without that type of understanding our work would be doubly difficult."

On shipboard she discovered a pile of State Department briefings, which she read systematically. Without her knowledge the other delegates met and assigned her to Committee 3, which would deal with humanitarian, cultural, and educational matters. Eleanor assumed that because she was a woman they were keeping her off committees dealing with economic and political topics—the cultural committee seemed safest. But, she later wrote, "I kept my thoughts to myself and humbly agreed to serve where I was asked to serve."

In London Eleanor quickly established herself as one of the hardest-working and best-informed UN delegates. She never missed a meeting for any reason. When King George and Queen Elizabeth invited her to lunch, she accepted gracefully but told them she would have to leave early in order to attend a subcommittee meeting. By chance the humanitarian committee turned out to be more important than anyone had anticipated. At the end of the war tens of thousands of displaced persons—many from the Ukraine, Poland, Czechoslovakia, Latvia, Lithuania, Estonia, and other regions controlled by the Soviet Union—were left in temporary refugee camps in Germany. The Soviets claimed that some of these men and women were traitors and should be returned to their homelands for punishment. The preliminary discussions on this issue took place in Committee 3.

The opposition, including the United States, favored leaving the refugees free to choose their own homes. John Foster Dulles asked Eleanor "rather lamely" if she would present the case for the refugees. "Mrs. Roosevelt," said he, "the United States must speak in the debate. Since you are the one who has carried on for us in this controversy in the committee, do you think you could say a few words to the Assembly? I'm afraid nobody else is really familiar with the subject."

Eleanor had learned to reply to such condescending remarks with a tender sarcasm too subtle to arouse hostility. She described her answer in these words: "'Why Mr. Dulles,' I replied as meekly as I could manage, 'in that case I will do my best.'"

Her adversary in the debate was Andrey Vyshinsky, a skilled orator who had conducted the great Moscow purge trials of the 1930s. He delivered a speech that lasted late into the night, hoping to delay the vote until some of the opposing delegates went home. When it came time for Eleanor to speak, she realized that the support of the South American representatives would be crucial, and so she talked about Simón Bolívar's stand for freedom in Latin America. The delegates listened and stayed to the end. Late at night the General Assembly voted against forcing the refugees to return to their homelands.

At the end of the session Dulles and Vandenberg admitted to Eleanor that they had fought her appointment as a UN delegate but declared that they had found her "good to work with." This was a personal triumph for Eleanor, and the refugee vote was a political triumph for the United States. But what did the triumph mean? What were the refugee camps like? Although Eleanor had been instrumental in determining the fate of thousands of displaced persons, she had never even seen a refugee camp. Instead of heading home at the end of the UN session, she decided to visit Germany.

Eleanor left England early one morning in an Air Force plane. The young pilot and copilot told her, "rather proudly," that they would show her the effects of Allied bombing. Sunrise found them over Germany, which until a few months before had been fighting the bloodiest war in history. The land below was occupied now by Allied troops. The plane swung low over several German cities: Cologne, Frankfurt, Munich, Berlin. Eleanor had known some of these places before the war. Now they lay in ruins—mile after mile of rubble where houses had once stood. She felt that "nobody could have imagined such utter, horrible destruction." These ruins were the product of Allied air power, and the bombing had ended the war in Europe. But Eleanor felt only pathos. "I thought," she wrote, "that nothing could better illustrate the sickening waste and the destructiveness and futility of war than what I was seeing."

Eleanor saw more of the war's human cost when she walked among the ruins of Berlin. She stood by the

Brandenburg Gate—once the symbol of Germany's greatness, now a bomb-damaged ruin—and saw "the degrading sight of men and women and children dealing in the black market." They ambled back and forth over the broad square, clutching pitiful articles in their hands. Watching their faces Eleanor felt that "they would sell anything for food, and doubtless they had."

Of the several refugee camps that Eleanor toured, the most memorable was Zilcheim, a Jewish camp outside Frankfurt, where the refugees had built an earthen hill on top of which they placed a stone monument "To the Memory of All Jews Who Died in Germany." As a young woman Eleanor had disdained Jews, but her attitude had changed with her personal growth. Her journey into humanity made her more sensitive to the needs of women and blacks and taught her to recognize the dignity and the suffering of Jews in America and abroad. At the beginning of the war she had urged Franklin to receive more Jewish refugees into the United States. Now she was standing among the survivors of the Holocaust.

Eleanor could see grief in the faces of the men and women in the Jewish camp; each "seemed to represent a story more tragic than the last." An old woman who had lost her family knelt in the mud before Eleanor and threw her arms around her legs. "Israel," she murmured, "Israel, Israel." A boy of twelve approached Eleanor. He had wandered into the camp holding his younger brother, about six, firmly by the hand. He did not know his own name or where he lived or what had happened to his parents. "He was just there," Eleanor wrote, "taking care of his younger brother." He wanted to sing for her, and so she and her guides stopped to listen. Then standing in the mud of the dirty refugee camp the orphan raised his small head and sang "A Song of Freedom." For a moment all the world was that small boy, and "no one listening could speak." Eleanor, who had been an orphan when she was twelve, with a younger brother, in a place that was not home, listened intently to the song that was sung for her.

A few days later Eleanor was back in New York City, far from refugee camps and bombed-out cities. The first UN General Assembly was over, and with it, she assumed, her career as a delegate. She wrote President Truman to thank him for "an unforgettable experience" and turned her attention to letters, lectures, and friends. But the feverish activity of the previous weeks left a deep impression. She recalled the faces of the women in the black market and the old woman who grasped her legs and cried, "Israel, Israel." She recalled too the earnest delegates in London at the birth of an organization she and Franklin had dreamed of for almost three decades. She knew that Europe's veteran diplomats were skeptical about the United Nations and its future. But as she told herself "again and again" on the plane back from Europe, "There was also hope in the air. There had to be hope."

Eleanor's retirement from the United Nations was brief. Harry Truman reappointed her as a delegate in 1946 and in addition chose her as the American representative to the UN Human Rights Commission, which was established to draft an international bill of rights. Completing that document was her chief goal during the next two years. She became chair of the Human Rights Commission, and on that and other committees she grew to be one of the most skilled diplomats at the United Nations.

Her statecraft was a unique blend of idealism and realism. She believed that the human condition could be improved and that international agreement on human rights would contribute to that improvement. She also recognized that different nations had different views on human rights and that each delegate at the UN would represent his or her country's interests as well as those of other nations. The United States would want a bill of rights emphasizing political freedoms: free speech, freedom from arbitrary arrest, the right to a fair trial. In these areas the Americans enjoyed more freedom than the Soviets. The Soviet Union would emphasize the economic freedoms enjoyed by Communists: the right to a decent standard of living, good medical care, and adequate housing. Other nations would want to emphasize freedoms that prevailed in their own countries and avoid those that they feared. As chair of the Commission on Human Rights she mediated between the conflicting views of Russians, Chinese, Indians, English, Canadians, and other peoples.

The meetings of the Human Rights Commission took place in Geneva, Paris, and Lake Success, New York. Eleanor kept one basic objective before the delegates: that the United Nations should state clearly which human rights should exist in member nations. "Hopes have been aroused in many people through the ages," she wrote, "but it has never been possible for the nations of the world to come together and try to work out in co-operation such principles as will make living more worthwhile for the average human being."

Sitting at the head of the conference table with seventeen other delegates, Eleanor reminded some observers of a "favorite aunt," others of a mother figure. Often her remarks exuded gentleness and femininity. Eleanor could be humble: "I am probably the least learned person around this table," she would say, "so I have thought of this article in terms of what the ordinary person would understand." She could flatter the male ego: "Now, of course, I'm a woman, and I don't understand all these things, and I'm sure there's a great deal to be said for your arguments, but don't you think it would be a good idea if . . ." She could compliment her colleagues while quietly calling attention to her own usefulness: "The writing of a preliminary draft of the bill of rights," she declared in her column, "may not seem so terrifying to my colleagues in the drafting group . . . all of whom are learned gentlemen. But to me it seems a task for which I am ill-equipped. However, I may be able to help them put into words the high thoughts which they can gather from past history and from the actuality of the contemporary situation, so that the average human being can understand and strive for the objectives set forth."

In such ways Eleanor played the role of a deferential and well-meaning woman, somewhat at loss in a man's world. But beneath her humble demeanor was a strength she had gained from thirty years of public service—a toughness that was honed now by the demands of her UN job and by the knowledge that she was on her own. When the need arose, she could cast off all pretense of tenderness and whip her committee into line. She chaired a meeting as expertly as if "'out of order' was born on her lips," one observer commented. Another said she showed a remarkable combination of naiveté and cunning. She was credited with being "exceedingly practical, and even tough, though in an outwardly dreamy and idealistic way."

Her major problem in leading her committee to complete a declaration of rights was the tendency of Soviet delegates to use every issue as an opportunity to denounce the West and praise Communism. Eleanor had none of the exaggerated fears of Americans who felt that the Soviet Union was completely evil or that the Communists were on the verge of taking over the United States. She could respect the Soviet delegates as individuals, acknowledge the achievements of the Communist countries, and advocate a UN seat for Communist China as the de facto government of the Chinese people. But she regarded the Soviet Union as young, brash, and opinionated, and she recognized that the Russians would struggle for every point they could win in the UN and in the world at large. During the deliberations of the Commission on Human Rights, the USSR blockaded Western access to Berlin and established Communist regimes throughout Central Europe.

Eleanor believed the proper response to the Soviets in the UN was to "have convictions; be friendly; stick to your beliefs as they stick to theirs." In response to a Russian delegate's portrayal of injustice in America, she suggested that the USSR and the United States submit themselves to investigation by a neutral agency to determine in which country human rights were more respected. Her practical need was less to defend America against Soviet criticism than to direct the attention of all the delegates away from mutual recrimination and toward the business of drafting the bill of rights.

Typical of her approach was her reply to a Yugoslav delegate on the UN Social, Humanitarian, and Cultural Committee who had accused the United States of warmongering. "The time has come for some very straight thinking among us," Eleanor replied. "The ultimate objective that we have is to create better understanding among us, and I well acknowledge that this is going to be difficult. . . . Now, I don't expect the millennium immediately, but I do expect and hope and pray that we are going to see a gradual increase in good will rather than a continual backwards and forwards of telling us what dogs we are and how bad we are. I see no use in that at all. I am weary of it all, and all I can say to my colleagues is that I hope we can work with good will." By refusing to waste time answering diatribe with diatribe, Eleanor encouraged her fellow delegates to look to their business of discovering which ideals they shared. By combining firmness and tact, she was able to win points without making enemies of her opponents.

One of Eleanor's greatest challenges was in simply coaxing the delegates to work the long hours necessary to keep their business flowing smoothly. One reporter described her as a "super-mother, presiding over a large family of often noisy, sometimes unruly but basically good-hearted boys, who now and then need firmly to be put in their places." At the Human Rights Commission's 1947 meeting in Geneva she persuaded her colleagues to attend day and evening meetings from the start of the session. She was soon denounced—in fun, she hoped—as "a merciless slave driver." One evening near the end of the session the Soviets invited the Human Rights delegates to a cocktail party where vodka flowed freely. Eleanor could not attend because of a speaking engagement.

She returned to the conference room for the eight o'clock meeting. Only one other delegate, General Carlos P. Romulo of the Philippines, was there. He and Eleanor sat alone around the big table and chatted. At eight-twenty no other delegate, adviser, or secretary had arrived, and Eleanor reflected that "this was no less than mutiny." Finally at eight-thirty there was a commotion at the door, and "the lost sheep began arriving." Eleanor observed that "they were in a happy if unhurried mood, and a little shaky on their feet." "They took their accustomed places," she wrote, "leaned back in their chairs and gazed at me with pleased, rather foggy eyes."

She planned first to dispose of a simple matter and called on General Romulo to speak. Like her, he had been delivering a lecture while the delegates were drinking, and he spoke precisely and soberly on the issue. "Is that clear to everyone?" Eleanor asked the dazed delegates. An Australian representative, an old-school colonel, said it sounded confused to him. And so Eleanor reviewed the matter succinctly. Was it all clear now? she asked somewhat irritably. The colonel rose, "possibly with some slight difficulty," and made Eleanor a courtly bow. "Yes, Madame Chairlady," he said in a deep voice, "It is all just as clear as mud." Knowing the vodka had won the evening, she pounded her gavel on the table and declared, "The meeting is adjourning until tomorrow morning!"

With that one exception the Human Rights Commission stuck to a rigid schedule throughout the Geneva meeting and completed its work, as Eleanor had hoped, before Christmas. As she was walking toward her office, the Soviet delegate, Alexander Bogomoloff, overtook her and said, "Madame, I have never worked so hard at any international conference." Eleanor gave him a confiding smile. "I am glad," she said, "that you have discovered that even in a bourgeois democracy, as you insist on calling the United States, some of us know how to work." The Soviet delegate "laughed heartily," and they parted.

During the two years when the Human Rights Commission was drafting a declaration of liberties, Eleanor kept up her other activities as journalist, political propagandist, and lecturer. In her mid-sixties now, she was as vigorous as a young woman and followed a remarkable schedule. She arose early in the morning, flipped over her mattress, and remade her bed. She began the day with long walks, leaning forward like a skier, at so fast a pace that guests who tried to keep up often failed, and only the Scottie Fala was her constant companion. One winter day two and a half feet of new snow lay outside the cottage at Val-Kill. The two-mile drive to the main highway was unplowed, and Eleanor had an appointment that afternoon at a Poughkeepsie radio station. The manager called, offering to send a sleigh for her. No, he must not trouble himself, she replied, and she set off walking through the thigh-deep snow. At the main road she hitched a ride for the five-mile drive into Poughkeepsie. Later that evening she hiked back to the cottage, commenting that the return trip was easier because the trail had been broken.

Eleanor was just as energetic when she lived in her Washington Square apartment. At the lower end of Fifth Avenue, the square was a mixed neighborhood where expensive apartments and old hotels mingled with the buildings of New York University, tenement houses, and a sprinkling of Italian stores and restaurants. On pleasant days the square swarmed with "loafers, young stickball players, amateur artists and chess experts hunched over their boards." Eleanor lived in an apartment on the west side of the square from which she looked out onto trees and a half-dozen "graceful old buildings whose high windows and ancient brick walls made an attractive picture that frequently appealed to Greenwich Village artists." In New York City, as in the country, she began each day with a long walk accompanied by Fala. Many women might have been frightened to go out alone on the streets, but Eleanor was never bothered except one evening when a sailor "who had probably consumed too many beers" took her for a younger woman. Eleanor commented wryly, "He quickly discovered his mistake."

Her apartment was relatively small, but in it Eleanor managed during one UN session to host dinners for all the UN delegates and their spouses. She believed that friendly informal contacts among the members—with or without vodka—was one of the best ways to ensure goodwill in committee meetings. So in one six-week period she gave eighteen dinners, entertaining nine people at each. The setting was inelegant, for the guests ate with their plates in their laps. But Eleanor's goodwill was infectious in the small apartment and also at Val-Kill, where she had hot-dog picnics for the UN delegates.

During the early sessions of the United Nations Eleanor came to represent the humanitarian spirit that was one of the underlying goals of the international organization. When she approached the podium to deliver a speech at the 1948 meeting of the General Assembly, the other members rose to give her a standing ovation. She was the only delegate ever so honored. In that year the Commission on Human Rights completed the Universal Declaration of Human Rights and submitted it to the General Assembly at its Paris meeting. While in Paris Eleanor delivered a lecture at the Sorbonne in which she declared that she had been mistaken in thinking that the limits of her patience were reached in raising a large family—presiding over the Commission on Human Rights required even more forbearance. The document came before the General Assembly for final approval during a session that lasted late into the night of December 10, 1948. It was adopted with eight abstentions and two delegations absent; the other delegates voted their unanimous approval. That night Eleanor jotted this note: "Long job finished."

The Universal Declaration of Human Rights contains many traditional Anglo-American concepts, such as Article 9, declaring that "no one shall be subjected to arbitrary arrest, detention or exile." And it includes the economic freedoms advocated by the Communists. "Everyone," Article 25 states, "has the right to a standard of living adequate for the health and well-being of himself and of his family, including food, clothing, housing and medical care. . . ."

Eleanor said that it was only a beginning. She and other delegates hoped that some day it would be backed up by international treaties and enforcement agencies. But "in the meantime," she wrote, "a great satisfaction should permeate the thoughts of all men, for the great documents declaring man's inherent rights and freedoms, which in the past have been written nationally, are now merged in an international, universal Declaration." Many of the great historic charters of freedom found their way into the Universal Declaration of Human Rights—the Magna Carta, the Bill of Rights, the Communist Manifesto. There is also much of Eleanor Roosevelt in it. The opening lines—"Recognition of the inherent dignity and of the equal and inalienable rights of all members of the human family is the foundation of freedom, justice, and peace in the world"—were ideas that had appeared in Eleanor's youthful compositions and in her mature political writings such as *The Moral Basis of Democracy.* "There is a spring that flows for all humanity. . . ."

The Universal Declaration of Human Rights has no standing in international law. It is more like the American Declaration of Independence than the Constitution in that it is a moral rather than a legal document. The UN delegates began work on human rights "covenants" to be approved by international treaties and have the force of law, but most nations resisted the idea of giving so much power to the UN, and the covenants were not even drafted until 1966. In the meantime the Universal Declaration acquired far greater importance than had been anticipated as a worldwide standard for human rights. It became the cornerstone for the constitutions of many newly independent nations in the 1950s and 1960s. Nobel laureate Alexander Solzhenitsyn said it was the "best document" ever produced by the UN, and UN Secretary-General U Thant called it "the Magna Carta of Mankind."

Through her role in the United Nations Eleanor Roosevelt added to her worldwide reputation as a friend of humanity. When the UN met in Geneva, police had to hold back the crowds that flocked to see her. Her lecture at the Sorbonne during the Paris meeting was attended by several thousand Parisians eager for a glimpse of "the First Lady of the World." Eleanor received many invitations to visit other countries. When her son Elliott visited the Soviet Union, he was met by Premier Nikita Khrushchev, whose first comment was, "When is your mother coming?"

Eleanor would eventually accept Khrushchev's invitation and those of many other heads of state. For several years she circled the globe almost annually. She was particularly eager to visit the new countries of the Third World because in the UN she was made aware of how hostile much of the Third World was to the United States and to white people in general. UN delegates were shocked by the treatment of blacks in America, and several believed that the American government was more eager to eradicate hunger in Europe than in Asia and Africa.

A trip in 1952 to Pakistan and India was typical of Eleanor's contacts with the Third World. As her plane landed in Karachi she was surprised to see a crowd of ten thousand Pakistanis awaiting her. She was escorted to a cart pulled by a camel and led a parade of 127 brightly decorated camel carts through the streets of the capital. Her sponsors in Pakistan were members of the All-Pakistan Women's Association, and they conducted Eleanor to a number of sessions in which women discussed their rights. Simply by her presence Eleanor gave encouragement to women seeking fuller equality.

Eleanor flew on to Bombay, where a crowd of a thousand Indians greeted her. She stood in an open touring car with her head bowed and her hands folded in a traditional Hindu greeting while the crowd shouted, "Eleanor Roosevelt Zindabad—long live Eleanor Roosevelt!" As the car was about to leave, the enthusiastic Indians asked her to stand again. She did, but was so overcome by emotion that she nearly collapsed and had to be assisted by an aide. She addressed the Indian parliament, standing at the edge of the rostrum, pocketbook in hand. And she visited the shrine of India's greatest humanitarian, Mahatma

Gandhi. The problem of one part of the world, Eleanor said, is "the problem of all."

From her personal contacts with people throughout the world, Eleanor came to understand the ambitions and frustrations of the Third World as well as any other American. She referred to the citizens of the new nations as "the proud, emerging peoples, who live on hope, as we did during the Depression." In 1953 Truman's administration came to an end, and President Eisenhower did not reappoint Eleanor to the United Nations. She continued through personal diplomacy, however, to make contact with people in other countries and became a leader of the American Association for the United Nations.

During the 1950s Eleanor Roosevelt was also a major force in the Democratic Party—standard-bearer of Democratic liberalism and guardian of the legacy of Franklin Delano Roosevelt. At the 1952 presidential convention she electrified the delegates with an address in which she quoted from an undelivered speech Franklin wrote just before he died: "We must cultivate the science of human relations. . . ." The words could as easily have been Eleanor's.

In 1952 and 1956 Eleanor supported Adlai Stevenson for the Presidency. She admired his fine intellect and developed a warm friendship with him. In 1956, at age seventy-one, she followed him from caucus to caucus at the convention, delivering short pro-Adlai speeches. After he was nominated, she spent two months touring the country on his behalf. In both elections the Republicans won easily. After his defeat in 1956 Eleanor wrote Stevenson a perceptive and kind note. "The love affair between the American people and President Eisenhower," she said, "is too acute at present for any changes evidently to occur."

In her seventies Eleanor's hair was gray; it was cut short or pinned close to her head. Her arms were plump, and she was beginning to look somewhat like the old lady in a shawl she had once expected to become. But she continued to follow a rigorous schedule of exercise and public appearances. At seventy-one she arose at seven, did sit-ups, and moved "at the speed of light." She delivered a hundred speeches a year and kept fifteen to twenty appointments a day. She liked to associate with young people and often entertained some of her twenty-four grandchildren and great-grandchildren at Val-Kill. She was known to most of her progeny by the French name Grandmère. One of them asked Tommy Thompson, "Who is Grandmère?"

"Why, she's your grandmother, of course," Tommy answered.

"I know that," he replied, "but who is she? Daddy listens to what she says. You do what she tells you to do. Everybody stands up when she comes in. Who *is* Grandmère?"

Eleanor had attained such a heroic stature that her grandson was understandably confused. And yet, as in the past, she drew her greatest comfort from her personal relationships. "The people I love," she said, "mean more to me than all the public things." Some of the old friends were still close by. Joe and Trude Lash were her frequent companions in Hyde Park and New York City. Hick moved to Hyde Park and was usually the first person Eleanor called whenever she came up to Val-Kill. Eleanor lost one of her best and most useful friends in 1952 when Tommy, her secretary for thirty-one years, died. Eleanor said, she was "the person who made life possible for me." Fortunately, Eleanor found in Maureen Corr another secretary-friend who could keep up with her still furious pace of correspondence and appearances.

Eleanor's best friend, her essential friend, during her years alone was a handsome physician named David

Gurewitsch. They became acquainted in 1947 when they chanced to sit next to each other on a plane taking Eleanor to Geneva for a UN meeting. The plane was delayed for several days in Ireland by the fog, during which time the physician was ill, and Eleanor nursed him. David was one of the hardworking but inwardly lonely people to whom Eleanor was drawn. His father had committed suicide before he was born, and his mother never recovered from the loss.

David was a good deal younger than Eleanor, but there developed between them a relationship that stimulated both. In David's words, their friendship began when, during their first meeting, "I heard much about Mrs. Roosevelt's life and she, in turn, learned about some of the vicissitudes of my life, of my hopes and ambitions." During the following years they exchanged hundreds of letters, and David was Eleanor's frequent companion at dinner and the theater. She felt alive and womanly in the company of this handsome young man, and he, in turn, was fortified by her "rocklike strength." Esther Lapp told him years later, "You were dearer to her, as she not infrequently said, than anyone else in the world. Yes, she not only loved you, she was in love with you." Like her relationships with Hick and with Joe, this friendship involved an intense caring that bordered on romantic love. Both the tenderness and the pathos of her attachment were apparent when she gave him a photo of herself as a younger woman, with the inscription, "To David, From a Girl He Never Knew."

Eleanor may have reflected at times as they sat together in the theater or took walks at Val-Kill that if they had been born in another time, David might have been the ideal husband she never had. But like her other loves, this love would never be complete. One day she learned that David planned to marry a beautiful dark-haired young woman named Edna. Eleanor turned pale when she heard the news, fearing that the marriage would end her close ties with David. But as with other disappointments, she was able to adjust. She befriended Edna Gurewitsch, and eventually the physician and his wife joined Eleanor in buying a house in New York City that they made into two apartments. As Eleanor's personal physician, David continued to accompany Eleanor on her travels and remained her closest friend. She said their relationship was the most "meaningful" of her friendships.

The personal dynamics among the three of them were exemplified when the Gurewitsches and Eleanor went on a nine-day vacation to Puerto Rico. Eleanor almost did not go, feeling she would be intruding on David and Edna. Maureen Corr called Edna to warn her that Eleanor was wavering. Edna then casually told Eleanor over a glass of Dubonnet how much she wanted her to come. "Mrs. Roosevelt," she said, "I'm so glad you're going to Puerto Rico with us. You know David is a difficult person to take away for a rest. He always has to be doing or exploring something, and if you are there, you will help me keep him interested."

They went to Puerto Rico, and at age seventy-five for the first time in her adult life Eleanor spent more than a week without major responsibilities. She read Arthur Schlesinger's third volume on the New Deal, and she went on walks with the Gurewitsches. As she watched David walking a rail over a stream, she said to Edna, "Look at David. Remember, Edna, the nicest men in the world are those who always keep something of the boy in them. Franklin was like that."

In her mid-seventies Eleanor remarked, "At present I look like Methuselah, but I feel no older than my youngest friends." In a two-year period, 1957–1958, she made two trips to the Soviet Union and received Premier

Khrushchev at Hyde Park. During her 1957 trip she visited the Premier in his villa at Yalta. He greeted her on his porch, a boisterous, portly man with a close-shaved head, wearing a jacket and an open shirt. Somewhat shorter than Eleanor, he looked like a jolly farmhand and she like a benevolent grandmother. They sat on the porch for several hours at opposite sides of a table and debated the relative merits of the capitalist and Communist systems.

"As certainly as it takes nine months to make a baby," said Khrushchev, "as certainly Communism will rule the world." Eleanor firmly disagreed. After a while they adjourned for lunch with the Khrushchev family. As Eleanor prepared to leave, the Premier asked, "Can I tell our papers that we have had a friendly conversation?"

"You can say that we have had a friendly conversation but that we differ," Eleanor replied.

Khrushchev enjoyed his sparring with the "First Lady of the World" and visited her at Hyde Park the next year, where they continued their debate. After leaving, he sent Eleanor a stack of books, with markers indicating passages that bolstered his arguments.

In 1960 Eleanor again backed Adlai Stevenson for the Democratic presidential nomination, but Stevenson did not enter the primaries, and a young Senator from Massachusetts, John F. Kennedy, became the party's standard-bearer. After Kennedy's inauguration Eleanor went with the Gurewitsches to an inn in Tucson, Arizona, for a brief holiday. Energetic as ever, she beat her friends at croquet—apologizing always for doing so. In Tucson the three friends watched John Kennedy's first press conference. Eleanor was impressed.

With Kennedy in office Eleanor began to receive more invitations from Washington. She was once more appointed a UN delegate; she chaired Kennedy's Commission on the Status of Women, and she sponsored hearings in

Washington where young civil rights workers testified about police harrassment in the South. After the American-sponsored Bay of Pigs operation failed to overturn Fidel Castro's Communist government in Cuba, Eleanor was appointed to the "Tractors for Freedom" committee that arranged an exchange of American tractors for the soldiers captured in the abortive invasion.

Seemingly there would be no end to the story that Eleanor had declared was over seventeen years before. Born in the horse-and-buggy age, Eleanor was living at the dawn of the space age. Long a crusader for civil rights, she was alive on the eve of the great Washington March and Martin Luther King Jr.'s "I Have a Dream" speech. Many of the humanitarian reforms Eleanor had called for would be enacted during the next decade. And she was almost a part of that new age.

But in 1960 Eleanor often felt ill and turned out to be suffering from a deadly disease known as aplastic anemia. At times she was able to lead a normal life; at times she was disabled by her infirmity. In 1962 it was discovered that she was suffering also from a rare form of bone-marrow tuberculosis. She went to the hospital in the fall of 1962 and came home to die. On her first night at home she insisted on entertaining David and Edna Gurewitsch for dinner. They sat at her bedside for a few minutes with plates in their laps, pretending that nothing had changed, but she was terribly weak. A month later, on the evening of November 7, 1962, Eleanor Roosevelt died.

A hearse arrived at her apartment in the dark, and David went down to ride with Eleanor's body. Edna heard the hearse door slam, and it pulled away from the house. Watching from an upstairs window, she saw the long black car stop for a red light. How strange, she thought, that the traffic lights were still functioning.

After Eleanor's death the extraordinary character of her life became all the more apparent. Not only was she one of the most influential people of the twentieth century, but she also possessed a remarkable ability to "walk with kings and keep the common touch." She could be as friendly to a soldier in a hospital as to the Queen in Buckingham Palace; and she could involve herself in important administrative business, such as chairing the UN Commission on Human Rights, yet still spend hours writing letters to strangers who wanted her advice or comfort. The epitaphs written for her over the years are extraordinary in their consistent veneration. "Because of her life," wrote William Chafe, "millions of others may have experienced a new sense of possibility." Adlai Stevenson declared, "She would rather light a candle than curse the darkness, and her glow has warmed the world." A wonderful Herblock cartoon shows a cluster of cherubs in heaven looking shyly from behind their clouds at an approaching stranger. Awestruck, one of them remarks, "It's her. . . ."

In 1958 Donald Meyer wrote a review of the third volume of Eleanor's autobiography, *On My Own*, in which he quoted a comment she made upon visiting a primitive Ettu village in Japan: "How important it is to recognize that there is a bond among all peoples." "That is what Mrs. Roosevelt's life has been," wrote Meyer, "the recognition of bond." Eleanor Roosevelt's life was rich in the bonds of friendship and love. But only a few intimates realized that her sense of kinship was created by a continuing struggle against despair. Sensitive as she was to moments of communion with other human beings, Eleanor was equally sensitive to the distances between one human being and another. The woman who became a friend of the whole world slept alone most of her life.

Sometimes Eleanor showed David Gurewitsch the hidden side of her personality. They went on long walks in the evenings, and Eleanor revealed her sorrows and anxieties. Responsive to her needs, David would help Eleanor regain the equilibrium from which she addressed the world. But on these walks her desperation was so great at times that she seemed almost suicidal. "Behind tranquillity," Eleanor wrote, "lies conquered unhappiness." She might have added that unhappiness is never completely overcome.

And yet Eleanor's life was certainly a triumph. The sensitivity she took into the world had been a hallmark of her family for three generations. Her grandfather, "Greatheart," had practiced on a local scale a traditional form of philanthropy, endowing a newsboys' home and a great museum. Eleanor's father and brother had been as compassionate as Eleanor but lacked the toughness to make a mark on the world. Eleanor's Uncle Ted had passed legislation intended to improve the lot of the average American, but the hero of San Juan Hill was not noted for personal warmth. It was ironic that the man who said, "Speak softly and carry a big stick," received a Nobel Peace Prize for sponsoring negotiations that ended the Russo-Japanese War, but his niece—who deserved the prize as much as any human being in the twentieth century—never did. She more than anyone else in that remarkable clan deserved the name Greatheart.

A plane circling New York City on the day of Eleanor Roosevelt's death would have discovered a place miraculously transformed from the city where she was born seventy-eight years before. The five-story buildings had given way to skyscrapers rising as much as a thousand feet into the air. The Brooklyn Bridge was joined by other large bridges crossing the East River and the Hudson. In New

York harbor, far below, steamships had replaced the graceful schooners, and on the city streets automobiles had replaced horses and buggies. Gliding down toward the airport the plane might pass over the cluttered streets of suburban Hempstead, where her father had played polo and ridden to hounds in the green countryside, and where he built a house called "Half-Way Nirvana" for his beautiful wife and for the golden-haired girl he taught to be compassionate.

# Study and Discussion Questions

### Introduction

1. How does Youngs justify his decision to devote roughly equal time in this book to Eleanor Roosevelt's early years and to her later years? How can the life of an obscure child be as important as the life of a world-famous adult?

2. We are told also that the book is about a personal as well as a public life. Does the personal life sound like a mere digression from the "more important" public life? Or is it possible that by learning about the personal life we will have a greater understanding of the public life?

3. In a choice of styles, Youngs promises to focus on *episodes* that are useful in revealing people, places, and events of the past. He writes, "My own telling of Eleanor Roosevelt's life is as much a work of evocation as explanation." Why is it important that the past be *evoked* as well as described and explained?

### Prologue: The South Pacific, 1943

1. The book begins by taking us to a time in Eleanor Roosevelt's adult life. Why not just begin in chronological order, as the next chapter does? How does this "prologue" about a journey to the wartime South Pacific set the scene for the story we are about to read?

2. The prologue focuses on one episode in Eleanor Roosevelt's life. In what ways does this wartime episode introduce us to Eleanor's values, personality, and influence as a whole?

3. In what ways does Eleanor Roosevelt act out her values during the South Pacific journey—in press conferences, among soldiers, elsewhere?

4. How did others react to Eleanor Roosevelt? What did they find more notable about her?

## Chapter 1: A Victorian Family

1. What were the similarities and differences in the upbringing of Eleanor's parents, Anna Hall and Elliott Roosevelt? What were the similarities and differences in Anna's and Elliott's own temperaments?

2. What were the characteristics of the New York aristocracy into which Eleanor Roosevelt was born? What were the notable features of the lifestyles and values of the aristocrats? In what ways was public service a part of that life style?

3. What were the qualities and the failings of each of the Roosevelts, Anna and Elliott, as parents?

4. In what ways was Eleanor Roosevelt's childhood different from most other children of her time? On the other hand, what experiences—good and bad—did she have that children in other social classes might also enjoy or endure?

5. Which of her early childhood experiences would you expect to be most important in shaping Eleanor's life?

6. In understanding the life *as a whole* of a public figure, what is the value of examining as closely as this chapter does, that person's family roots?

## Chapter 2: The Legacy

1. In what ways was the tragedy of Elliott Roosevelt's life created by the rules of Victorian society? In particular, how did that society influence (wrongly perhaps) his expectations of

himself-what he would do and achieve-in the world of work? And how did social norms determine what would happen to him when he "went astray?"

2. How did Theodore Roosevelt influence his brother's life?

3. What were the qualities and the flaws of Elliott Roosevelt as a parent that were revealed during the last few years of his life?

4. What were the qualities and the flaws of Anna Hall Roosevelt as a parent that were revealed during the last few years of her life?

5. What "legacy" did each of Eleanor Roosevelt's parents pass on to her? Do you think that Eleanor would have become the same person in later life without undergoing such a tragic childhood? Is it possible that these events enabled her to be more sympathetic as an adult to the plight of men and women suffering from poverty, discrimination, and injury?

## Chapter 3: Growing Up

1. What was the character of the Hall household, the place where Eleanor Roosevelt spent her early adolescence? In what ways did Eleanor's own personality and values appear during her life with the Halls?

2. In what ways did Eleanor come into contact with ordinary men and women during her years with Mary Hall?

3. Eleanor writes that Marie Souvestre "shocked" her into thinking. In what ways did Eleanor's experience with Souvestre, Allenswood, and travel in Europe contribute to her education?

4. Why did Eleanor return to America rather than continue her schooling at Allenswood? What role did the social values of that era play in determining her path?

## Chapter 4: Eleanor and Franklin

1. Marie Souvestre hoped that Eleanor Roosevelt would achieve some kind of meaningful existence when Eleanor returned to New York—that her character would not be undermined by "social dissipations." What were some of the creative outlets for a woman's talents in 1900? How did Eleanor's work at Rivington Street Social House take her into that creative world? And why did Eleanor eventually have to give up social work?

2. What was the nature of Eleanor and Franklin's courtship? What attracted each to the other? What did each expect from their marriage?

3. How did Eleanor and Franklin's honeymoon experience in the Dolomites suggest both their capacity for intimacy and also differences in their temperaments that might eventually cause problems?

4. Kitty Gandy was apparently unrestrained by the social conventions that limited the creative outlets for socially elite women like Eleanor Roosevelt. In what ways did Kitty's life reflect that greater freedom?

5. What were the important features of Eleanor's early married life to Franklin? What were the pleasures of her life as a young bride? In what ways and for what reasons did she feel herself confined and thwarted by her role as a married woman? What role did Franklin's mother, Sara Roosevelt, play in her early married life?

6. Evaluate Eleanor's role as a mother: in what ways did convention and circumstance determine the role she played (and did not play) in raising her own children? What were her accomplishments and limitations as a parent?

## Chapter 5: A Politician's Wife

1. What were the important lessons that Eleanor and Franklin learned about American politics during Franklin's legislative career in New York? How did Franklin win his first election? What did the Roosevelts' experience with Tammany Hall teach them about political machines?

2. As a political wife Eleanor Roosevelt came to realize that something in her "craved to be an individual." In what ways had her life to that time limit her individuality? What avenues, if any, were open to her to allow her to become more of an individual?

3. What were the strengths and weaknesses in Eleanor and Franklin's marriage during his early years as a politician?

4. In 1913 Franklin Roosevelt went to Washington as Assistant Secretary of the Navy. What was Eleanor's role in Washington in the public life and as a homemaker?

5. In what ways did Eleanor expand her horizons during her early years in Washington? In what ways was she still limited by conventional behaviors and conventional thought?

## Chapter 6: Grief

1. During the Great War Eleanor Roosevelt came to understand the world as wounded: her own personal world and the world as a whole. A statue called "Grief" came to symbolize for her a way of responding to those wounds. What was the history of the statue itself? What was its importance to Eleanor?

2. In what ways did the war draw Eleanor Roosevelt into a new set of activities? How did these activities draw her beyond the limits of her previous life? In what ways did it bring her into contact with men and women who were not part of her "social circle"?

3. How did Franklin Roosevelt's affair with Lucy Mercer affect the life of Eleanor Roosevelt? In what ways did it (and did it not) change her relationship with her husband and mother-in-law? How did it influence her personal growth and understanding of the world?

4. The mother of one of the wounded soldiers Eleanor Roosevelt visited at St. Elizabeth's hospital credited Eleanor with going to the hospital with "a spirit of love." Youngs' claims that during this period Eleanor "found her capacity for love strangely enlarged." Evaluate this statement.

5. Another way of understanding the importance of the war years in Eleanor Roosevelt's growth is contained in her statement that she was "thinking things out for myself and becoming an individual." Review the ways that Eleanor's individuality had been thwarted during the previous years and ways that it was now coming to the fore.

## Chapter 7: Public Service

1. Franklin Roosevelt's polio influenced the course of his life and of Eleanor's. Frances Perkins said that being crippled gave Franklin "humility of spirit and a deeper philosophy." What evidence do you see in this chapter to support that statement?

2. Her husband's polio required Eleanor to be more active and self-reliant as a parent. What are some examples of the new domestic roles she filled and talents she developed?

3. During the 1920s Eleanor Roosevelt also became much more active in public life. What was her role in the Democratic Party, the League of Women Voters, the Women's Trade Union League, the Val-Kill furniture factory, and the Todhunter School?

4. With these activities Eleanor began to develop a political philosophy and a set of positions on important policy issues of her time. What was her position on the World Court, child labor, and women playing roles in public life? What did she think of women who held that public life was properly a sphere for men only?

5. Eleanor Roosevelt also came into contact with other women who were active in the world. Who were these women and what values did they share with Eleanor?

6. In 1928 Franklin Roosevelt reentered politics. How did the events of that year affect the fortunes of his friend Al Smith and Franklin himself? What did Eleanor fear she would lose in becoming the First lady of New York?

7. How did Eleanor and Franklin function as partners—both domestically and politically—during his tenure as governor of New York? How accurately did Eleanor characterize their marriage in the interview published at that time, "What Is a Wife's Job Today?"

8. How did Eleanor Roosevelt experience the possibility of becoming the First Lady of the land? Why was she so apprehensive about the prospect?

## Chapter 8: First Lady

1. In a variety of ways Eleanor Roosevelt observed closely the impact on America of the Great Depression. What are some notable examples of the hardships caused by the Depression as revealed in this chapter?

2. Eleanor had feared that she would lose her own autonomy in the role of First Lady-traditionally a ceremonial position, but in fact she used that role more effectively than any other first lady, before or since, to affect public policy and public opinion. How do the following demonstrate her resourcefulness: Arthurdale, the "Gridiron

Widows," the Marian Anderson concert, "My Day"? What are other examples of her influence?

3. Lorena Hickok was Eleanor Roosevelt's closest friend during the early years of her time in the White House. What was the texture of their personal friendship; that is, what did they offer each other as companions? How did Lorena contribute to Eleanor's understanding of the state of the Nation during the Depression?

4. Later in life Eleanor Roosevelt wrote of her White House years: "It was almost as though I had erected someone a little outside myself who was the President's wife. I was lost somewhere deep down inside myself." How could she say this, and what did she lose in becoming First Lady?

## Chapter 9: The Democratic Crusade

1. In *The Moral Basis of Democracy* Eleanor Roosevelt set forth her understanding of democracy. In this book she emphasized the ideal character of the citizens of a democracy. Describe the ways that Eleanor herself lived up to the ideal or addressed the problem noted in each of the following quotations from the book:

   - "Our own success, to be real, must contribute to the success of others."
   - "No one can honestly claim that either the Indians or the Negros of this country are free."
   - "Hunger and thirst, lack of decent shelter, lack of certain minimum decencies of life can be eliminated if the spirit of good will is awakened in every human being."
   - Democracy is "a method of government conceived for the development of human beings as a whole."
   - Democracy encourages "a sense of brotherhood, a sense that we strive together towards a common objective."
   - "Somehow or other human beings must get a feeling that there is in life a spring, a spring which flows for all humanity."

2. The coming of the Second World War reshaped life in the White house. How did it affect Eleanor Roosevelt's daily life? What kinds of activities did she undertake in taking part in the war effort? What was the importance of her wartime journeys to England and to the South Pacific (as described in the preface)?

3. During the war Eleanor continued her efforts on behalf of African Americans. What did she do to promote civil rights? How did some Americans, opposed to equality, react to her efforts?

4. During the war Eleanor and Joseph Lash became close friends. Under what circumstances did they meet? Why did Eleanor particularly admire Lash?

5. On April 12, 1945, after serving longer in office than any other president, Franklin Roosevelt died at Warm Springs of a cerebral hemorrhage. How did Eleanor and how did the nation as a whole react to his death?

## Chapter 10: On Her Own

1. During her "years alone" Eleanor Roosevelt continued to be an important *presence* in American life. What did she do on a day-to-day basis to present her views to the public? What was her attitude toward Joseph McCarthy and his brand of anti-communism?

2. As a delegate to the United Nations Eleanor Roosevelt showed great sympathy towards the refugees, displaced by the turmoil of the recent war. How did she express that sympathy in the debate *about* the refugees, and how did she make contact *with* actual refugees?

3. Arguably the most important public document of the twentieth century is the Universal Declaration of Human Rights. Remarkably, in an age when many nations did not even allow women to vote, and when women's rights were sharply curtailed in the United States, it was a

woman, Eleanor Roosevelt, who presided over the drafting of this document. What was Eleanor's contribution to the document (a) as an astute committee chairperson presiding over a diverse and sometimes cantankerous collection of delegates, and (b) as an idealist who believed deeply in the importance of the document?

4. During her final years Eleanor Roosevelt remained active in public affairs. In what ways did she express her ideas in Democratic politics and in meeting with foreign statesmen? What was the importance of David Gurewitsch for Eleanor during these years?

5. After Eleanor Roosevelt's death many thoughtful statements were written celebrating her life. Adlai Stevenson wrote one: "She would rather light a candle than curse the darkness, and her glow has warmed the world." Which of the epitaphs cited in this chapter do you consider most appropriate?

6. In what ways does Eleanor Roosevelt's Statement, "Behind tranquility lies conquered happiness," suggest the central struggle of Eleanor's own life?

7. What is J. William T. Youngs's own attitude towards Eleanor Roosevelt, as revealed in these pages?

8. What epitaph would *you* write for Eleanor Roosevelt?

# A Note on the Sources

Eleanor Roosevelt was a good writer, and her own letters, articles, and books are the best source of information about her life and thought. The handiest of these sources are the three volumes of her autobiography: *This Is My Story* (1937), *This I Remember* (1949), and *On My Own* (1958). They are also available in a one-volume edition titled *The Autobiography of Eleanor Roosevelt* (1992). Together these volumes form one of the most candid and engaging autobiographies ever written. They are redolent of Eleanor's charm and reveal her sense of humor, her feeling for a good story, and her ability to analyze her own character honestly. Occasionally, however—as in evaluating her own early childhood or her feelings for Franklin during courtship—she reads into the past feelings that occur later. Other sources then are valuable in rounding out the picture presented in the autobiographies.

Eleanor wrote many other books containing her ideas on a wide range of subjects. These include *Your Teens and Mine* (1961), *If You Ask Me* (1946), *It Seems to Me* (1954), *This Troubled World* (1938), *The Moral Basis of Democracy* (1940), *India and the Awakening East* (1953), *It's Up to the Women* (1933), *Tomorrow Is Now* (1963), *My Days* (1938), and *You Learn by Living* (1960). She wrote a daily column, "My Day," which was printed in many newspapers across the nation; its subjects range from square dancing and stargazing to national and international politics. Her monthly magazine column, "If You Ask Me," appeared in *Ladies' Home Journal* from 1941 to 1949 and then in *McCall's* until 1962. Consisting of prosaic advice on growing up, courtship, marriage, in-laws, and other domestic matters, these columns are full of Eleanor Roosevelt's good-natured humanity.

Her ideas also appear in scores of magazine articles. A bibliography listing these is available at the Franklin D. Roosevelt Library in Hyde Park. It runs to thirty-three pages and suggests the broad range of Eleanor Roosevelt's interests during a forty-year period. The articles include "Servants" (*Forum,* January 1930), "Ten Rules for Success in Marriage" (*Pictorial Review,* December 1931), "What Are the Movies Doing to Us?" (*Modern Screen,* November 1932), "On Girls Learning to Drink" (*Literary Digest,* January 7, 1933), "Subsistence Farmsteads" (*Forum and Century,* April 1934), "The Unemployed Are Not a Strange Race" (*Democratic Digest,* June 1936), "Should Wives Work?" (*Good Housekeeping,* December 1937), "On Teachers and Teaching" (*Harvard Educational Review,* October 1938), "Flying Is Fun" (*Collier's,* April 22, 1939), "What's Wrong with the Draft?" (*Look,* July 15, 1941), "Shall We Draft American Women?" (*Liberty,* September 13, 1941), "Women at War in Great Britain" (*Ladies' Home Journal,* April 1943), "Abolish Jim Crow!" (*New Threshold,* August 1943), "What Kind of World Are We Fighting For?" (*Canadian Home Journal,* January 1944), "Women's Place After the War" (*Click,* August 1944), "For an International Bill of Rights" (*Democratic Digest,* July 1946), "What I Think of the United Nations" (*United Nations World,* August 1949), "Education of an American" (*House and Garden,* August 1953), "Negotiate with Russia; Never Use the H-Bomb" (*Time,* August 30, 1954), "Children of Israel" (*Midstream,* August 1955), "F.D.R. as Seen by Mrs. Roosevelt" (*Wisdom,* January 1958), "Where I Get My Energy" (*Reader's Digest,* March 1959), "My Advice to the Next First Lady" (*Redbook,* November 1960), "What Has Happened to the American Dream?" (*Atlantic,* April 1961), and "I Remember Hyde Park" (*McCall's,* February 1963).

Eleanor Roosevelt's writings appear also in several anthologies. *The Wit and Wisdom of Eleanor Roosevelt* (1996), edited by Alex Ayres, is a volume of quotations on a variety of topics including business, education, and leadership. David Emblidge has compiled a three-volume collection of Eleanor Roosevelt's newspaper columns titled *Eleanor Roosevelt's "My Day"* (1989–1991). Emblidge has authored a one-volume anthology of these columns titled *My Day: The Best of Eleanor Roosevelt's Acclaimed Newspaper Columns, 1936–1962* (2001). Eleanor Roosevelt's correspondence with Lorena Hickok includes some of her most revealing letters, personally and politically. Some of these have been published in *Empty Without You: The Intimate Letters of Eleanor Roosevelt and Lorena Hickok* (1998), edited by Rodger Streitmatter.

The Franklin D. Roosevelt Library houses many collections of papers relating to Eleanor Roosevelt. The most important manuscripts consulted for this book were Anna Eleanor Roosevelt: Papers, 1884–1964; Roosevelt Family: Papers Donated by the Children, 1686–1959; and the Lorena Hickok Papers. These collections consist of several thousand boxes of letters, diaries, newspaper articles, schoolbooks, and other materials and include letters by Eleanor Roosevelt's parents, mother-in-law, and children. Unfortunately, some manuscript sources that would enable us to know Eleanor and Franklin better have been destroyed or are inaccessible. In 1937 Eleanor burned the courtship letters Franklin had written her, declaring that they were too personal to share with the public. Franklin's letters to Lucy Mercer and Eleanor's early correspondence with Lorena Hickok are not currently open to the public. But the many manuscripts that are available exhibit Eleanor's personality and values, enabling us to reconstruct the story of her troubled childhood, to follow her "career" as a young bride, to see her grow into maturity. In many cases, too, they give us glimpses of her inner life—of the personal struggles that make this world leader into the most human of human beings.

Among the most valuable secondary works on Eleanor Roosevelt's life, the most comprehensive are a number of books by her friend Joseph Lash. His *Eleanor and Franklin* (1971) and *Eleanor: The Years Alone* (1972) constitute a detailed and thoughtful general biography. Lash's *Love, Eleanor: Eleanor Roosevelt and Her Friends* (1982) and *A World of Love: Eleanor Roosevelt and Her Friends, II* (1984) focus on Eleanor's friendships and provide an interpretation of his own role and Lorena Hickok's role in Eleanor's life. His *Eleanor Roosevelt: A Friend's Memoir* (1964) is a personal history of her life during the twenty-three years he knew her.

Ruby Black's *Eleanor Roosevelt: A Biography* (1940) is an informal account by a journalist friend. Alfred Steinberg's *Mrs. R: The Life of Eleanor Roosevelt* (1958) is another general biography. James R. Kearney, *Anna Eleanor Roosevelt: The Evolution of a Reformer* (1968), and Tamara K. Hareven, *Eleanor Roosevelt: An American Conscience* (1968), focus on Eleanor's role in politics. Jason Berger examines her role in foreign affairs in *A New Deal for the World: Eleanor Roosevelt and American Foreign Policy* (1981). Stella K. Hershan investigates Eleanor's influence on others in *A Woman of Quality* (1970). Eleanor Roosevelt's life and career are also receiving attention in scholarly articles. A collection of essays titled *Without Precedent: The Life and Career of Eleanor Roosevelt* (1964), edited by Joan Hoff-Wilson and Marjorie Lightman, contains three general assessments of Eleanor's life: "Biographical Sketch" by William H. Chafe, "E.R. and Reform" by Tamara K. Hareven, and "E.R. and Feminism" by Lois Scharf. (Other essays in *Without Precedent* are listed below.) One of the finest Eleanor Roosevelt scholars and a contributor to this volume, Blanche Wiesen Cook, published *Eleanor Roosevelt, Volume I, 1884–1933* (1992) and *Volume II, The Defining Years, 1933–1938* (1999). This and Cook's subsequent volumes promise to be the definitive biography of Eleanor Roosevelt. See also Stella K. Hershan, *The Candles She Lit: The Legacy of Eleanor Roosevelt* (1993), and Maurine Beasley, *Eleanor Roosevelt and the Media: A Public Quest for Self-Fulfillment* (1987). Maurine Beasley, Holly Shulman, and Henry Beasley have edited *The Eleanor Roosevelt Encyclopedia* (2001), an invaluable reference work.

Several members of the Roosevelt family have written personal accounts of the First Lady. Elliott Roosevelt collaborated with James Brough in writing *An Untold Story: The Roosevelts of Hyde Park* (1973), *A Rendezvous with Destiny: The Roosevelts of the White House* (1975), and *Mother R: Eleanor Roosevelt's Untold Story* (1977). James Roosevelt worked with Bill Libby on *My Parents: A Differing View* (1976). And a Roosevelt grandson, John Boettiger, tells the story of his mother, Anna, in *A Love in Shadow* (1978). Anna's relationship to Eleanor is also documented in *Mother and Daughter: The Letters of Eleanor and Anna Roosevelt* (1982), edited by Bernard Asbell.

Eleanor Roosevelt's life has been chronicled in several books of pictures. Richard Harrity and Ralph G. Martin, *Eleanor Roosevelt: Her Life in Pictures* (1958), Helen Gahagan Douglas, *The Eleanor Roosevelt We Remember* (1963), and Joseph Lash, *Life Was Meant to Be Lived: A Centennial Portrait of Eleanor Roosevelt* (1984), survey her whole life. A. David Gurewitsch's *Eleanor Roosevelt: Her Day* (1973) consists of photos taken by Gurewitsch during his long friendship with Eleanor.

Many of the books written about Franklin Roosevelt contain information about Eleanor. The most thorough, scholarly, and readable account of Franklin Roosevelt's life is the multivolume biography by Frank Freidel: *Franklin D. Roosevelt: The Apprenticeship* (1952), *The Ordeal* (1954), *The Triumph* (1956), and *Launching the New Deal* (1973). Other fine sources are *Roosevelt: The Lion and the Fox* (1958) and *Roosevelt: The Soldier of Freedom* (1970), both by James MacGregor Burns.

Our understanding of Eleanor Roosevelt's life is assisted at many points by the growing body of literature on women in America. *Notable American Women, 1607–1950* (3 vols., 1971), edited by Edward T. James, and *Notable American Women: The Modern Period* (1980), edited by Barbara Sicherman and Carol Hurd Green, contain biographical sketches of many women with whom Eleanor associated. Page Smith's *Daughters of the Promised Land: Women in American History* (1970) is a narrative overview. Eleanor Flexner's *Century of Struggle: The Women's Rights Movement in the United States* (rev. ed., 1975) is the definitive account of the women's movement for the years 1800–1920. *A Heritage of Her Own* (1979), edited by Nancy Cott and

Elizabeth H. Pleck, is an excellent collection of essays on women's roles in the family and in the outside world. Other valuable sources include Mary P. Ryan, *Womanhood in America: From Colonial Times to the Present* (rev. ed., 1980); Carol Ruth Berkin and Mary Beth Norton, *Women of America: A History* (1979); Gerda Lerner, *The Majority Finds Its Past: Placing Women in History* (1980); Sheila M. Rothman, *Woman's Proper Place: A History of Changing Ideals and Practices, 1870 to the Present* (1978); Elaine Tyler May, *Great Expectations: Marriage and Divorce in Post-Victorian America* (1980); and two books by William H. Chafe, *The American Woman: Her Changing Social, Economic, and Political Role, 1920–1970* (1974) and *Women and Equality: Growing Patterns in American Culture* (1978). In *At Odds: Women and the Family in America from the Revolution to the Present* (1980), Carl N. Degler describes the conflicting demands of work and the family in American history—a leading theme in Eleanor Roosevelt's own life and writing.

The world changed greatly during the seventy-eight years of Eleanor's life. By 1962 little was left of the old New York in which she was born, but many sources are available that help reconstruct the environment of her early life. Among the most useful are Dixon Wecter, *The Saga of American Society* (1937); Henry Collins Brown, *Fifth Avenue Old and New* (1924); Allen Churchill, *The Upper Crust* (1970); Benjamin Blom, *New York: Photographs, 1850–1950* (1982); Jeffrey Simpson, *The Hudson River, 1850–1918: A Photographic Portrait* (1981); Raymond J. O'Brien, *American Sublime: Landscape and Scenery of the Lower Hudson Valley* (1981); and two novels by Edith Wharton, *Old New York* (1924) and *The Age of Innocence* (1920). Eleanor published her father's letters in *Hunting Big Game in the Eighties: The Letters of Elliott Roosevelt, Sportsman* (1933). We catch glimpses of Anna Roosevelt in a book written after her death by three anonymous friends: *In Loving Memory of Anna Hall Roosevelt* (1893). Two biographies focusing on Theodore Roosevelt's youth provide further insights into the Roosevelt family and the "black sheep" Elliott: Edmund Morris, *The Rise of Theodore Roosevelt* (1979), and David McCullough, *Mornings on Horseback* (1981). In "The Paradox of Eleanor Roosevelt: Alcoholism's Child," in *Virginia Quarterly Review* (1987), Hugh Davis Graham argues that her father's alcoholism was the root cause of her personal insecurity.

Several monographs describe the Victorian culture within which Elliott and Anna enjoyed their greatest triumphs and their ultimate downfall: Jackson T. Lears, *No Place of Grace: Antimodernism and the Transformation of American Culture, 1880–1920* (1981); Peter C. Cominos, "Late Victorian Sexual Respectability and the Social System," in *International Review of Social History* (1963); Charles E. Rosenberg, "Sexuality, Class and Role in 19th-Century America," in *American Quarterly* (May 1973); Ann Douglas, *The Feminization of American Culture* (1977); Barbara Welter, "The Cult of True Womanhood, 1820–1860," in *American Quarterly* (Summer 1966); Nancy Cott, "Passionlessness: An Interpretation of Victorian Sexual Ideology, 1790–1850," in *Signs* (Winter 1978); Peter Gay, *The Bourgeois Experience: Victoria to Freud, Vol. I: Education of the Senses* (1984); and Phyllis Rose, *Parallel Lives: Five Victorian Marriages* (1984).

Descriptions of Eleanor and Franklin's early married life appear in *F.D.R.: His Personal Letters, 1905–1928* (1948), edited by Elliott Roosevelt. Their letters to Sara from Europe in 1905 and from Campobello in 1907 are especially enlightening. The setting and atmosphere of their sojourn in Cortina is suggested by the following works: S. H. Hamer, *A Wayfarer in the Dolomites* (1926); Mona Wilson et al., *Grand Tour: A Journey in the Tracks of the Age of Aristocracy* (1937); Gabriel Fauré, *The Dolomites* (1925); Herbert Warren Wind, "The House of Baedeker," in *The New Yorker* (September 22, 1975); and Karl Baedeker's many tour guides.

Sara Roosevelt is the subject of a biography by Rita Halle Kleeman titled *Gracious Lady* (1935). In *All in the Family: The Story of Sara Delano Roosevelt and Her Daughter-in-Law, Eleanor Roosevelt* (2004) Jan Pottker paints a sympathetic portrait of Sara. Eleanor Roosevelt wrote a brief description of Louis Howe and others who influenced her in "The Seven People Who Shaped My Life," in *Look* (June 19, 1951). On Hyde Park, see Clara and Hardy Steeholm, *The House at Hyde Park* (1950). Campobello is described in Stephen O. Muskie's *Campobello: Roosevelt's "Beloved Island"* (1982) and Allen Nowlan's *Campobello: The Outer Island* (1975). Francis Parkinson Keyes portrays social life in Washington, D.C., in *Capital Kaleidoscope: The Story of a Washington Hostess* (1937). And the life of poorer Washingtonians—people Eleanor came to know during the Depression—is discussed in James Borchert's *Alley Life in Washington: Family, Community, Religion, and Folklife in the City, 1850–1970* (1980). Eleanor's life during the period of the Lucy Mercer affair is the subject of *Eleanor* (1979), a novel by Rhoda Lerman. The book is a fascinating but sometimes misleading attempt to reconstruct Eleanor's life during these difficult years.

The changes in Eleanor's life during the 1920s are indicated by a variety of sources. Richard Thayer Goldberg, *The Making of Franklin D. Roosevelt: Triumph over Disability* (1981), describes Franklin's rehabilitation after he contracted polio. In *Invincible Summer: An Intimate Portrait of the Roosevelts* (1974), Kenneth Davis portrays Eleanor

Roosevelt's friendship with Marion Dickerman. Lorena Hickok gives an account of her relationship with Eleanor in *Eleanor Roosevelt: Reluctant First Lady* (1962), and her own life is the subject of Doris Faber, *The Life of Lorena Hickok, E.R.'s Friend* (1980). During the 1920s a dramatic change occurred in the pattern of Eleanor's friendships. Prior to that time her closest friends had been members of her own family and social set. The importance of this type of friendship in reinforcing the traditional role of women is described in Carroll Smith-Rosenberg, "The Female World of Love and Ritual: Relations Between Women in Nineteenth-Century America" (in Cott and Pleck, *A Heritage of Her Own*). Eleanor's most rewarding friendships in the 1920s were with women who were active in the world outside the family. Blanche Wiesen Cook has written a perceptive article explaining the importance of such associations in the growth of women like Eleanor Roosevelt: "Female Support Networks and Political Activism: Lillian Wald, Crystal Eastman, Emma Goldman" (in Cott and Pleck, *A Heritage of Her Own*). Lillian Faderman's *Surpassing the Love of Men: Romantic Friendship and Love Between Women from the Renaissance to the Present* (1981) provides a historical framework for evaluating Eleanor's friendships with other women. Donn W. Parson, in his Ph.D. dissertation, "Entering the Public Sphere: The 1920s Rhetoric of Anna Eleanor Roosevelt" (1995), discusses Eleanor's efforts to persuade women to enter the "unladylike" arena of politics.

Three useful interviews with Eleanor were conducted in this period by Rose Feld (*New York Times*, April 20, 1924), Diana Rice (*New York Times Magazine*, December 2, 1928), and M. K. Wisehart (*Good Housekeeping*, August 1930). Elisabeth Israels Perry's "Training for Public Life: E.R. and Women's Political Networks in the 1920s" (in *Without Precedent*) is a fine essay on Eleanor's political apprenticeship with the Women's City Club in New York. Susan Ware's "E.R. and Democratic Politics: Women in the Postsuffrage Era" (in *Without Precedent*) follows Eleanor's political role from the 1920s through the 1950s.

Eleanor's life and influence as First Lady is the subject of several essays in *Without Precedent:* "E.R. and American Youth: Politics and Personality in a Bureaucratic Age" by Winifred D. Wandersee; "E.R. and Black Civil Rights" by Joanna Schneider Zangrando and Robert L. Zangrando, "'Turn Toward Peace': E.R. and Foreign Affairs" by Blanche Wiesen Cook, "E.R. and Ellen Woodward: A Partnership for Women's Work Relief and Security" by Martha H. Swain, "Helen Gahagan Douglas and the Roosevelt Connection" by Ingrid Winther Scobie, "E.R. and the Issue of FDR's Successor" by Richard S. Kirkendall, and "E.R.

as First Lady" by Abigail Q. McCarthy. See also Lois Scharf, *Eleanor Roosevelt: First Lady of American Liberalism* (1987); Anita Danker, "Government Policy and Women in the Workplace Through Depression and War," in *New England Journal of History* (1988); and Paula F. Pfeffer, "Eleanor Roosevelt and the National and World Woman's Parties," in *Historian* (1996). Both Pfeffer and Scharf argue that Eleanor was a social reformer but not a feminist.

For a general account of women's activities in this period, see Susan Ware, *Beyond Suffrage: Women in the New Deal* (1981), and Frances M. Seeber, "Eleanor Roosevelt and Women in the New Deal: A Network of Friends," in *Presidential Studies Quarterly* (1990). Susan Ware tells the story of one of Eleanor's most important political allies in *Partner and I: Molly Dewson, Feminism, and New Deal Politics* (1987). In *Farewell to the Party of Lincoln: Black Politics in the Age of FDR* (1983), Nancy J. Weiss argues that Eleanor's influence was great in bringing blacks into the Democratic Party. On Eleanor Roosevelt and civil rights, see also Allida M. Black, "Championing a Champion: Eleanor Roosevelt and the Marian Anderson 'Freedom Concert,'" in *Presidential Studies Quarterly* (1990). Lorena Hickok's vivid descriptions of the victims of poverty are available in *One Third of a Nation: Lorena Hickok Reports on the Great Depression* (2000), edited by Richard Lowitt and Maurine Beasley.

The texts of the First Lady's press conferences are published in *The White House Press Conferences of Eleanor Roosevelt* (1983), edited by Maurine Beasley. Lorena Hickok's perceptive and colorful accounts of the Depression are collected in *One Third of a Nation: Lorena Hickok Reports on the Great Depression* (1981), edited by Robert Lowitt and Maurine Beasley. Elsie Ripley Clapp, who directed the Arthurdale School from 1934 to 1936, tells about her work in *Community Schools in Action* (1939). Two memoirs by servants suggest the flavor of life in the Roosevelt White House. The housekeeper, Henrietta Nesbitt, published her recollections as *White House Diary* (1948), and a White House maid and seamstress, Lillian Rogers Parks, collaborated with Frances Spatz Leighton in writing *The Roosevelts: A Family in Turmoil* (1981). On Eleanor in World War II, see Doris Kearns Goodwin, *No Ordinary Time: Franklin and Eleanor Roosevelt: The Home Front in World War II* (1994); M. Glen Johnson, "The Contributions of Eleanor Roosevelt and Franklin Roosevelt to the Development of International Protection for Human Rights," in *Human Rights Quarterly* (1987); Monty N. Penkower, "Eleanor Roosevelt and the Plight of World Jewry," in *Jewish Social Studies* (1987); and Timothy P. Mega, "Humanism and Peace: Eleanor Roosevelt's Mission to the Pacific, August-September, 1943," in *Maryland Historian* (1988).

During her years alone Eleanor was the subject of many fine magazine articles, suggesting her enormous prestige. Among the best are "Number One World Citizen" (*New Republic,* August 5, 1946) by Ralph G. Martin; "The Years Alone" (*The New Yorker,* June 12 and June 19, 1948) by E. J. Kahn Jr.; "First Lady of the U.N." (*New York Times Magazine,* October 22, 1950) by Elizabeth Janeway; "Eleanor Roosevelt at a Youthful 70" (*New York Times Magazine,* October 10, 1954) by Robert Bendiner; "Eleanor Roosevelt Today" (*Look,* April 17, 1956) by Laura Bergquist; and "Mrs. Roosevelt at a Remarkable 75" (*New York Times Magazine,* October 4, 1959) by James MacGregor Burns and Janet Thompson Burns. William E. Leuchtenburg's *In the Shadow of FDR: From Harry Truman to Ronald Reagan* (1983) describes Eleanor's influence in Democratic politics after Franklin's death. Edna P. Gurewitsch tells the story of her husband's friendship with Eleanor in "Remembering Mrs. Roosevelt: An Intimate Memoir," in *American Heritage* (December 1981). Subsequently, Edna Gurewitsch expanded her memoir into a book, *Kindred Souls: The Devoted Friendship of Eleanor Roosevelt and Dr. David Gurewitsch* (2002). In *Casting Her Own Shadow: Eleanor Roosevelt and the Shaping of Postwar Liberalism* (1996), Allida M. Black argues that Eleanor was "a consummate liberal power broker." Mary Ann Glendon tells the story of Eleanor Roosevelt's most important legacy to human rights in *A World Made New: Eleanor Roosevelt and the Universal Declaration of Human Rights* (2001).

For a book-length annotated listing of Eleanor Roosevelt literature, see *Eleanor Roosevelt: A Comprehensive Bibliography* (1994), compiled by John A. Edens.

*Eleanor Roosevelt: A Personal and Public Life* is also available as a Books on Tape recording read by Donada Peters.

# Index